The Effective Teaching of
Religious Education

THE EFFECTIVE TEACHER SERIES

General editor: Elizabeth Perrott

THE EFFECTIVE TEACHING OF RELIGIOUS EDUCATION

BRENDA WATSON

LONGMAN
London and New York

Longman Group UK Limited,
Longman House, Burnt Mill,
Harlow, Essex CM20 2JE, England
and Associated Companies throughout the world.

Published in the United States of America
by Longman Publishing, New York

© Longman Group UK Limited 1993

First published 1993

ISBN 0–582–08707-4 PPR

British Library Cataloguing-in-Publication Data

A catalogue record for this book is
available from the British Library

Library of Congress Cataloging-in-Publication Data

Watson, Brenda.
    The effective teaching of religious education / by Brenda Watson.
        p.   cm. -- (The Effective teacher series)
    Includes bibliographical references and index.
    ISBN 0-582-08707-4
    1. Religious education--Study and teaching. I. Title. II. Series.
BL42.W37 1993   92-41217
291.7--dc20   CIP

Set by 7E in 10/12pt Times
Printed in Malaysia by TCP

To Hilary, for unstinting support
of many kinds
during the writing of this book

CONTENTS

LIST OF TABLES

LIST OF FIGURES

EDITOR'S PREFACE

This well established series was inspired by my book on the practice of teaching (*Effective Teaching: a Practical Guide to Improving your Teaching*, Longman, 1982), written for trainee teachers wishing to improve their teaching skills as well as for in-service teachers, especially those engaged in the supervision of trainees. The books in this series have been written with the same readership in mind. However, busy classroom teachers will find that these books also serve their needs as changes in the nature and pattern of education make the in-service training of experienced teachers more essential than in the past.

The rationale behind the series is that professional courses for teachers require the coverage of a wide variety of subjects in a relatively short time so the aim of the series is the production of 'easy to read', practical guides to provide the necessary subject background, supported by references to guide and encourage further reading, together with questions and/or exercises devised to assist application and evaluation.

As specialists in their selected fields, the authors have been chosen for their ability to relate their subjects to the needs of teachers and to stimulate discussion of contemporary issues in education.

The series aims to cover subjects ranging from the theory of education to the teaching of mathematics and from primary school teaching and educational psychology to effective teaching with information technology. It looks at aspects of education as diverse as education and cultural diversity and pupil welfare and counselling. Although some subjects such as the legal context of teaching and the teaching of history are specific to England and Wales, the majority of the subjects such as assessment in education, the effective teaching of statistics and comparative education are international in scope.

Elizabeth Perrott

AUTHOR'S PREFACE

In a recent radio discussion someone commented: 'religion answers the questions no-one asks'. In a sense this book might be seen as a sustained response to that remark. For behind it lies an insight which religious education can ill afford to ignore. The remark, however, also reveals serious confusion both as regards the nature of religion and the role it plays in the lives of those who have genuine commitment to it. Furthermore, the comment should be challenged concerning its accuracy. There is much evidence to suggest that people continue to find religion a source of endless fascination, provided that certain assumptions and barriers to thinking about it are removed. This is where religious education can play a major role.

The mere mention of RE, however, raises important questions: Why have RE in schools? Isn't it just indoctrination? Can anyone teach it? Can it be relevant to today's pupils? How should world religions be taught? What about the place of Christianity? Is RE assessable? How does it relate to worship in schools?

I try to deal with all these issues in this book. RE is an area of great complexity and controversy, and attempts to simplify too much can be damaging. Clear guidelines, however, can help teachers cope with this, and turn the very difficulties themselves into the means of tacking against the wind, like sailing a yacht.

I believe that RE takes off for pupils – and for teachers too – when it launches out into the deep. Attempting to hug the shores and play safe results in either mildly entertaining or positively dull RE, both of which risk being marginalized in pupils' attitudes by the superficiality which even young children detect, though normally at an unconscious level.

The book is written with the needs of specialist and non-specialist teachers in mind, in both primary and secondary schools. The intention is to integrate theory and practice so that the discussion of ideas is closely related to what is feasible in the classroom. I therefore hope that the book will prove an encouragement and stimulus to all who either care about religious education or find themselves obliged to teach it and want to do it professionally as well as possible.

ACKNOWLEDGEMENTS

I gratefully acknowledge my debt to the Farmington Trust for making the writing of this book possible, and especially for all the help and encouragement given me by Colonel Robert Hornby. The thinking expressed in its pages is the result of innumerable conversations with colleagues and pupils over the years, and to them all I give thanks. I would especially mention Professor Edward Hulmes whose rigorous engagement with the issues surrounding religious education has been profoundly stimulating to me. I also want to thank Dora Ainsworth for the many insights shared in our discussions together, and Elizabeth Ashton who has offered perceptive comments on the manuscript as well as being a source of inspiration in many other ways too. I acknowledge helpful conversations on Chapter 7 of the book with Dr Terry McLaughlin of the Department of Education, University of Cambridge. I am very grateful too to Catherine and Hilary Elgar for their valuable help with the figures. Finally, a note of sincere appreciation to Helen Gibson, without whose calm efficiency and friendly presence in typing the text the work would have been impossible.

We are grateful to the following to reproduce copyright material:

Julie A. Gage for the poem 'Lavender Lily'; Tim Tiley Ltd for the final verse of 'The Blind Man and the Elephant' by Katherine Earl.

CHAPTER 1

The effective teaching of RE

The crucial role of the teacher

The most fundamental factor in effective RE, as in the effective teaching of any other subject, is the teacher. Guidelines, syllabuses, books, aids of various kinds, all depend upon the teacher who actually applies them within the classroom situation. The teacher is in control of the way that the intended learning is handled. The same topic, with the same age and ability range of pupils, and the same general style and method of teaching, can yield entirely different results, depending upon the teacher. One lesson can really take off, and another be dead.

Material which I have tried out in schools with different teachers has yielded fascinatingly different results. I think of one particular school working with a scheme on 'The World of Nature and Belief in God' in which the same slides were shown, the same background material given to teachers, and the same amount of time allowed for discussion in the four different classes of 9–10 year-olds, each of which was similar in composition with regard to ability and home background. The same materials produced exciting work from one group, ordinary and rather drab work from another, and moderate interest in the other two. The difference was that the teacher in the first group *really* related to the material and to the children, and she had understood the underlying purpose and challenge of RE and was able to *point up* the discussion, listening carefully to what the children said and leading them on in their thinking. She was, from what I saw, an extremely effective teacher of RE.

What makes an effective teacher of RE?

What do you think would be the profile of an effective RE teacher, whether in the primary or in the secondary school? These are some of the responses teachers have made:

1. able to establish good rapport with pupils;
2. has charisma;
3. is good at organizing;
4. is a survivor;

5. keeps in touch with what's happening in other subjects and in pupils' backgrounds;
6. has a quality of openness;
7. has long teaching experience;
8. has good qualifications in the subject;
9. has strong religious faith;
10. has enthusiasm for the subject;
11. has a sense of humour.

How did the particular teacher mentioned above match up with this list? 1, 3, 5, 6 and 7? Yes. 4 – A survivor? Yes, in the sense that she was not a person who just reacted and went along with the system, but was prepared to be independent and assess situations for herself. 10 – Enthusiasm? Yes, for whatever she was teaching – she believed that, provided she was involved and interested herself, her pupils would be too.

But regarding 2 this teacher was not especially charismatic – in fact more self-effacing than naturally the centre of attention. Point 7 – long teaching experience? Moderate, about eight years, but hardly any of that in RE. Point 8 – qualifications? None in religious education. 9 – strong religious faith? No, she was an agnostic.

This teacher, therefore, was not an RE specialist in any sense. She was indeed inexperienced in teaching RE having been unhappy with what she had hitherto been expected to present. But the credits she did have outweighed such difficulties. She in fact demonstrated what I have elsewhere argued (Watson 1987: 14–16) is at the basis of all education worthy of the name – a quality of five-fold respect, namely for oneself – a proper self-affirmation; for all other people as persons like oneself; for the total environment in which we find ourselves, both natural and cultural; for beauty, delighting in experiencing a sense of awe and wonder; and finally respect for truth which, however difficult to attain, needs to be like a beacon beckoning us forward. These constitute, so to speak, the raw materials for effective education per se.

Provided there is a basic commitment to education, therefore, her example offers real hope to the many teachers, in both secondary and primary schools, who find themselves having to teach RE with much less knowledge and experience of the subject to back them than they would wish.

For her it worked because of one other factor – her ability and willingness to engage at some depth with the concepts, ideas and questions evoked by the material. If a concept presented difficulties for children in understanding, she did not, gladly or reluctantly, resolve to postpone trying to communicate it – she thought of ways round, using such devices as homely examples and visual stimuli. She had taken the trouble first to find out what she could about the topic from the notes given, and had thought about it carefully, so that in a real sense she was herself involved in what was happening in the classroom.

She believed in openness, in giving space to pupils, and actually practised this. She told me that perhaps her agnosticism was a help in this respect, because, while she respected the faith of religious people and found religious ideas fascinating, she was not tempted to be dogmatic about what she believed.

Is religious faith a hindrance or an asset for RE?

There is in fact a flaw in such reasoning, because a dogmatic kind of agnosticism is possible: agnosticism just as much as religious faith rests on its own assumptions which can betray key-hole vision. Furthermore a strong case can be made for arguing that religious commitment is the only way to understand the depths of religion which from the outside may remain sheer enigma. As in the teaching of science or music, for example, the scientist or the musician has far more to offer than the non-scientist or the non-musician.

Nevertheless, we do well to remember that if education is thought of in terms of enabling pupils to take responsibility for their own ongoing self-education through life, the more limited experience that the teacher may have can nevertheless be deployed in a professionally helpful way. Similarly the teacher and the knowledge itself, as well as the teacher's religious or non-religious faith, can often get in the way of pupils' learning. This is especially so in the case of a subject which, like RE, arouses strong emotions.

Basic attitudes essential for both specialist and non-specialist RE teachers

It is obvious that experience and knowledge of the subject yield dividends in the classroom. Especially in secondary schools, considerable sophistication is called for in order to sustain the interest of older and often religiously alienated pupils. In both primary and secondary schools there is a need for as highly qualified teachers as possible to act as coordinators, helping and encouraging those whose main expertise lies elsewhere.

RE does, however, have to call on the services of many non-specialist teachers. I would like therefore to reassure them, as well as those specializing in the subject, that most teachers who are willing to try to teach RE well *can* do so. This is based on my conviction that certain basic attitudes and interests are present in almost all people – both teachers and pupils – and that these provide the raw material for effective RE.

An outstanding American teacher of music speaks from her own experience of young children (Upitis 1990: 2): 'We have one strong factor in our favor in taking on the task of helping people become musicians, and that is, in some form *all of us are already musicians.*' In thinking about this I concluded that the basic requirements for teaching music – in addition to certain skills essential to any effective teaching of any subject – are a basic sense of rhythm and pitch, delight in organized sound and ensemble work, and a real interest in developing children's own creative powers.

Figure 1.1 represents what I see as the equivalent for teaching RE and shows how these qualities are related to the attitude of five-fold respect discussed above (p. 2). Although these qualities may appear as a formidable list, they are mostly present in people, even though for many reasons they often remain undeveloped. The purpose of education,

Figure 1.1 **Basic requirements for effective religious education**

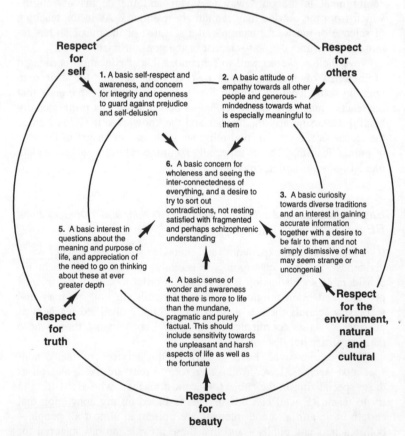

The outer circle represents the attitude of five-fold respect essential for education; the inner circle, attitudes stemming from each which are essential pre-requisites for effective religious education.

and of RE in particular, is to help these aspects to grow, relating them to basic religious concepts and basic skills for discernment. Whether formally qualified or not, the effective teacher in the classroom will seek to exemplify such qualities. These are not optional.

What is effective RE?

This is an interesting question in itself, quite apart from how to achieve it. Here is a selection of characteristics of effective RE which I have heard many times. You may like to compare it with a list of your own.

1. class control;
2. interest shown by pupils;
3. exam results;
4. reinforces nurture within a particular religious tradition;
5. encourages religious conversion;
6. develops openness and tolerance towards other religions;
7. level of information retained about religions;
8. helps pupils to become kind and compassionate;
9. promotes good citizenship;
10. develops strong sense of social justice;
11. lack of complaint about having to attend school worship;
12. encourages willingness to question everything.

The first two of these points are the ones which most immediately concern the teacher, together often with the third, that of exam results and assessable performance which is a priority forced upon teachers by society as a whole.

The fourth and fifth relate to a long-standing debate about the purpose of RE – this is the 'confessional' approach which starts off from the assumption of the truth of a particular religious viewpoint and seeks to nurture pupils within, or strongly encourage them towards accepting, that viewpoint. Points 6 and 7 advocate what is regarded by many as an opposite way of looking at the purpose of RE. Known as the phenomenological approach to RE, it is the one currently in the ascendancy in many schools, whereas the confessional approach is the one which is more traditionally associated with RE.

Points 8–10 show how RE has frequently been understood as primarily moral education. This remains one of the strongest reasons why so many parents still want their children to have RE even though they themselves have long since given up having much to do with religion. This has also been a way of escaping from the serious clashes which historically have taken place between different Christian groups involved in education and which remain a distinct possibility in the multi-faith situation.

The link with school assemblies (11) is very important for some RE teachers. For others, what they see as the opposite approach to worship, that of questioning, (12) should be the fundamental criterion for judging effective RE.

This list, therefore, raises important questions with regard to the purpose of RE, style of teaching, and the content of what is taught. These issues will be teased out in the course of this book: thus Chapter 4 will attempt to adjudicate between different views of the role of RE. All I shall do at this stage is to give a summary of how I see effective religious education.

Qualities which effective RE develops

Figure 1.1 on page 4 drew attention to six qualities which the whole of the curriculum ought to be encouraging. RE can be judged effective to the degree that it helps pupils develop:

1. a basic self-awareness;
2. a basic attitude of empathy;
3. a basic curiosity towards diverse traditions;
4. a basic sense of wonder;
5. a basic interest in questions about the meaning and purpose of life;
6. a basic concern for wholeness.

We can apply these to the purpose of religious education in this way: to help pupils

1. *A basic self-awareness*

(a) to reflect constructively about religion without being over-whelmed by prejudice, whether religious or non-religious;
(b) to see and understand the kind of assumptions about religion present in their environment and in society as a whole, and be prepared to think about these and not automatically either reject them or take them over;
(c) to develop trust in their own powers of perceptiveness and intuition, provided that this trust is balanced by openness towards the insights of others and the findings of fresh evidence;
(d) consequent on this, to develop willingness to modify, change, enlarge, or revise, what has so far been thought and felt about religion.

2. *A basic attitude of empathy*

(a) to appreciate the power and attractiveness of religion and be able to get on the wavelength of religious people;

(b) to be aware in a meaningful way of the kind of experiences and arguments upon which religious people base their convictions;

(c) to learn fluency in the language of affirmation, both of others as people and of what is meaningful and important to them. It is especially important with regard to those people whose views are very different from one's own.

3. *A basic curiosity towards diverse traditions*

(a) to appreciate and delight in diversity and know enough about different religions not to offend the susceptibilities of people, and to be able to give respect to them as persons without marginalizing their religious commitment – to be able therefore to contribute towards a harmonious society;

(b) to perceive the crucial area of common-ground between almost all major religious traditions, and that differences and disagreements are only meaningful against that background of what is held in common.

4. *A basic sense of wonder*

(a) to foster their capacity for imagination which can give rise to vision, realizing that reality can be greater and other than it often seems – so that they appreciate that a flat two-dimensional approach to life is not the only option available;

(b) to understand that religious faith expresses itself in a variety of forms, many of which are close to the arts, and to realize also that religious language is mostly used in symbolic or metaphorical ways;

(c) to appreciate the emotional power of religious commitment and how this can be beneficial or harmful.

5. *A basic interest in questions about the meaning and purpose of life*

(a) to challenge secularist assumptions and to appreciate that religious truth-claims cannot be easily dismissed;

(b) to understand what is distinctive about religion, that is, what it essentially concerns, and be able to distinguish between that and features of it which can vary and perhaps be dispensed with altogether;

(c) to realize in particular in how many different ways religion can masquerade as something else, and fail to be what it claims to be;

(d) to appreciate the highly controversial nature of religion and of almost everything that is said about it by anyone, whether religious or not;

(e) to have a firm grasp of criteria by which to evaluate precise examples and manifestations of religion in practice;

(f)   to appreciate the force of the question-mark with regard to the ultimate divide between religion and non-religion, and to appreciate the reality of the dilemma, and the ways in which religion needs to be questioned for its failures, negative attitudes, hypocrisy and externalism.

6. *A basic concern for wholeness*

(a)   to be able and willing to reflect in depth about the totality of life's experience and the views one comes across.
(b)   to be able to appreciate the interlinking of everything and the force of cumulative evidence, and that what is done and learnt in school cannot be divorced from what happens outside;
(c)   to appreciate that religion challenges head-on any view that regards knowledge as something only arrived at by reasoning and scientific experimentation;
(d)   to be concerned about conviction for or against religion, but to be open to evidence and to experience – not to have the answers all neatly sewn up, but to see life as a journey of exploration with exciting prospects and a sense of fulfilment in actually moving forward and, if necessary, changing in order to accommodate fresh insight.

Effective teaching

What the teacher needs – in addition to developing these points which are appropriate for pupils – is professional awareness of the nature of RE:

1.   that it is crucial to draw attention to fundamental assumptions in our society, and to keep open for pupils the options of accepting, modifying or rejecting these views (Chapters 2–3);
2.   that the purpose of RE is pupils' self-education, engaging in depth upon the meaning and truth-claims of religions in a way which is relevant to their total experience of life (Chapter 4);
3.   that space needs to be given in which pupil involvement has a chance to develop, together with creativity, a sense of wonder and the cultivation of inner quietness (Chapters 5 and 6);
4.   that teachers need to model a positive, fair and balanced approach to the diversity of religious traditions and outlooks, and the controversy which these can generate (Chapter 8);
5.   that in a spirit of critical affirmation it is important to develop skills of evaluation and criteria for discernment (Chapters 7 and 9);
6.   that the crucial need is to put persons first, to establish genuine relationships which are affirming of pupils, believing that they

have something to give, and so listening to them and responding to them – and in the light of this to encourage their capacity for self-assessment (Chapter 10);

7. that the distinction between education and dogmatic teaching is all-important and that, provided this is borne in mind, opportunities for stillness and possible worship can be an invaluable aid to education (Chapters 6 and 11);

8. that RE can relate in a dynamic and creative way to all other areas of the curriculum (Chapters 12 and 13).

The content of RE

Nothing has been said so far about precise content, for example, which world religions should be included, or whether the focus should be mainly on Christianity, how far non-religious stances such as Humanism should feature in RE, or what to do about the occult, and so forth. Nor has anything been said about precise method.

This is deliberate because:

1. The most impeccable and well-prepared content, and the most exciting and suitable method, will fail as RE unless plugged in to what is its central purpose as outlined above. Furthermore, if this is really understood, this purpose can be achieved through a great variety of approaches with regard both to content and method. The teacher can adapt almost any and every available item. Even something from the day's newspaper can be all that is needed as an effective starting-point, just as the latest or the most interesting work done in other subject areas of the curriculum may be used. Materials that happen to be available in the school, including even seriously inadequate ones, can be brought into play and yield educationally valuable material if approached from a point of view of real understanding on the teacher's part.

2. What is essential or helpful or inspiring for any one pupil, group of pupils, or class will vary enormously, and therefore effective RE is inescapably dependent on the teacher's skills and perceptiveness within a particular situation. There are no blue-prints which can be given. Even agreed syllabuses, drawn up for a particular locality, only suggest ideas and very general outlines; if given in any detail they will be more or less inappropriate for this particular pupil or this actual class.

3. There has to be a freshness about teaching – it cannot be pre-arranged and pre-packaged, for that almost always loses the attention of pupils, even if not also of the teacher. Teaching must be alive and it can only be alive in the present moment – it is time-consuming to try to make stale bread palatable, and why

bother when fresh bread is available? Fresh bread is the interests, concerns, questions and problems of the moment which pupils bring and which the teacher as a person brings.

4. The teacher always has to operate within a number of constraints such as agreed syllabuses, governors' wishes, heads of department, parental pressures, and so on, which mean that he or she is the only person who is competent to decide on content and method. Other people, such as the author of a book, do not have the right to do more than offer suggestions which are a few among the thousands possible.

5. The possible content of RE is so enormous, and the possible interpretation so varied, that the idea of a core content and suitable method of conveying it is utterly unrealistic. Attempted cores turn out to be highly simplistic generalisations that satisfy very few people, but carry many dogmatic messages which are in fact controversial and so therefore masquerade as being objective. Selection itself – the choice of this material rather than that – can be a hidden form of indoctrination and the more so if it comes in the garb of so-called publicly agreed authority. So it is better that variety and flexibility are maintained with freedom to respond to current needs and interests.

The need to look at theory

Because teaching RE effectively depends upon understanding the nature of RE and developing those skills and attitudes essential to it, there is a certain amount of theory to be mastered. This can sometimes be rather hastily dismissed as irrelevant to the classroom. But time spent with a map at the beginning of a difficult and complicated journey is time well-spent – failure to do so can be disastrous, causing much frustration and waste of time and the real possibility of never reaching the destination at all.

Impatience is justified if theory moves off into the stratosphere, so to speak. Provided, however, that it is properly grounded, failure to engage with it may be termed irresponsible. This is because the effectiveness of RE depends first and foremost on the teacher perceiving the underlying challenge it presents, and why, so that what is negative can be countered.

There is another important reason for attending to theory: it needs to be shared with pupils. Edward Hulmes, who has contributed one volume to the Effective Teacher Series on *Education and Cultural Diversity* (Hulmes 1989) has many times noted that RE is for teachers as much as for pupils. I would want to add that the theory of RE is for pupils as well as for teachers. This is the only way in which indoctrination can be avoided and any real understanding of religion conveyed. We cannot expect pupils to learn the sophistication necessary for handling difficult concepts if we constantly draw a veil over them and shut pupils off from the real debate. Pupils as well as teachers should be aware of secularist tendencies in what is taken for granted in our society and in the educational world, and they should realize that these are not beyond being questioned. Again, they need to appreciate the problems posed by the fact that there are so many different religions, and be alert to possible responses. It is also most important that the abuse of religion with its destructive consequences is faced, and that pupils are helped towards levels of discernment.

A consideration of these basic issues is the theme of Chapters 2 and 3.

CHAPTER 2

RE – Erratic boulder?

Geographers speak of a rock deposited by the Ice Age perhaps hundreds of miles from its place of origin as an erratic boulder, and it often seems to me that that is how RE appears in the landscape of today's schools. What is it doing there – strange, alien, even threatening? Of fascination to some, most would prefer to have it taken away or at least effectively cordoned off so that its presence could largely be ignored.

Fifty years ago most people would not have thought of RE in such terms. They would have preferred the analogy of the soil which supports vegetation and the wherewithal to live. Very few seriously asked how education could flourish without the sustenance provided by religion. This was why religion was the one subject required by British law to be taught in schools. Even in the 1988 legislation, RE has been referred to as 'basic', although in most people's minds any substance to that interpretation has long since evaporated.

What kind of picture does 'RE' conjure up in your mind? Often when people have enquired about my subject area, my reply is greeted with a polite, 'Oh!' followed by a change of conversation. To them RE is an embarrassment, something to avoid, forget or oppose. Lurking behind their response are images of RE reflecting past experience: 'dull', 'irrelevant', 'soft option', 'load of nonsense', 'dangerous – trying to get at people', 'morals and all that', 'a training in prejudice', 'an anachronism in the modern world', 'the odd one out in schools', 'to do with the God squad'. But a few say, 'fascinating', 'tremendously important', 'really stimulating', 'central to the curriculum', 'exciting', 'fun'.

Wherever you may locate your own particular response, I want in this book to discuss what is involved in giving RE the positive and creative image which it should have by virtue of the importance of its subject-matter, the challenging controversy it can generate, and the depth of feeling to which it can appeal. Religion is one of the most powerful sources of human motivation, and can therefore, even in a utilitarian age, be seen as 'useful' for attaining socially acceptable ends.

These very assets of course, if improperly handled, become liabilities. The uses to which religion can be put are not always beneficial – indeed can be very damaging indeed. The controversial element can lead to intolerance, bigotry and bitterness. Similarly depth of feeling can become equated with prejudice, and the arousal of emotions in schools can become indoctrination. Even a sense of the importance of its subject-matter can generate the pious 'holier-than-thou' tone of voice, so much detested and ridiculed – probably quite rightly – by our society.

In Western societies like Britain awareness of the possible or actual dangers of RE is more to the fore than appreciation of its potential assets. Effective teaching of RE has to battle against unfavourable odds and can be severely damaged in the process. The suggestion that it might occupy 10 per cent of curriculum time in order to do justice to it and its importance in general, and for all other subjects in particular, is normally greeted with frank incredulity. 'That's ridiculous – of course there's no hope of that.'

Features of Western society today

In order to manoeuvre intelligently within this state of affairs it is necessary to refer to the overall context in which RE operates. Here we find that the pressures against taking religion seriously are considerable, despite much that is extremely positive and creative to which RE can and should relate. Here is a list of some of the facets of life in the late twentieth century which should be RE-friendly. You will probably want to add many more.

1. impact of science in increasing knowledge;
2. achievements of technology in reducing drudgery;
3. more widespread opportunities for enjoyment of life;
4. revolution in communications;
5. increased pluralism of society;
6. concern for human rights;
7. stress on the importance of individual integrity and personal responsibility;
8. renewed interest in the spiritual dimension to life;
9. impact of the 'Green Movement';
10. awareness of and concern about global evil and suffering;
11. acceptance of religion as a phenomenon and some resurgence of religious feeling.

The marginalizing of religion

Yet all these facets also carry negative implications with regard to religion.

The success of science in extending the frontiers of knowledge has led to scepticism about religion
The achievements of science have encouraged the view that scientific

method provides the *only* route to genuine knowledge. As religious beliefs cannot be proved scientifically they are to be doubted, for it is assumed that religion is just a matter of subjective opinion. This assumption will be examined in detail in Chapter 3, as it is so pervasive and damaging, and RE must be able to discuss the degree to which its basis is faulty.

The achievements of technology have promoted the distractions of a utilitarian approach to life
The spectacular achievements of technology have dazzled people into awe at the marvels of human inventiveness and mastery over the natural world; as well as promoting an unprecedented emphasis on mechanical and organizational efficiency. This has greatly encouraged a utilitarian attitude to life, and inflated the notion that human beings are the measure of all things. Both of these developments have tended to have the effect of dulling sensitivity to religion.

The attractiveness of a materialist way of life in encouraging consumerism, individualism and hedonism or the pursuit of pleasure
A materialist way of life is enjoying a heyday. This shows itself in a variety of ways: in the all-consuming craving for more money and possessions, more power and social status, and more pleasure and entertainment. In such an environment it is hard to take religion seriously which requires that all these things – good as they may be – must take second place to the cultivation of spiritual values and the worship of God, not gods. It is not that these things are in themselves opposed to religion, but the possessiveness and distractedness which they tend to promote are.

The restlessness of constant change and novelty, promoting activism
Technology has brought speed of travel, and the almost instantaneous dissemination of information from one part of the world to another, such as has been unheard of in the history of the world. It has created a world of mobility: of rapid and constant change, with attention focused mainly on novelty or utility – a world eager to break free from tradition which has become irrelevant to a restless, fast-moving age. Although this can help religions come together, their traditions are under threat. It also affects religions in another way: religious sensitivity needs stillness in order to develop – a stillness almost impossible for most people in today's noisy world.

Pluralism leading to relativism
Increased pluralism has brought different problems for religion, notably that of yet another -ism – relativism. Out of bewilderment at such diversity of views and the need to promote some level of harmony between them, the view has been quite widespread that

differences are *entirely* due to cultural context and are not therefore contradictions to be resolved. This on the surface may not seem to be hostile to religion, but it causes severe re-interpretation encouraging many people to regard religion as little more than a culturally derived dressing-up game. How justified such a view is will be looked at in Chapter 3.

A pragmatic basis for the human rights movement
The emphasis in the human rights movement supported by this relativism is more and more in the direction of a hidden pragmatism. There is a marked reluctance to arguing why people should be accorded such rights – 'It just is so and things work better if you accept it – racism for example causes instability and prejudice and violence, so it must go'. Religious support is normally little called upon – indeed the record of most religions with regard to these issues is not regarded as good, and so it is not surprising that many see religion as the suppressor of human rights rather than as their advocate.

Personal responsibility seen as the pursuit of autonomy and individualism
This relates also to the newer concern for a holistic way of life which takes personal experience, integrity, health and good relationships seriously. Religion is often castigated for encouraging an attitude of dependence upon authority or tradition, which is at loggerheads with the attitude of taking responsibility for oneself. Religion has been accused indeed of keeping people docile and naive. Assertiveness training has rarely featured much in religious traditions. They have often not promoted the idea that human nature is basically sound if encouraged, but rather emphasized the need for a concept of divine grace. This does not seem to fit in at all with the demand for autonomy.

The spiritual dimension seen as separate from religion
It may seem that the movement just discernible towards 'spirituality' would be wholly to the benefit of religion, yet it is not necessarily so. The word spiritual has become for many fundamentally dissociated from religion and so serves to encourage an alternative, one that is more attractive because lacking both definition and the incubus associated with religion. The search for spirituality can become diverted also into cults or fascination with the occult, and if it avoids these dangers it can become simply another form of aesthetic experience and move away from the major religious traditions, so that the arts become a kind of substitute for religion.

The 'Green Movement' is often critical of religion
The 'Green Movement' is not necessarily the friend of religion – it can displace it as understood within the great religious traditions, giving

rise to a neo-paganism which challenges them. It is deeply critical in particular of the exploitation of the earth which it often considers the three semitic religions are guilty of pursuing – Judaism, Christianity and Islam. Christianity especially has come in for great criticism as being the major religion in the history of Western civilization.

The problem of global evil and suffering can be seen as an indictment of religion

Concern about the destructiveness of human nature is paralleled by awareness of the enormity of global evil and suffering, aggravated by the potential powers now within human grasp, and has been augmented by the speed and change of life and the challenges and displacements this brings. All this, often broadcast by the media too, has had a detrimental effect on religion causing the age-old cry of the heart, 'If there is a God why all this suffering?' to be raised with ever-greater seriousness and urgency. The dilemma is worse still in that religion often appears to be inextricably and centrally involved in the perpetration of crime and the proliferation of human misery and damage to the environment.

Damaging criticism of organized religion

The shortcomings of organized religions in having within their ranks and amongst their leadership large numbers who do not live up to their beliefs have had a serious effect on attitudes towards religion. A huge battery of criticism is levelled against religion including charges of hypocrisy, smugness, dogmatism, narrow-mindedness, imperialism, naivety and prejudice. Criticism of religious institutions, leadership and policies is rife, and religious people have on the whole been tardy in responding creatively to justified charges and pointing out the inappropriateness of false charges; an approach of burying one's head in the sand has been a characteristic of many religious people. Hatred of religious bigotry, and of the violence and injustice it can produce, is a major reason for people turning their backs on religion. This question will therefore be discussed in some depth in Chapter 3.

The radical secularism of society

All these factors fan the bias against religion and produce a fundamental obstacle for RE – that of the radical secularism of Western society. What I mean by this is the prevalence of the assumption that religion does not matter because it is not true – it is an illusion. God is banished and the spiritual dimension to life, if there is one, is simply an aspect of human personality which human beings create for themselves.

In such a society it is not 'done' to admit to taking religion seriously. David Hay, who was director of the Religious Experience in Education Project at Nottingham University, draws attention to the taboo about religion in British society. Research conducted at the Alister Hardy Research Centre suggests:

a culturally mediated prejudice. It is based on a conviction that religious ways of interpreting reality simply must be mistaken because they appear to conflict with, or be irrelevant to, cherished and successful scientific paradigms. It too easily discards the spiritual dimension of human experience as attributable to some kind of personal or social pathology and it creates a taboo a bit like the one there used to be about sex.

(Hammond *et al.* 1990: 205)

A question of vocabulary: secularist and secular

It is important to note at this point two very different ways in which the word 'secular' can be used. One meaning relates to this-worldly matters – how things get done, efficiency, practical points, anything to do with what we see, hear, touch, feel and taste, how we find out about these things, and so on. But the word can also be used to denote the idea that religion does not matter because it is not true.

The distinction is a very significant one, because all the great religions of the world have emphasized how important it is that religion and life are bound up together, that religion does not hive off into some remote corner unrelated to the real world; all religions do bother about the secular in the first sense of the word – about how life is actually lived and what people are and do, and not just about what they say and believe. But if secular is used in the second sense, as meaning the abandonment of religion, it is obviously the enemy of religion. Its presence will indicate hostility towards religion and make it very difficult for people to take religion seriously.

Some Christian theologians (e.g. Macquarrie 1968: 20f) have tried to indicate the difference between these two uses of 'secular' by coining specific terms: secularity and secular as referring to the straightforward neutral sense, and secularism and secularist to the anti-religious stance. Although this distinction is not widely known, I think it is a most helpful one because when words mean radically different things it is useful to have some way of distinguishing them outwardly.

Is society really completely secularist?

The widespread presence of secularism does not mean that religion is totally eclipsed or reduced to the status of a literally insignificant minority interest. The legacy of Christianity in the West is still at work. Its roots are tenacious and most people still wish to acknowledge the ideal of Christian values, as George Carey, Archbishop of Canterbury, noted at the 1991 2nd Malvern Conference, 'I would deny that Britain is post-Christian – I think that people have basic Christian values which they would be very reluctant to let go.'[1]

You may like to consider how far you agree with this view.

Michael Polanyi draws attention to the way in which people can unconsciously share certain basic assumptions or beliefs even if, at a conscious level, they express something else. He suggests a reason for this – the power of habit: 'People can carry on a great tradition while proposing a philosophy which denies its premises. For the adherents of a great tradition are largely unaware of their own premises, which lie deeply embedded in the unconscious foundations of practice' (Polanyi 1964: 76).

He considers that our society is a secularist one, not in its values but in its rejection of the beliefs supporting those values. In this way we may be able to see that he would both agree and disagree with the Archbishop's statement. Values enshrined within Christianity are still widely held, but this does not mean that Christianity is believable in for the vast majority. The vehicle may still be moving forward under the impact of the initial push, but if the source of the pushing is removed, how long will it continue in motion? Are there other pushing agencies available, and if so will they push in the same direction?

This poses the interesting question which only the future can resolve: how long can values survive without the beliefs which sustain them? Peter Fuller, the atheist art critic who died in 1990, pursued the question rigorously as to how art can flourish in a secular society. The discontinuity with religion which he saw as the dilemma of modern art he takes for granted, and even a cursory knowledge of twentieth-century art confirms this. He asks, 'Can work be reinvested with its spiritual-aesthetic dimension when tradition has in fact gone, and we have lost the illusions of faith?' (Fuller 1990: 297).

Impact of secularism on schools

It would be surprising if education escaped being profoundly influenced by secularism. Schools may, and often do, challenge society, but they cannot avoid also reflecting it in the same way as revolutionaries normally rebel only against some of the characteristics of a society – others they have internalized too deeply.

In schools the assumptions of society show themselves in three ways: through what has been called the explicit, the implicit and the nul curricula.

The explicit curriculum

The explicit curriculum refers to what is openly expressed as the intention of the school, and to what is actually taught – the content per se which is put across.

In the majority of schools this is mostly devoid of any reference to religion; it is carved up either into subject areas which by definition rule out any necessary reference to religion, or into topics or integrated approaches which normally have little specifically religious content. The subject area RE continues to have low status. The position is still worse because, in many schools, most of the RE time available is spent on content only marginally linked with religion: on moral and cultural education of one kind or another or social studies in which the information conveyed about different religions tends to be of a largely sociological nature, describing other people's customs and beliefs.

It is difficult to avoid the conclusion that with regard to the explicit curriculum, RE has to fight for its life – constant vigilance is the necessary price it pays for retaining any foothold at all in a curriculum groaning under the weight of other priorities. In the majority of schools RE is, for political as well as pragmatic reasons, there by sufferance – occupying time which most teachers would quite happily see spent on something else of more pressing importance.

The implicit curriculum

The implicit curriculum is what is received through the total impact of what actually happens in school. It covers attitudes, relationships, behaviour, selection of content, manner of teaching, way of speaking to pupils, and so forth. The implicit curriculum includes the messages conveyed by the ethos of the school and the total approach to pupils, as well as to how the explicit curriculum is delivered.

One powerful message put across by the curriculum in most schools is that knowledge can be divided into compartments. This has the effect of divorcing religion – like other subjects – from the rest of the curriculum. If practical considerations make it desirable to put RE with another subject, then the one chosen is usually humanities or social studies, it being taken for granted that religion is an aspect of what people believe. It is assumed to have nothing to do with, for example, science, maths or PE.

We need to remember that the implicit curriculum works especially through style of teaching. Pupils can pick up many notions from the very methods we use. Thus discussion lessons can often give the impression that everything is just a matter of opinion – there need be no rigour, for 'it's all subjective anyway'. Talk of problem-solving becomes translated into a message to pupils that all matters of controversy can and should be resolved; the idea that not everything is a problem to be solved is barely entertained. The use of role-play can similarly often give the impression that facades are more important than being oneself, acting a part more significant than reflective evaluation.

Thus the implicit curriculum rests on beliefs and values also – not necessarily the same as those behind the explicit curriculum, for there is often considerable double-talk and hypocrisy, mostly unintentional but sometimes not. The existence of a powerful taboo against religion in society as a whole, together with the lack of opportunity given by the explicit curriculum for questioning the taboo, ensures that most of this implicit curriculum operates against religion – against its being taken seriously at all.

The nul curriculum

The nul curriculum exists by reason of the fact that it does not exist – it is what is conveyed by omission, avoidance, bypassing, as well as by ridiculing, criticizing, and putting-down. Its allies are boredom, distraction, prejudice and narrowness of outlook. It refers to excluded knowledge, failure to give pupils opportunities to appreciate, areas left out of consideration, ideas not addressed, concepts not offered or discussed. Pupils cannot think about or develop sensitivity and discernment concerning what they are in deepest ignorance about, even as not to appreciate that there is anything of which they are ignorant is an even greater indication of the degree of deprivation. It also relates to the way in which subjects are not presented – to processes and procedures and methods which are rarely or never employed. This is not neutral – it indoctrinates more successfully than anything else. As Maria Harris has noted:

The point of including the nul curriculum is, of course, that ignorance – not knowing something – is never neutral. If we do not know about something or do not realise what is addressed can be understood in another manner or seen through another lens, it skews our viewpoint; it limits our options; it clouds our perspective.

(Harris 1988: 20–1)

Religion is most notable by its absence, and, where it appears, by the omission of any serious discussion of its truth-claims. A good example of this is the way in which the national campaign against AIDS has been conducted. It is on the whole assumed that any religious considerations are irrelevant. Indeed it is remarkable how little the question of any revision of a hedonist philosophy of life has even been raised, never mind taken seriously and discussed. Concern about moral or spiritual or religious attitudes of responsibility with regard to sexual activity has been conspicuous by its absence. The problem of AIDS is seen as mechanistic, and therefore mechanistic solutions are all that are offered.

The scales are not neatly balanced as between secularism and religion in our society. In most societies the world has known, the balance has been in favour of religion; in ours it is the other way round. This is the background against which RE has to happen.

Failure to meet the secularist challenge

Reaction against the privileged status of religion

It is interesting to note that there appears to be great resistance to acknowledging the full impact of secularism on schools. The real situation RE has to contend with is now very different from how many, perhaps most, people have generally thought it to be. Historically, the Christian churches had exceptionally close links with education: indeed in the early nineteenth century almost all the impetus for setting up schools and teacher-training establishments and extending schooling to all children came from the churches. The teaching of religion was always a feature of the curriculum, and until 1988 was the one subject legally required.

In recent decades there has, however, been more and more chafing at this privileged position. That the subject was in fact normally accorded Cinderella status mattered little to the many who objected to its being there at all. The charge of indoctrination has been regularly levelled against it with great force, especially because of the holding of assemblies for worship which is still required by law. Many have accused schools of trying to prop up ailing churches and fill empty pews, and Christian teachers in particular have been assumed to be heavily biased, teaching for commitment to their particular brand of religion and intolerant towards other religions and other world views. In his book *Better Schools: a Values Perspective* (1990) Clive Beck devotes a chapter to religious bias alongside chapters on racism, ethnic bias, sexism and class bias. There is no mention at all of secularist bias. The omission is significant: the danger is perceived as entirely pertaining to religious believers, and illustrates very well the hold which a secular view has on him and on the educational world in Britain and in the United States.

Indoctrination into secularism

Most people do not in fact recognize the secularist bias precisely because it *is* ubiquitous and so forcefully put across. It has often and justly been observed that real indoctrination goes undetected except by those who for other reasons have cause to question the content of the beliefs and values into which they are being pushed. Most people in our society have no cause whatever to question the truth of what is put across in the teaching of science, English or history, for example, and therefore the indoctrination which can go on there is largely unheeded. The fear and suspicion of religious indoctrination is a most powerful indicator of the opposite trend being uppermost. Most people have not been indoctrinated into religious faith but into a questioning or ignoring of religion as basically superseded if not actually false.

David Hay calls for a 'de-indoctrination' from secularism (Hay 1990: 109). He summarizes the kind of attitudes and assumptions towards religion which a majority of children when they arrive in school for the first time will be likely already to have assimilated.

They will have some feeling that the sacred books of the religions are really fairy stories, that religious people are out of date and a bit silly, that the clergy are figures of fun. All of this will have been picked up from a multitude of cues within the family – coyness in speaking about religion, sentimental talk at Christmas-time that equates religion with belief in Santa Claus, contempt for the hypocrisy (real or imagined) of religious officials, and the equation of religion with fanaticism and political reaction. Where children do not carry these assumptions inside them, it is because they have been brought up in an enclave that is struggling against the weight of secular pressure.

(Hay 1990: 96–7)

This is the situation which RE must address.

The task for RE

For many – perhaps most – children, their schooling does not greatly increase their understanding of religion. A large comprehensive school in an area little affected by a multi-faith presence could report colossal ignorance of the most elementary 'facts' concerning Christianity. Thus in a class of 31 fourth-formers, 14 pupils did not know in any terms however simple, the significance of Good Friday nor 9 of Easter Sunday; 21 could not name one book in the New Testament and 27 one book in the Jewish Bible.

What is even more instructive was the reaction of staff and visiting RE specialists to this information. It did not trouble them much. Such 'facts' are unimportant. From one point of view I agree – I do not think we should be concerned about teaching a basic kit of factual information. Does it really matter that pupils know Jesus had 12 disciples and what their names were? But what *is* serious is what this kind of ignorance reveals about the level of understanding concerning religion which they have. What Good Friday and Easter Sunday stand for is not something to be taught as such but something which pupils with any understanding at all of Christianity would automatically acquire en route. The equivalent level of ignorance in another subject might be not to know the name of Shakespeare or anything at all about evolution or to have any skills of basic measuring or to know that Asia is a continent. It is not these facts per se which are important, but the lack of experience of literature, science, mathematics and geography that ignorance of these facts betrays.

RE has a most important and wide-ranging task to fulfil. It cannot do this unless it first challenges the secularist assumption so endemic in our society.

Note

1. Reported in the *Malvern Gazette*, 19 July 1991, p. 1, under the heading 'Elgar's Malvern held the key'.

CHAPTER 3

Giving religion a chance: the formidable case against secularism

The acknowledged purpose of RE is to help pupils towards an understanding of religion so that they can reflect on it in an informed way. But they cannot do this if their minds and emotions are already sealed tight against it – if they assume that religion is outdated and not worth studying.

As the previous chapter showed, many aspects of growing up in today's world encourage such a dismissive attitude to religion. In order therefore to teach RE effectively, we need to be very clear about how shaky the secularist stance actually is, and how strong is the case for an openness towards religion.

It is a matter of practical importance that teachers can argue this case. Specific work on it in secondary schools is often essential in order to break down resistance to the subject. Many 'awkward' classes become much less so if some exploration in depth is attempted of the kind of points discussed in this chapter.

It is important also that awareness of this argument informs what primary school teachers do concerning RE. In all sorts of situations it is called for, not only with children, but with other staff, parents and governors.

RE is on a much stronger wicket than it is usually given credit for, provided it is open in character. I shall return to this point at the end of the chapter on page 35.

The nature of assumptions

Two preliminary points need to be made before setting out the argument against secularism.

First, we all have to live and act *as if* we were sure and *as if* we had reliable knowledge. We have to stand somewhere as we decide the next step forward. Yet whether we think of ourselves as secularist or as religious, we cannot be absolutely certain in such a way that our certainty cannot be challenged by other people. Delusion is possible for everyone: *feeling* certain does not mean that therefore the world is as we think it is. All of us can make mistakes.

The unavoidable fact of the matter is that both religion and secularism are stances. To vary the analogy, not to be religious is already to have invested money in what is as high a risk venture as an investment in religion.

Secondly, it is impossible to prove assumptions, but this does not mean that we are just locked into a position for ever. Experience of life, and genuine discussion with people of other views, can enable us to add to, and revise, and even occasionally to give up, aspects of the stance which we have adopted so far. What is needed is a willingness to be open to fresh possibilities – to be prepared for a constant voyage of exploration.

We need to look at assumptions, seeing whether we think they really are justified, and if so, do they really lead to the positions which we at the moment think they lead to. For example, if we think that a basic assumption is that people matter as persons, and that this is justified, then what follows?

(a) does this entail a secularist view of the universe and of life as a whole?
(b) does it leave the options open for religion?
(c) does it maybe lead more naturally to a religious view of the world?

The case against secularism

At this point we can move to the case against secularism. RE needs to sow seeds of doubt into the current widespread acceptability of secularism. Suggestions are made in Chapter 13 on how the possibility of a different perspective can be approached in the classroom, and it might be helpful to read these two chapters in conjunction.

In Chapter 2, 11 aspects of contemporary society which can cause trouble for religion were outlined. Three of these are of major significance: scientism, relativism and religious intolerance. The others are largely dependent on them.

Secularism based on a mistaken view of science

Figure 3.1 offers a possible starting-point for explaining why science has for many people ruled out religion. The root problem here is the question of how we can arrive at absolutely certain and reliable knowledge. Scientific method, using experiment and reasoning, has led to a marvellous extension of knowledge. But it has also led to assumptions which cause religion to be ignored, doubted and re-interpreted.

This is because of certain -isms or hardened stances. The diagram gives three:

Figure 3.1   The fact-belief divide

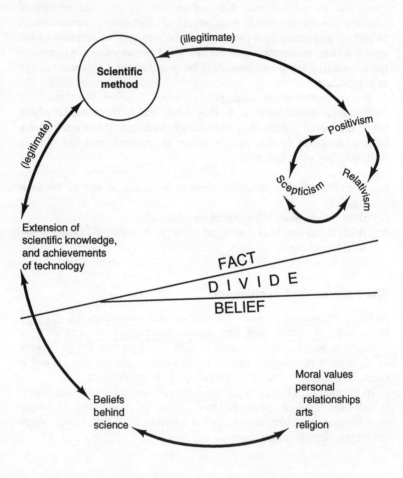

1. *Positivism* is the name given to the philosophy based on the principle that all claims to knowledge must be scientifically provable – there must be 'positive proof'. This philosophy was developed first in the seventeenth century and it has become increasingly influential ever since.
2. *Scepticism* is the familiar name given to the appropriateness of doubting the reliability of something until it is proved beyond shadow of doubt.
3. *Relativism* is a stance which assumes that opinions which cannot

be tested scientifically are just subjective and relative to the particular context giving rise to them, to cultural upbringing and different individual and group experience.

All these -isms together set up a serious fact/belief divide whereby facts are regarded as objective, reliable and unbiased, and values, principles and beliefs as subjective, unreliable and probably biased. On the doubtful side of this line come most of the things which people care most about – matters associated with personal relationships, the arts, moral issues and religion.

The fact/belief divide is powerfully at work today as for example the debate on the original National Curriculum proposals with regard to the teaching of history and geography has amply attested.[1] The way that many politicians and others have called for the teaching of 'facts' and wish to throw out all matters relating to 'mere opinion' such as environmental concerns, shows how unaware many people are that there is any problem with regard to the reliability of facts or the possibility of there being evidence supporting beliefs and values. The fact/belief divide is simply taken for granted.

Yet the positivism which is ultimately responsible for it is deeply flawed in three ways: it is *illogical, unscientific* and *exclusivist.*

It is illogical
It contradicts itself. It claims that proof is necessary for knowledge, yet cannot prove itself to be true. It appeals to reason, but in order to reason we have got to take something for granted as a starting point and this cannot be proved. Another way of expressing the same idea is that logic is like kicking a ball – it may go in a straight line, but if the direction is wrong it will not help the team to win the game.

But how do we know in which direction to head? There is no proof on which to draw reliably for that. It rests on what is bound to be, to some extent, subjective assessment, as in playing a game when there are rules and communal experience to draw on, but ultimately it depends on the players' awareness and skill.

It is unscientific
Positivism contradicts actual scientific experience and findings. Many leading scientists do not consider that science can give absolutely reliable and unchallengeable knowledge.[2] Increasingly today, they are accepting that scientific pronouncements have an unavoidable element, not only of subjectivity, but also of informed guesswork about them. This is because of the nature of the world which is so complex and has what appears to be an inbuilt indeterminism or chance.

An anecdote told by a scientist well summarizes this element of randomness: 'When I visited the European Medium Range Weather Forecasting Centre they told me, 'We can predict the weather accurately provided it doesn't do anything unexpected'' (Stewart 1989: 131). To insist therefore that science provides cast-iron knowledge is to *believe* in a mirage. Science cannot provide that kind of certainty.

Furthermore, it is often overlooked that we can only apply scientific method to a tiny fraction of the impressions upon which we act. This very selectivity of what the scientist chooses to notice and work upon is another reason for saying that science is to some extent subjective.

Besides this, the whole process of scientific investigation is based on a series of assumptions which the scientist makes, very often at an unconscious level. If those assumptions were seriously challenged the scientist would not be able to operate. (See suggested reading in Chapter 13, p. 202 n. 1.)

It is exclusivist

A positivist view of science excludes an enormous area of life. Scientific method is obviously extemely valuable for finding out about things amenable to observation, experiment and logical progression of thought. To say however that this route supplies the *only* reliable way to knowledge is grossly to overstep its boundaries. It is in fact to be very dogmatic and to try to say something about every other way of knowledge, and every other thing to be known. For by insisting it is the *only* way to knowledge it is dismissing other ways as unimportant, irrelevant and probably misleading.

This is a wide agenda. Where is the scientific evidence to support so wide an onslaught? The intrusion of the single word 'only' is a serious fault.

This challenge of scientific method to ways of knowing is probably more significant today than the well-publicized clashes between religion and science associated with Galileo and with Darwin. It was indeed Darwin's wife, Emma, herself a scientist, who pointed out the real danger in the use of scientific method when she asked him: 'May not the habit in scientific pursuits of believing nothing till it is proved, influence your mind too much in other things which cannot be proved in the same way? and which if true are likely to be above our comprehension?'[3]

Doubt can play a very useful role in resisting credulity and naivety, but to argue that only if you doubt can you arrive at the truth (a position of scepticism) is to disregard the question of what is to be known. In getting to know a person for example, to insist on doubting everything he or she does and says all the time will soon put an end to any effective relationship – doubt is simply not appropriate. We get to know people by accepting them, by trusting them – the opposite of doubt – and by 'giving them the benefit of the doubt' indeed, unless exceedingly strong evidence to the contrary presents itself.

Exclusivism frequently occurs unintentionally but nevertheless effectively through the teaching of separate subject areas which tends to give the impression that they offer a complete explanation of something.

Secularism based on relativism

The fact that religion won't just go away – that it is a phenomenon to be explained – has led those influenced by positivism to explain religion as entirely a matter of social and cultural conditioning and outward show: basically religion is a kind of cultural dressing-up game. This is a view of religion which is seen as primarily like fashion – what people 'put on'. Such 'sartorial' religion is taken seriously indeed, because it deals with deep human needs, desires and questions, and the level of conditioning can be deeply internalized. It can nevertheless be seen as a kind of charade whereby societies have in the past been held together but which, as a charade, is replaceable by something not involving the pretence element. For there is no truth-element involved in religion. It is all a matter of cultural focusing.

Relativism draws attention to what Aristotle noticed long ago: 'Fire burns both in Hellas and in Persia; but men's ideas of right and wrong vary from place to place.'[4] People brought up in different places and having different life experiences will come up with different opinions. If they had been born into a different culture they would have believed something quite different.

Before responding to this objection against religion it is important first to acknowledge the insights it brings – insights often neglected in earlier centuries. Just as Figure 3.1 draws attention to the proper use of science, so there is something extremely valuable and 'right' about a relativist approach, provided it does not overstep itself and pretend it has the whole truth. These insights include awareness of:

1. an amazing diversity of views – even within one society this is so, and even more so on a global scale;
2. the importance of context in understanding why people are as they are, and believe as they do, and assume what they do;
3. the possibility of self-delusion: we *could* be conditioned into mistaken views;
4. the importance of non-judgemental attitudes towards people;
5. a style of education which encourages individual learning skills rather than teacher-dominated presentation of content. As such it seems particularly appropriate for a time of rapid change and the need to unlearn dogmatism.

These insights are muddled, however, if the little word 'only' creeps in to the way in which they are expressed. 'What you believe is *only* a matter of where you were born, and what people around you believe.' The short maxim, 'It's *all* relative' expresses the same exclusivism. In this way beliefs and values are denied their claim to be real knowledge.

There are at least three strong arguments against relativism as a stance which it is important that we help pupils to understand.

It is illogical

Relativism actually bows itself out. For if all opinions are relative, then the view that all opinions are relative is itself relative and therefore not true in itself. So if it is true it is false.

This is like the puzzle which can quite infuriate children as well as adults: one side of the paper has written on it: 'The sentence on the other side of this piece of paper is not correct', and the other side has this sentence, 'The sentence on the other side is correct'. Which side is right?

The point is of course that the puzzle itself is false in setting up an impossible situation. Similarly, the relativist stance does not work unless it makes an exception of itself which denies its own principle.

In my experience children in primary schools as well as older pupils not only can see this point, but also enjoy doing so – they find it intriguing.

It is exclusivist

Relativism as a stance ignores what is central to religion – its truth-claims. It assumes that there can be no evidence worth discussing concerning the truth of religious beliefs.

This is to misrepresent religion. Religious faith is based on what is believed to be true. Within Judaism, Christianity and Islam, faith is a response to what is claimed as revelation about the nature of reality. Within religions of Indian origin, such as Hinduism, Buddhism and Sikhism, certain views of reality being as it is are taken for granted, such as *dharma* – the existence of a moral law, and *karma* – the impact of this on individuals according to how much they fulfil or fail to fulfil *dharma*, and *samsara* – the process of reincarnation. These are not regarded as just ideas in the mind, or a figment of the collective imagination, but as true.

The attractiveness of the cultural explanation of religion is that it appears to account for the diversity in religious practices and beliefs without the necessity to get involved in controversy. Cultures are like colours – we can have any number on our palette without any problems. We don't need to enter the troubled waters of religious truth-claims. Yet as the sociologist Peter Berger has pointed out, while a sociological perspective on religion is extremely illuminating, fascinating and insightful, it can be misread as an argument against religion (Berger 1969: 9). It can seem to offer a completely adequate explanation of religion which bypasses what religious believers have always insisted upon as the truth. Such matters become safely and clinically bracketed away into the equation: knowledge = understanding of religious people (who believe x, y, or z). The possibility that knowledge = understanding of x, y or z is ruled out.

This is to be just as dogmatic as relativists accuse religious people of being. It is to risk leaving out what religion is really about, rather like music without sound, or mathematics without numbers.

It could be destructive in its consequences

The pervasiveness of a version of religion as culturally cosmetic subtly does a lot of harm to people; it can be very dismissive and hurtful, marginalizing what makes a religious person tick. This can have the effect of isolating that person and creating the ghetto mentality. It can also cause self-crisis in which the mainspring of a person's belief system is called into doubt and inwardly crumbles without anything strong and important to take its place.

Fear of this happening is a prime reason for some religious people's failure to relate to other people's views; they therefore take refuge in intransigent attitudes often referred to by other people as fundamentalist or extremist. Often, therefore, relativism produces, through reaction to it, precisely what it sets out to destroy: increased dogmatism.

More often the impact of dogmatically held relativism on other people is to cause them to waver, feel uncertain and drift into what they feel they can be sure about – mostly in Western society a materialist attitude to life, or perhaps pursuing a lifestance which thinks it has avoided value judgements. Of course it has not; for example, with regard to moral issues, the typically relativist view that there are no absolutes is itself a stance based on assumptions which it is possible to challenge.

It is also a potentially destructive one. Put in a nutshell, it puts the whole concept of justice into jeopardy. If all is relative, then protest against racism, sexism and so forth is at root an arbitrary subjective one – why shouldn't somebody be racist if all is a matter of mere opinion or expediency? If there are no absolutes or eternal values, then the moral imperative behind such movements evaporates into thin air.

The appeal to human rights, which has provided the primary motive power behind freedom movements throughout the world, has a non-discardable moral aspect to it which denies the relativist stance. This moral underlay even shows itself in the fervour and intensity with which relativists dismiss those who disagree with them as 'dogmatic'.

Values are necessarily grounded in belief. The relativism of values seems so sensible and convincing until we reflect on what this implies, namely that what we feel passionately about with regard to truth or justice or purpose of life has no justification apart from the fact that we happen to think like this.

This consideration leads us on to the third major argument supporting secularism, that based on a lively concern for justice, peace, goodwill and genuine respect for people.

Secularism based on hatred of religious intolerance

A major reason why people decide to have nothing to do with religion is that, in the name of religion, much injustice, violence and bigotry has been perpetrated. An example is the writer, A.N. Wilson, whose rejection of religion was on account of its encouragement of so much evil. An extract from his booklet, printed in *The Observer* on 2 June 1991, caused it to receive a record mailing from readers, many of whom supported his 'boo-ing' of all religious leaders as so many cackling geese.[5]

This is so widespread a reason for rejecting religion, present in all strata of society and amongst all types of people, young and old, that any RE which fails to help pupils think clearly about it is seriously deficient.

I want to express this point very strongly indeed. The sentimentality conveyed by the careful selection of only 'nice' aspects of religion to present to pupils causes them to see it – and perhaps believe in it – as just a fairy story unrelated to the real world. For in the real world there is a nasty side to religion, and religious people can become ogres. Religion is responsible for much injustice affecting ordinary everyday life as well as newspaper-headline material. Religious people often too easily run away from this, but school RE must not.

Various considerations however undermine the force of this objection to religion. To dismiss religion because of its potential for evil is to risk being onesided and exclusivist, committing a logical error, failing to appreciate the nature of religion, and mistaking the real culprit responsible for such unedifying behaviour. I shall discuss each of these considerations in turn.

A one-sided and exclusivist view

This objection to religion is highly selective in what it chooses to notice about religion; it ignores all its beneficial aspects. Religion has been, and is, capable of sustaining some of the finest civilizations the world has seen, and it has attracted many of the most brilliant and high-minded people who have ever lived. To ignore what has been regarded as central by such civilizations and persons can hardly claim to be a fair and objective approach.

If religion has produced its hypocrites and bigots, it has also produced people like St Francis and Sri Ramana (see Chapter 6). To notice only the bad, when there is so much good, may be seen as a jaundiced view.

A logical error

There is no necessary connection between evil and religion, either a logical one or on factual grounds. To argue that religion *can* go wrong, and therefore should be rejected, is like saying that because surgery *can* go wrong, therefore all surgeons should be pensioned off. Eggs can become poisoned, therefore eggs should no longer form part of a staple diet . . . !

To blame religion for what could be people's failure to live up to it is not logical. Just because the vicar down the road is selfish and insensitive, I am not justified in concluding that therefore religion is bad. Another explanation of the vicar's selfishness is possible, namely that he does not live up to his religion and is therefore a poor representative of it.

In fact this is the case because Christianity does not teach, 'Thou shalt put thyself first'. If the vicar thinks it does he is mistaken.

Appreciating the nature of religion

If the risk of eating eggs being poisoned is extremely high, then we should be justified in rejecting eating them. People who oppose religion on the grounds of its intolerance and bigotry think that the risks are very high. This is where we need to turn to the factual evidence.

This indicates clearly that religion has no monopoly of evil. The blatant example of Stalin has vividly shown the world this. It suggests therefore that there is another explanation for such behaviour. The diagnosis is misleading if it gives the impression that there is a straight connection between the expression of religious belief and bigotry.

It is essential to appreciate that when religious people show bigotry, intolerance, narrow-mindedness, violence and all other such forms of evil, they are in fact betraying the religion which they say they uphold. They stand condemned by the very tenets of their religions unless that religion is in itself a perverse and cancerous development which will in time kill what gave it birth in any case. All the great world religions have very high moral codes which reach out towards a quality of authentic selflessness and love for all others which is the antithesis of selfishness and hatred. (See Chapter 8 on this.)

The sternest critics of religion have often been found within religions. Religious people themselves, because of the strength and depth of their religious convictions, have appreciated most thoroughly the extent of the abuse of religion. This is because such bigotry and violence are the result not of being too religious, but of not being religious enough, of superficiality, of mistaken ideas about what religion is about. As Edward Hulmes quoted in his book in this series, *Education and Cultural Diversity:*

The great teachers of religion have always had to get rid of the useless lumber which accumulates in its progress – the rigid dogmatism, the narrow legalism, the mechanical rites, the silly superstitions which may become a substitute for religious life.[6]

Many religious people are as worried as non-religious people about the abuse of religion. Speaking about the resurgence of interest in religion which many people see in the world today, the Chief Rabbi, Jonathan Sacks, asks 'Whether religious revival might be not a refreshing breeze but a destructive hurricane.' He goes on to note how 'revolutionary leaders have enlisted religious passion . . . it is an explosive combination. War becomes a holy struggle against the demonic other. Terror is sanctified. Hatred becomes a form of piety' (Sacks 1991: 79).

The real culprit
It is not religion, nor its truth-claims, that is the trouble, but rather attitudes of selfishness and possessiveness – of thinking of religion or of truth as an entity which we have and somebody else does not have.

The distinction between religion and exclusivism is crucial. People can believe in something strongly without assuming that therefore other people are wrong to believe something else. Apparent contradictions often turn out to be paradoxes – insight relating to different circumstances and experiences. What never fails to harm is pride in being right. People may actually be right but that is not an excuse for smugness, and non-interest in what anybody else thinks except to knock them down and force them to acknowledge the superiority of one's own views.

When this happens, the rightness of the belief or value or action is not infrequently forgotten altogether and ignored. The nineteenth century headteacher who knew he was right that God loved everyone, and would therefore thrash any boy who did not acknowledge that, had in fact paid almost no attention whatever to the content of his belief. A moment's reflection would have helped him to see the folly, cruelty, and hypocrisy of trying to force someone to acknowledge this.

Many people suffer from the same disease of thinking they must be right all the time, and they must push their rightness onto other people. This is what does the damage – not religion – for it can be seen in all walks of life wherever people are emotionally involved. Because religion appeals so strongly to the emotions and to life commitment, it is a special temptation for religious people. (See Chapter 8 for further discussion of this.)

Conclusion: giving religion a fair hearing

The argument developed in this chapter is of vital importance for the teaching of RE because it concerns deep-seated anxieties with religion which people have today. These must be addressed in such a way as to help pupils to see that the questions are open ones, worthy of their attention throughout life. Religion deserves a fair hearing, and effective RE will see that it gets that. It deserves it because:

1. Unlike positivism and relativism, it is not based on an illogical position. It does not assume any proof demonstrating its validity, and therefore it cannot be knocked down for not offering it. Of course religion can be challenged, but there are plenty of sound reasons *for* religion.[7]

2. To consider religion carefully is not to be dogmatic and exclusivist, but actually the opposite, for it allows an important area of experience – both communal and private – to be explored instead of being ignored or reinterpreted in terms inappropriate to it. Religion is thus allowed to speak for itself.

3. Religion *can* be creative. It can afford motivation as hardly anything else can, and its influence can help both society and individuals to a fuller and more satisfying form of life.

Whether school RE reflects the obvious case for it depends upon the openness with which it is approached and the style of teaching adopted. And this brings us to the next chapter.

Notes

1. E.g. the statement by Kenneth Clarke on 14 January 1991 following final proposals from his curriculum advisers – reported in *The Times*, 15 January 1991, by David Tytler under the heading 'Geography lessons to deal in facts, not opinions, Clarke rules'.

2. See, e.g. Peter Hodgson, 1986, *The Implications of Quantum Physics*; Ian Stewart, 1989, *Does God Play Dice – the New Mathematics of Chaos*; Fritjof Capra, 1982, *The Turning Point – Science, Society and the Rising Culture*.

3. Quoted from Irving Stone's biography of Darwin *The Origin*, in Jonathan Fisher, 1986: 33.

4. *The Nicomachean Ethics*, V (vii) 2.

5. A.N. Wilson in 'Why I have given up religion'. An extract from his 1991 book *Against Religion: why we should try to live without it*, extracted in *The Observer*, 26 May 1991: p.49f. The following week's edition (2 June 1991) carried a full page of comments 'For or against God?' – 'one of our biggest postbags in recent years', p. 21.

6. Quoted from H.J. Paton, 1955, *The Modern Predicament* in Hulmes 1989: 150.

7. Further reading might include for example: Gillian Ryeland (ed.), 1991, *Beyond Reasonable Doubt*; A booklet by Richard Swinburne, 1986, *Evidence for God*; Peter Vardy, 1988, *And if it's true?*; Richard Holloway, 1988, *Crossfire – Faith and Doubt in an Age of Certainty*; John Houghton, 1988, *Does God Play Dice? A Look at the Story of the*

Universe; Brian Hebblethwaite, 1988, *The Ocean of Truth – A Defence of Objective Theism*; Also, Short Occasional Papers (Farmington Institute in Oxford) e.g.: Russell Stannard, 1985, 'Science, psychology and the existence of God'; John T. Watson, 1986, 'Recovery of belief in God'.

CHAPTER 4

The purpose of RE

Secularist influence within RE

The secularist assumption is challengeable, as we have seen, and thus the ground is cleared for a serious consideration of religion. Yet much of the RE of the past 30 years has been strangely reluctant to offer the challenge.

To some extent this is because secularist attitudes have invaded RE, as they have influenced the thinking of many religious people in general, often in unsuspected ways because of the level of secularist indoctrination in our society.

RE teachers have responded positively to many of the insights of the modern world but in the process they have sometimes allowed the pendulum to swing too far to the other side. Table 4.1 sets out a number of features of RE which illustrate this trend. Thus for example many have deemed it necessary – in order to make RE relevant, acceptable and interesting today – to downplay work on religious vocabulary and explicit beliefs. This has led to considerable confusion as to what religion is anyway, because any necessary reference to the divine, to God, to the transcendent has been removed from it. This has not encouraged clear thinking on a number of other points of vital importance to RE, such as the question of openness and religious commitment presumed by many to be incompatible.

A close look at the points listed in Table 4.1 will show the level of confusion operating. Thus the two columns of section 2 are not opposites in the way that the two columns of section 1 appear to be. Furthermore, the points under the first column of section 2 have many inbuilt inconsistencies. An emphasis, for example, on observable practices does not fit neatly alongside an emphasis on implicit religion.

Effect on Teaching
All this has profoundly affected those who teach RE in both primary and secondary schools, some of whom really do not seem to know what the subject is about. The goal-posts seem constantly to be moving – indeed they are often told there are no goal-posts. It is a bit like trying to paint a picture with no picture frame at all in mind – endless possibilities mean confusion and distraction and difficulty in applying oneself to anything.

*Table 4.1   **Features of recent religious education***

Section 1: *Important and helpful features*

educationally open	NOT	indoctrinatory
promoting understanding	NOT	engaging in propaganda
multi-faith and global	NOT	narrowly Christian or parochial
skills	NOT	ill-understood facts
relevance	NOT	impersonally academic
relating to whole of life	NOT	isolated

Section 2: *Debatable – over-swing of pendulum?*

implicit	NOT	explicit
affective	NOT	cognitive
religion today	NOT	historical perspective
experiential	NOT	theological
studied neutrality	NOT	commitment
world religions	NOT	Christianity
observable practices	NOT	what is at the heart of religion

In practice of course, faced with a class of pupils, decisions have to be made, so people settle for what is on offer without any real consideration of the overall value or purpose. The pressure of this or that requirement or directive, together with the environment in which one happens to be, for example working under an agnostic headteacher, or a staunch Christian one, or with an enthusiastic multi-faith team, etc., governs what happens.

I certainly want teachers to respond closely to the situation in which they are – but they need to be clear about the overall function of RE, what it is about, in order to respond in a way which is meaningful so as not to be just taken over by the latest influence.

The purpose of this chapter is to aid this by:

1. looking at the main views on offer about the proper focus of RE and;
2. setting out a possible *rapprochement* between these approaches which tries to bring together what is good about them, and add what they all tend to omit.

Three views of the purpose of RE

There have been broadly three quite different approaches to RE which are still discernible today. Any one person may hold aspects of each together, though not necessarily in a way which is successfully integrated.

The confessional model

The traditional answer given as to the purpose of RE has been nurture within a particular faith. In Western civilization this has generally been considered to be Christianity, as this is the religion which has most powerfully moulded the values and beliefs on which society is based, just as in a Muslim country for example the religion to be handed on would be Islam. This approach recognizes the seriousness of failing to induct pupils into the heritage of a great tradition.

The recent debate concerning the role of RE in the new legislation of 1988 has shown how powerful this attitude towards religion still is among politicians, the church and the public at large. Many fear the collapse of a society which is not undergirded by religious principles to which the young are trained to commit themselves.[1]

The dogmatic attempt to hand on religious faith through education is very much alive within religions other than Christianity also. Indeed the presence of a significant number of people of other faiths in our society has given fresh courage to many Christians to try to reassert the 'confessional' approach to RE. If for example Muslims want to bring up their children within their own faith, perhaps in Muslim schools, surely it is time – so the argument runs – to reverse the anti-confessional trend and teach Christianity as true?

Almost all the advocates of the confessional approach today would in fact distance themselves from the kind of RE that this has often produced in the past. They would mostly agree with the list of 'helpful' features in Table 4.1, on page 38, and acknowledge that the confessional approach should not engage in those in the righthand column. But they would still insist that induction into a tradition is right – it should be teaching religion not just teaching *about* religion in a way which distances it and effectively marginalizes it. They would also assume the validity of the religious starting-point, and while acknowledging that faith should never be *forced* onto people – that freedom is essential for real religious awareness to develop – they are nevertheless sure that they are right and that no teacher will be misleading the young if they teach religion straight.

Although therefore most advocates of a confessional approach have taken on board quite a lot of the criticism against old-style RE understood as indoctrinating, narrow, academic and meaningless to the vast majority of pupils, they have not gone far enough in meeting certain objections.

Objections to the confessional approach

These objections include the need to start where people are and relate to the pressures placed on them. As discussed in Chapter 2, the world in which RE has to happen is a pluralist, secularist one and only a minority of the population acknowledge that religion is an important part of their lives. To meet the needs of pupils growing up in such an environment, RE must not assume any religious faith – it has to start much further back with questions of why there is such a phenomenon as religion. And it must help pupils to come to their own commitments as they live their lives in a world of confusing, diverse and often conflicting values and beliefs.

A second objection is that it still has not taken the point seriously enough about the rights of pupils to autonomy and freedom in reflectiveness and choice of commitment. This point was acknowledged even 150 years ago by a far-sighted Baptist parson, John Howard Hinton. The way he expressed it, quaint to us today, nevertheless neatly points up the dilemma:

If one government has a right to require that children be religiously educated, so has another, so have all (whether . . . in Constantinople Islamism, or Pekin Confucionism . . .). Would all this be right – this forcible impregnation of the minds of millions upon millions of children, with or without the consent of parents, with these systems of error, all called religion?[2]

To the objection that Christianity is true while the others are false he replied significantly, 'It may be so said, we think so; nothing more.'

He took his argument further than that based on the existence of the pluralist society whether of his day or ours, and drew attention to the crucial question of truth-claims which cannot be publicly demonstrated in such a way that reasonable people may not disagree.

A third objection to the confessional approach is that it assumes that religion provides the adequate answer to the dilemmas facing society. 'If people had been taught to believe in God then this or that calamity would not have happened.' Yet, as has already been discussed in Chapter 3, it unfortunately is the case that religion *can* become a powerful ally of thuggery, violence, aggression, intolerance and denial of human rights. Just to invoke God's name for what one chooses to do is no guarantee whatever that the thought, word or action really is God's will, or is creative and positive as opposed to being destructive and negative. Christians need to remember the words recorded of Jesus: 'Not everyone who says to me on that day, Lord, Lord, shall enter the Kingdom but those who do the will of the Father' (Matthew 7:21). This remains a pertinent warning for all who profess religious faith, or who argue that religious commitment by itself can save the world.

The saying draws attention to the crucial distinction between outward words and behaviour and inner integrity and authentic devotion – a distinction which RE must share with pupils. (See Chapters 7 and 8 for further discussion of this.) This distinction may be unclear to religious believers themselves, and consideration of this possibility suggests a fourth objection to the 'Confessional' model for RE: it does not have to, but easily can, unless great care is taken, result in a narrowing of perspectives. What is communicated can easily be a view that ignores other religions, or that interprets them inadequately within terms of a comparison with one's own, or that accepts them without trying to relate to them so that they exist in a kind of schizophrenic soup in the mind and emotions.

In Britain this kind of attitude has led to considerable animosity between some supporters of teaching Christianity in schools and some supporters of a multi-faith approach. An unfortunate and unnecessary bifurcation has taken place, the latter group overreacting to the perceived dogmatism and parochiality of the former. I shall return to this after looking at the other two models (see pp. 46–48).

The Highest Common Factor model

This is a term which I have coined myself. It indicates the kind of approach to RE which wants to nurture pupils in values, attitudes and interests associated with religion, yet which can be acceptable to the widest number of people, including those who are not religious. It looks for the Highest Common Factor (HCF) and seeks to promote that.

Those unhappy with the 'confessional' model, mostly in its Christian form, have over the years sought to escape from the dilemma – unconsciously or consciously – by subtracting from the equation of RE all that is controversial and likely to cause trouble. They hope to nurture pupils in the rest.

What this HCF consists of has been seen in different ways. Traditionally it has meant some form of moral education to encourage pupils to develop attitudes of cooperation and concern for justice. A little religion is thought, furthermore, to be the way to reduce crime and promote a stable society.

Following the immense popularity of Goldman's analysis of the problems facing RE in the 1960s (Goldman 1964; 1965), the emphasis on moral education was given a partner, that of life-themes – general topics which could be seen in greater depth through helping pupils to appreciate their symbolic use within religion.

More recently, the quest for 'ultimate meaning'[3] has been understood to be at the heart of RE – and something which all can share in. This is generally linked to a sense of the importance of personal development, so that RE can play a significant role in PSE (personal and social education) courses. The induction into values and beliefs is here very low-key with the emphasis on personal search.

This approach has received considerable reinforcement recently in what is often referred to as 'the experiential approach to RE' (see Chapter 6 for detailed discussion of this) which focuses on helping pupils to relate to their own experiences and develop the skills they need to reflect on this in a meaningful way.

Objections to the HCF model

The main difficulty with the HCF approach, however interpreted, is that it tends to jettison most of what is distinctive of religion. This is not just a matter of irritating supporters of the confessional approach. It is that we tend to be left with an RE which effectively has lost its 'R'. We might just as well call it the Non-R RE model.

The widely accepted, and soundly based, educational aim of RE, advocated in almost all syllabuses and policy statements, is to help pupils achieve understanding of religion. It is difficult to see how avoiding teaching about what is distinctive of religion can help people gain an understanding of it!

The intentions may be fine, but when considering what is actually happening in schools where the HCF approach is practised – as it is in very many – it seems to fit the marvellously Jewish remark attributed to Sam Goldwyn: 'on the surface, profound, but deep down, superficial'. And the reasons, while many, are closely connected to the watering-down of any specifically religious content to a safe Highest Common Factor. This may provide calmer sailing but is it worth the trouble? Can we reach our destination of understanding of religion that way?

Furthermore, the rights of pupils to autonomy and self-responsibility are still not adequately protected under the new form of confessionalism. Certain principles and values are assumed to be unchallengeable and therefore to be nurtured. Many assumptions are made which pupils are not encouraged to question at all. This becomes clear especially to those who disagree with the content of the nurture. Thus, for example, Goldman has been accused of trying to instill Christianity – and his own particular brand of it – by the backdoor.

Another serious objection to this HCF kind of approach is that it fails to prepare pupils for the real world, helping them to appreciate the strength of religious conviction and extend to people of all kinds of religious persuasion, including those dubbed as 'fundamentalist' or 'extremist', real empathy and desire to understand their positions. The so-called open non-dogmatic approach not infrequently is arbitrary in its welcome, and conceals a strong form of commitment held sometimes with great intransigence.

There tends to be a lack of conceptual rigour in the way this HCF approach works in practice. Much RE writing in the past 20 years or so has centred on the raising of ultimate questions, and there has also been an insistence on developing in pupils skills of understanding and of handling these questions. This reflects the trend in education as a whole away from the imparting of so-called factual information towards a greater concern with process – with how we know. Yet despite this there has mostly in practice been little depth, little more than discussion of opinions with regard to these ultimate questions – what one disillusioned teacher called 'mutual exchange of ignorance'. Real attention to the quite sophisticated concepts with which religion is concerned has tended to be dismissed on the grounds that, apart from a select minority, pupils are incapable of any sustained thought, uninterested in such hypothetical and academically conceived ideas which in any case are mostly of historical interest and irrelevant to the modern world. Chapters 5 and 7 will especially try to address these issues.

The induction into beliefs and values separated from all that is religiously controversial or ill-fitting in a secularist, pluralist world, which the HCF model sees as the focus of RE, is performing a valuable educational service, but it is one which can and should be shared by the school as a whole, and every subject-area in it. RE should not be expected to bear the full weight of this responsibility, especially because if it does it cannot deal with what is distinctive and peculiar to it – there is not time, etc. Furthermore, moral education must be, and is seen by people to be, distinct from RE. Values have validity without any specifically religious component, so it is unhelpful – indeed dangerous for a secularist society – to link moral standards to religious commitment, or allow religious education to do the lion's share of moral education.

The interest in values education across the curriculum, e.g. in anti-sexism, anti-racism, and anti-elitism, and the impact of the 'Green Movement' in all subject areas, is in fact taking the mat from under the feet of such HCF RE. And it is better so, because all these value concerns do need to be pursued within other disciplines as within RE. This is helping many people see that RE should have something more distinctive to contribute to the values education of pupils than what can happen within the teaching of other subjects. How far the experiential approach offers something distinctive will be discussed in Chapter 6.

Although many would now see this HCF model as pushing RE into a backwater if it is pursued on its own, it is still a highly influential view, and is likely to go on being so for some time because Agreed Syllabuses on the whole encourage it.

They do so normally alongside another approach, the hope being that by putting the two ingredients together a synthesis will appear. Increasingly, such a synthesis is seen as important, indeed essential for proper motivation whether at teacher or pupil level, and for the health of RE in general.

The Phenomenological model for RE

The name 'phenomenological' betrays its origins in University departments, but in ordinary language this approach is usually referred to loosely as the multi-faith or world religions approach. The aim is to develop an attitude of tolerance and openness through the study of religions. A particularly influential way of studying them was outlined by Ninian Smart, one of the first members of the Shap Working Party which has been campaigning for this approach since the early 1970s: religions each have at least six dimensions: doctrinal, mythological, ethical, ritual, experiential and social. More recently he has added a seventh: the material and artistic dimension (Smart 1989: 12ff).

RE should aim at giving pupils information and understanding about all of these, bearing in mind the age and aptitude of pupils. Michael Grimmitt in his widely read book, *What can I do in RE?* (Grimmitt 1973), which advocated the dimensional alongside the existential approach to RE, advised intermingling the experiential, mythological and ritual dimensions and focusing on them in the primary school, adding the social and ethical together for lower Secondary, and finally bringing in the doctrinal with the upper forms of Secondary schools, as this dimension is the most difficult to cope with (pp. 50, 92f).

The aim of RE according to the phenomenologists is promoting respect for, and understanding of, religion and its significance for behaviour in such a way as to leave intact pupils' integrity – it is not educating into religion in any way, but educating about religion understood as more than information because involving a positive and creative approach to pluralism. Sometimes the phrase 'celebration of diversity' is used to point to the affective as well as cognitive impact which this approach would like to see in pupils.

Objections to the phenomenological model
There has been considerable criticism recently of this approach, even though it seems to be now so firmly entrenched in many schools. It has frequently been lampooned as the 'supermarket approach' to religion, or the 'Cook's Tour of World Religions'. While such phrases do not do justice to its many insights – to which I will return in Chapter 8 – there are nevertheless some serious weaknesses in the approach.

First, it can encourage superficial learning. This can be borne out by looking at many of the resources available – often well-produced, informative and written from a sympathetic point of view but lacking depth. As an example, I have before me a well-produced booklet,[4] interestingly and appropriately written, which confounds the young reader with factual details about Hindu mythology and customs. It could, however, easily leave the impression, especially with Western children, that religion is a matter of irrational feelings and sentimentality divorced from the real world and divorced from truth. It is not easy for twentieth-century children to see any profound link between the real world and the mantra described as 'magic syllables' and the action of the priest in 'bringing the goddess to life'. One teacher indeed summed up the book as portraying religion as a fairy story and a religious festival as like a birthday party.

Second, it easily misrepresents religion as something which can be neatly packaged up in sections. Themes like 'rites of passage' or 'festivals' can so attract attention to sociological aspects of religion, that the impression is given to pupils that religion is about how people organize themselves and give meaning to their lives – that the essence of religion is manufactured by societies and by people. The view that religion is a *response* to revealed truth, and the implications of this with regard to how we can be expected to find out about it, are not normally considered at all. In an article in the *British Journal of Religious Education* in 1989, Nicola Slee notes that in practice,

There is little respect for the claim of religious believers that it is a lifetime's work to come to know and be possessed by (note, not to possess) the truth of even one tradition. [She goes on to note that] . . . the needs of squeezing religions into manageable units can easily lead to unhelpful emphases on the superficial, the external and the exotic on the one hand, or the conservative, the established and the institutional in religious traditions on the other hand, at the expense of such less obvious and less accessible factors as the profound interiority of faith, the mundane ordinariness of discipleship, and the radical reforming zeal within traditions which challenges them to continually renew themselves. The inevitable over-simplification, if not actual misrepresentation, of the richness, complexity and dynamism of religious traditions can be deeply offensive to religious believers and can even lead to charges of racism.

(Slee 1989: 130)

I have quoted this objection at length because it is a very serious one. The failure of the phenomenological approach to teach skills of discernment, and to wrestle with truth-claims and the problems these present when they are conflicting, does not prepare pupils to cope with secularist objections to religion.

Thirdly, the phenomenological approach can easily convey relativism. The attempt to be fair to all traditions, by being equally tolerant of all and non-judgemental, can lead like a slippery slope from well-intentioned neutrality to profound scepticism about religion. For the descriptive approach carries hidden messages of the impossibility of any fair evaluation, for all such beliefs are subjective and relative to particular cultures. The 'sartorial' version of religion is smuggled in unawares, and with it radical doubt as to the truth of any religion.

As a college lecturer, Slee comments (1989 p.130) that this is what has happened for many of the students now coming up through secondary schooling, as several of her own students can testify.

Like the third objection to the HCF model, the fourth is that it fails to prepare pupils for the pluralist world with its confusions, contradictions and instability. Slee expresses it very clearly:

They need help in wrestling with the questions of identity, truth and commitment which the contemporary pluralism of beliefs and values poses more sharply than ever before and which are therefore very real and pressing questions for children of the secular century. Such questions will not and do not go away, whatever the philosophers of education dictate. Pupils *do* ask questions of truth, *do* seek to establish moral foundations for their lives, *do* quest for a spirituality which will assuage their own sense of rootlessness and hunger for meaning as well as teach them how to live compassionately and courageously on our fragile planet.

(Slee 1989: 130)

The need for rapprochement

Slee argues (p.131ff) that the time is ripe for a *rapprochement* between confessional and phenomenological approaches to RE, and many voices in the RE world would appear to agree with her. Robert Jackson, for example, envisages a 'middle way' as a 'study of religions conducted in such a way that it makes a distinctive contribution to the pupils' development of a coherent and personally satisfying set of beliefs and values' (Jackson 1987: 17). This echoes the Schools Council Working Paper 36 which in 1971 expressed the view that RE 'must include both the personal search for meaning and the objective study of the phenomena of religion. It should be both a dialogue with experience and a dialogue with living religions so that one can interpret and reinforce the other' (p. 43).

Overcoming false polarization

In order to achieve this middle way it is important that a false polarization is overcome. The debate over the Education Reform Act, and subsequent developments since then, such as the appeal by the London boroughs of Ealing and Newham against their local Agreed Syllabuses, has shown up the extent of this polarization. Many of those concerned about the ignorance and marginalization of Christianity in numerous schools have failed to state publicly what is insightful about the multi-faith approach, and those convinced of the appropriateness of the latter have tended to display similar insensitivity towards the former.

Things are, however, rarely so simple. In the first place there is much that is right about the confessionalist stance. Traditional Christian teaching has been removed from many schools and replaced by what may be in the minds of teachers clear and accurate material, but which is not infrequently received as a mish-mash of other religions and vague talk of spiritual development.[5] Ignorance of Christianity has in some areas reached monumental proportions.

Often there has been no concern at all that perhaps more can be expected educationally of the new Agreed Syllabuses. The omission of any reference to 'Jesus, God or the Bible anywhere', raised by Mr Harry Greenaway concerning the Ealing syllabus, does raise a serious question. As an editorial in the *British Journal of Religious Education* put it, 'It could equally be claimed that the syllabus is defective because it did not refer to Krishna, Allah and the Guru Granth Sahib anywhere.' [6] It could indeed.

The real matter is in fact that the vast majority of children in this country are growing up in a secularist culture which rules out religion altogether, and that those within faith communities are living in a world in which their faiths will be more and more subjected to secularist interrogation. Therefore it is no more satisfactory for Muslims or anyone else to have a syllabus which does not mention Allah anywhere than it is for Jesus, God and the Bible to be omitted. Furthermore, the problems, as well as the delights, of diversity of views exist, and we cannot pretend they do not. The confessionalist is typically too much aware of this problem, and the phenomenologist and supporter of the HCF approach is typically under-aware.

In the editorial mentioned above there was a significant reference to 'the poverty of the local environment' in 'an area where almost all the school population was Christian'.[7] This contains an unfortunate value judgement, not just upon the Christianity that precedes the reference, but on the whole concept of locality as somehow opposed to cosmopolitanism. We do well to remember that many can live incredibly full lives and develop a very extensive range of sympathy and understanding, who live only within a geographically and culturally restricted circle. The great composer Bach for example hardly ever left his native Germany. Also there are many who roam the world in an entirely superficial fashion, who are not really 'present' anywhere, who get bits and pieces of ideas from all over but who do not really understand them. The argument for multi-faith RE, which I support, must not get involved in negative judgements of this kind. People are not benighted and narrow and dogmatic just because they live in the Outer Hebrides or Gedney Drove End. These same characteristics can often be found – with far less excuse – in well-seasoned travellers who have had the privilege of sampling far and wide.

What we are really talking about of course is entitlement – sharing the privileges of being able to be in touch with other cultures. With this I agree fully. But we need also to remember that there is another entitlement – the privilege of feeling at home somewhere, of understanding something in depth, of being immersed in a culture. Many children exposed to global pluralism today lack this, and this is the underlying concern of those who support religiously confessional approaches to education. Many Jews, Muslims and members of other world religions are just as concerned about this as many Christians.

A further point can be made. There is no appreciation here that to teach Christianity *could* be a fine way of helping pupils towards that global perspective which I agree is desirable, and that the real issue is the superficiality or the depth of what is taught. To reduce RE to opposing camps of Christianity versus world faiths is belittling and damaging. Even if some people mistakenly do polarize the issue, those who claim to be more professional and enlightened should not. It is really unacceptable to see the position as simplified along the lines of Christian emphasis bad, world religions good. A much more positive way forward must be found, one which does justice to the insights of both sides, and which seeks to avoid the criticism which both sides must face as to how it is delivered in the classroom.

The need for balance
What this polarization shows up is a two-fold problem to be tackled:

1. The confessional concern for commitment to certain beliefs and values needs to be broadened. There is something intolerant and ungenerous about both the confessional and HCF models outlined above which fails to affirm the insights of those who start off from a different 'confession' of whatever complexion this might be. It must find a way of affirming the experience of others.
2. The phenomenological model needs to be deepened. It should acknowledge what is confessional about itself too which compromises it and opposes its intended outcome of openness and tolerance. These beliefs and values cannot for example remain in sole Olympian splendour as necessarily always more important than others.

A re-alignment is needed and some significant additions made to the RE programme. I believe such a *rapprochement* IS possible. If, for the sake of clarity, a name or label is helpful, we might call it 'Essentialist' RE.

Essentialist RE

This term emphasizes an approach to RE which concentrates on what is essential from several points of view, with regard to breadth, depth, relevance and time. (See Table 4.2). It assumes the importance of those qualities discussed in Chapter 1 (pages 6–8) and seeks to relate these to classroom practice.

Breadth – balance between the models
Essentialist RE takes seriously the concerns of well-intentioned people within the three major models outlined. The sevenfold purpose of RE

Table 4.2 Essentialist religious education

BREADTH
balance between the models of religious education

	Confessional 1. rootedness	HCF 2. moral education education	Phonomenological 3. encouraging tolerance and openness	
D E P T H	clear thinking yet open to a sense of wonder at that Mystery believed to be at the heart of reality	7. capacity to cope with controversy	accepts need for priorities and is brave enough to opt for doing a little well	T I M E
	4. religious concepts	5. search for commitment	6. discernment	

RELEVANCE
combines brain and heart, academic detachment
and personal involvement

as set out on pages 50–2 represents the basic thrust of the confessional, the HCD and the phenomenological models respectively in the three aims each given under Sections A and B.

Furthermore, the holistic emphasis on the interconnectedness of insights opposes isolationist views of religion and can help RE to be seen as 'basic' to the curriculum. (This is further discussed in Chapter 12, pp. 179–84.)

Depth – clarity as to what religion is
Essentialist RE seeks to go to the heart of the matter with regard to what religion really and distinctively is about. This is notoriously difficult – to attempt any definition of what religion essentially is. There has been a long-standing debate among philosophers and theologians. Often the 'essence' has been seen in terms which wider study of religions has shown to be too narrow or too idiosyncratic or in ways which undermine the significance of the external forms of religious traditions.

All turns on how the 'essence' is seen, and the kind of assumptions brought to bear on the endeavour. (This is set out in Chapter 5, e.g. p. 55, and Chapter 8, pp. 111–13.) Suffice it here to note that I do not mean that all religions are really saying the same thing; that differences do not matter, that they all have basically the same origins, or fulfil the same functions. Diversity, controversy and possible contradiction have to be taken seriously. It is important to note that in any case this question of the essence of religion is to be debated by pupils, not assumed for them. This is possible because the ability of even very young children to engage in reflective thought has now been recognized in many educational circles (see Chapters 5 and 7 for discussion of this).

Relevance – educational needs of pupils

Essentialist RE focuses on what is essential educationally for each pupil. Effective learning requires a certain simplicity of structure in which to contain the openness and indefiniteness of all genuine learning. Furthermore, this 'essence' needs to be capable of being infinitely adaptable according to the uniqueness of each person's experience and needs and interests. What is serious about so much school work generally is that so frequently it seems to fail to have any deep effect on life outside the classroom. The real needs of pupils are not being engaged with.

Essentialist RE therefore encourages a particular teaching style: a method which homes in on what is of central importance and relevance for each pupil. Not based upon any consensus of content, nor the expectation that teachers will do the same thing with all the class, this takes seriously the concept of the teacher as the manager of pupils' own learning instead of a purveyor of information and ideas.

Time – the need for priorities

This is a very practical consideration. All teachers are over-pressed with regard to what is expected of them, and none more so than those doing RE. We cannot do everything in a very limited time, so we must select what is essential on the fairest and most comprehensive basis possible: that is, what we think may help pupils to cope with, and make decisions about, things which happen to them – at any age and at any level; and also what will encourage responsibility concerning the effects they themselves have on others. I recently asked eleven experts on RE from widely differing backgrounds what they each saw as the major priority for RE. The results exemplify a coming-together through emphasis on what is essential (Watson 1992).

The purpose of RE

Essentialist RE stresses both the E and the R of RE. The purpose of education in general is to help each pupil to be responsible for his or her own self-education throughout life – holistically and with integrity. The purpose of RE is to help them genuinely to reflect upon religion, opening up for them the possibility of a self-chosen and real commitment, religious or otherwise, so that the individual can freely play his or her role in the wider community, whether this be the faith community or society as a whole.

RE needs to focus on:

A) *Responsibility to society*

1. inform about society, thus continuing the induction of pupils which they are already experiencing into the tradition which is theirs by virtue either of birth or of taking up residence in a country. In the former case help is needed to acknowledge the changing nature of society, and in the latter to become bi-lingual, as it were, in a deeper way. All Western societies have a heritage with religious roots – and still alive today despite massive conscious abandonment of the specifically religious aspect – and these roots are actually being strengthened by the multi-faith presence;

2. promote moral education in the sense of transcending the purely informational and inspirational in order to encourage pupils to play their part in maintaining an ordered and civilized society. The motivational power, as well as the explanatory role, of religion has always had an important contribution to make to moral education;

3. actively to fight prejudice and encourage an attitude of tolerance towards other people and openness to what is different from one's own outlook. The sympathetic and informed study of ethnic and religious minorities is crucial for the well-being of our multi-racial society.

B) *Educational concern*

4. develop and deepen pupils' grasp of religious concepts especially the key one of 'God'. Initiating pupils into theology is an essential part of RE, so that they may be on the wavelength of the major religions and be able – if they wish – to use their language and outlooks to make sense of their own personal experience. They cannot use a vocabulary which they do not know, nor relate to what they are in deepest ignorance of;

5. promote pupils' own search for a commitment by which to live and find meaning and fulfilment in wrestling with ultimate questions;

6. counter stereotyping of people and religions, and develop the capacity to discern the real from the sham, the inner meaning from the external expression, the central from the peripheral.

Finally, there is another aim which relates to both Sections A and B, and which none of the models has taken seriously enough:

Coping with controversy

7. help pupils to learn how to cope with controversy, complexity, confusion, and uncertainty within a safe environment, so that they

are able to manage these unavoidable aspects of life without trying to resort to premature certainty, dogmatism or exclusivism. This involves helping pupils so to develop skills of reflective thinking that they can be generously affirming of others without losing their own footing. The paradox of openness and criticism should be appreciated, together with learning how to draw conclusions from evidence.

Centering on five basic questions

Essentialist RE can retain all the important and helpful features listed in Table 4.1 without carrying the price-tag of those in the opposite column which are increasingly today being seen as unacceptable. It can do so by focusing on five basic questions which are expressed in Figure 4.1.

Figure 4.1   **Basic questions in religious education**

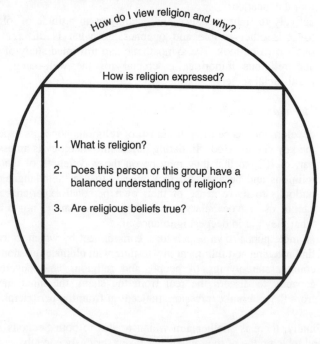

The circle symbolizes personal involvement by the pupil. Why use a circle?

The square symbolizes the way that religion is packaged up within words, actions and visual symbols. Why use a square? Why put the square inside the circle?

The circle and the square show the way in which the phenomenological and the personal aspects of understanding relate. The three questions in the centre concern the proper focus of RE, attending to what religious people may consider to be central to religion: the questions of definition, integrity and truth. This is not to be dogmatic about answers, but to encourage pupils to reflect on them, developing increasing knowledge and understanding of how religion is expressed, and learning how to make evaluation which is both personal and yet in touch with public enquiry.

A vital ingredient for exploring these five questions is imagination, and to that I now turn.

Notes

1. See, e.g. John Burn and Colin Hart, 1988, *The Crisis in Religious Education*.
2. Gladstone Tract 26 Letter from John Howard Hinton to Sir James Graham, London 1843, p. 11, to be found in St Deiniols Library, Hawarden.
3. 'Ultimate questions' is a much-used phrase concerned with what it means to be human. Read, *et al.* 1986, discuss this helpfully and give a comprehensive diagram of what is involved (on p.17): meaning, value, purpose, identity, origins, destiny and authority.
4. *Saraswati Puja* (by Sauresh Ray, 1985).
5. See e.g. John Hull, 1992, *Mishmash: Religious Education in Multi-cultural Britain: a Study in Metaphor* in which he defends the multi-faith position from such criticism. There has been a great deal of writing in recent years on these issues with evidence of some coming together. This is often associated with a concern for the curriculum as a whole. See e.g. M. Roques, 1989, *Curriculum Unmasked*, for a critique of education on Christian grounds, and a similar critique on religious grounds resulting from multi-faith seminars held at the Islamic Academy, Cambridge: *Faith as the Basis of Education in a Multi-faith, Multi-cultural country*, 1991. L.J. Francis and A. Thatcher, 1990, (ed.) *Christian Perspectives for Education* is a helpful compendium of views. How to address the reality of religious diversity is the subject of much literature: e.g. D. Rose, 1992, *Towards an Understanding of Religious Diversity in School*, M. Palmer, 1991, *What Should we Teach?* – *Christians and Education in a Pluralist World*, and B.V. Hill, 1990, 'Will and should the religious studies appropriate to schools in a pluralistic society foster religious relativism?' *British Journal of Religious Education*, vol. 12, no. 3: 126–36.
6. *British Journal of Religious Education*, 1991, vol. 14, no 1: 2.
7. Ibid. p. 65.

CHAPTER 5

Imagination and the development of religious concepts

Saying that imagination is essential for effective RE is perhaps like pubs advertising good food. No-one in their right mind would consider one offering bad or indifferent food! Our society pays lip-service at least to the idea of imagination in that the word 'imaginative' is normally regarded as a compliment – the opposite of 'dull'.

It is worth clearing up one not infrequent misunderstanding. Imaginative teaching is not what in the end matters – it is developing in pupils *their* capacity for imagination that counts.

Imaginative teaching does not necessarily produce the capacity for imagination in pupils. They can be overstimulated by variety, and often it is the teacher's ideas that are expressed and not the pupils'. Often, too, the teacher trammels the pupils too much within particular boundaries so that they are forced to go in the teacher's direction and not their own. Being an enabler of pupils' learning is an unselfish task and 'imaginative' teachers do not necessarily excel in qualities of humility and standing back and giving space to others.

Why, however, is it important that pupils' capacity for imagination is developed in order to understand religion?

Imagination is essential for getting on the wavelength of religious people

This use of imagination is probably obvious to everyone. The importance of practising empathy, especially with what may appear strange and uncongenial, is a major aspect of RE. This is not at all an easy task.

H.G. Wells wrote a story about a traveller in South America coming across a community of people who had all been born blind.[1] Imagine yourself as that traveller. How would you set about convincing these blind people about the blueness of sky, the greenness of grass, the beauty of painting? This kind of putting oneself in the place of another and attempting to portray and communicate something through a medium which is unsuitable to it is very essential for an understanding of religion.

The capacity for this use of imagination is closely related to attitudes of mind. Openness, and a spirit of generosity towards other people and what makes them tick, can enable very great barriers to be overcome. It is not easy, for example, for a modern Westerner to understand eastern religion or the Semitic thought-forms at the root of Judaism, Christianity and Islam. An imaginative 'thinking what I would think, if I was in their place' is something which has to be worked at.

Imagination is essential for understanding religious language and other forms of expression

It is easy for people to misunderstand religious language and ritual. There is a very strong tendency to take literally what needs imaginative interpretation. All the great religions affirm that at the heart of religion lies Mystery which nothing can adequately express: all religious forms of expression have the character of pointing towards this Mystery, and not describing it.

We need to appreciate that, as used in religion, 'mystery' does not indicate a problem to be solved. The kind of response which it calls forth is not a factual wonder *why* but a wonder *at*. It does not question as such, but accepts the givenness of mystery which arouses awe and even adoration.

It may be helpful to visualize the difference between the two approaches by envisaging two circles, the one is given a precise central dot which is clearly defined, the other does not express the centre but has a number of lines on the circumference of the circle which point towards the centre. The second approach to learning activates the imagination. It helps people to appreciate mystery by not defining too easily and sewing it all up. It has far greater fluidity and dynamism – it avoids the static quality of factual description.

There is no understanding of religion without appreciating that it concerns this second kind of expression and communication. Religious language is not primarily informational but inspirational in becoming more and more aware of the extraordinary ramifications of the few essential truths. This must be understood, really understood, for otherwise – whether or not we agree with the 'truths'– we are likely to misinterpret what religious people believe. For awareness of Mystery brings a paradox: at the same time that religious people claim to have knowledge of this Mystery they become more deeply aware that it is infinitely beyond any understanding. The function of religious language, ritual and art form is in fact to try to express the inexpressible as a way towards greater awareness.

Imagination is essential for gaining knowledge in religion

Imagination extends the possibilities of knowledge. Often people think of imagination as necessarily fantasy far removed from reality. Yet in fact imagination can be the means by which we can come to understand reality. It enables us to envisage what is not immediately present to the senses. Imagination is the capacity to make links and to see links – it is not discontinuous with reality, but is a way of understanding what really is there if only we can see it.

Einstein noted that imagination is more important than knowledge. He used to conduct what came to be known among his fellow-scientists as his 'Gedanken' (thought) experiments.

Russell Stannard, in a book on relativity written for children, explains how Einstein made his discoveries, not by finding new experimental results, but by drawing out the implications of what was already well-known.

> One of Einstein's ways of working things out was to take the laws of nature as they were understood at the time and imagine them in unusual fictitious situations – such as, for instance, trying to imagine what it would be like to catch up with a light beam. In this way he was led to discover that the old laws could not make sense of these situations. So this, in turn, led him to revise the laws of nature.
>
> (Stannard 1989: 120)

Elsewhere in the book Russell Stannard commented that, though such 'thought'-experiments are open to everyone, 'not many people think hard enough to produce one'.

Hard thinking is indeed required because the kind of information which science is dealing with and seeking to extend is quite literally mind-boggling. That light travels at the speed of five times around the earth in the time it takes to say *rice pudding* is indeed an amazing matter. The potential truths of religion are even more staggering to the imagination than straightforward empirical matters.

A great deal of 'making links' is achieved through the use of metaphor and analogy, for word-pictures can help us to move forward into fresh insights. Colin Gunton has recently written,

> It is now widely accepted that almost all intellectual advance takes place by means of metaphor . . . Metaphor is not mere ornament, but an indispensible means of articulating the shape of reality . . . They are the means of interpreting one part of the world by another.
>
> (Gunton 1992: 10)

A precise use of imagination with regard to religion is that without it a person can quite easily not even consider the possibility of there being truth in religion. For no-one can believe anything unless they previously know it to be *believable*. 'We are obliged to believe only what we think is consistent, without having any real choice in the matter' as a textbook on Logic puts it (Hodges 1977: 15). Imagination does not lead necessarily to belief, but belief cannot happen without the ground being prepared by imagination. This is why Cardinal Newman once remarked, 'It is not reason that is against us, but imagination.'[2]

The development of religious concepts

Imagination is, in all three aspects of its value for RE, intimately connected with the development of religious concepts. Inadequate concepts cause people:

1. to misinterpret religious people's behaviour and commitment;
2. to take literally what may have been intended metaphorically or symbolically;
3. not even to see the *possibility* of the truth of religious concepts.

Effective RE must therefore be concerned with the building-up of concepts which are worthy of a person's total development, emotional, experiential and intellectual, and which fairly represent what is at the heart of all great religious traditions. Only on this basis can people make the informed choice which is the hallmark of the educated person.[3]

An enormous task faces the RE teacher here. Two well-known quips make an important point: Xenophanes' famous remark in the sixth century BC, 'If oxen had gods they would look like oxen',[4] and Voltaire's sarcastic remark, 'God made man in his own image. Man has returned the compliment.'[5]

It is not difficult to illustrate the insight these sayings convey. This is reflected in such comments as that of the Russian astronaut Gagarin who said, 'I didn't see God in space', or of the scientist who says, 'You can't prove God exists', or of the literalist church-goer who says, 'If you don't go to church you are not worshipping God', or of the religious fanatic who says, 'God tells me what to do'. All these responses are based on a seriously inadequate concept of God as being literally like a man, best denoted by a small g: a god who is visible; a god who has physical properties like anything else in the world; a god who inhabits certain places and not others; a god who acts and behaves just like another person. Such concepts are unworthy of educated people and refer to anthropomorphism which has been misunderstood.[6]

Often indeed the concept is even cruder. A businessman commenting on an experience he had in a stockbroker's office in London when 'I saw a beam of light between me and my eyes' commented,

Although I wasn't a particularly religious person, I realised immediately that this must be the thing that people call God. There was never any question in my mind: there it was and I knew it. I had always had difficulty with the idea of a long-bearded god sitting on a throne on high, but because it came in the form it did, as an energy, I had no difficulty with it . . . [7]

The interesting point about this comment is that it indicates the degree of conceptual retardation from which an intelligent adult can suffer. The picture of an old man in the sky is not taught by any of the great religions – yet this may come as a surprise to many people today. Many adults have grown up in an environment in which they have picked up extremely infantile notions – notions which have never been challenged directly, but which, because of their almost total inadequacy and failure to square with other knowledge and experience, cause religion itself to be rejected as people become more sophisticated in other departments of life and other areas of knowledge.

Reasons for immature conceptual development in religion

Important research carried out at Oxford University by Olivera Petrovich (1989) suggests that such naivety is something which children learn from adults rather than being innate. In carefully structured interviews on the concept of God with three and four-year old children she found that if she began by asking them to distinguish between objects which were man-made and ones which were natural and then to speculate about origins in each case, a majority of the responses referred to the natural objects being made by God or an unknown power (almost half and half responses on this). When questioned further very few of them thought of this God or power as a man, but either as a person without a body or as something like air or gas, and a few said they did not know or that there was no God. The concepts therefore were for that age quite sophisticated, indeed quite sophisticated by many adults' standards as we have seen.

Petrovich found in her interviews with the children, that if she started off asking them about 'God', as a word which they had learned, the majority of them said that God was a man. She therefore deduced that crude anthropomorphism is something which children are taught, not necessarily intentionally, in fact probably not intentionally at all, but it is something which they pick up from the comments which they hear and the deductions which they make.

The possible distortions which people can pick up are numerous. In a famous book entitled *Your God is too Small* J.B. Phillips (1932) drew up a list of twelve inadequate concepts of God which people tend to carry around with them. These include such images as Parental Hangover, Resident Policeman, Managing Director and God-in-a-Box. It would not be difficult to draw up a similar set of misunderstandings from a survey of pupils in the classroom.

In almost every other sphere of knowledge and learning, the young child's highest intuitions are developed and allowed to mature – in mathematics, science, art, language-work, and so forth. But as regards religion, there appears to be a conceptual descent from an age of enlightenment in early childhood to one of childish lack of awareness in adulthood. Why is this?

Non-teaching in schools
Much school education has done little or nothing to try to correct these misunderstandings. There has been a major tendency, for example, to bypass and ignore the concept of 'God' altogether – a situation which leaves children where they were.

A prime reason for this neglect has been the impact of the theories of Piaget mediated in this country through Goldman in the 1960s. This has effectively banished explicit work on religious concepts in most primary schools, because children in those age-groups are deemed unable to think in abstract terms, but only concretely.

This prohibition, however has been based on what is highly questionable. Petrovich's research was a far-reaching critique of the assumptions, methods, and findings of Piaget. Her conclusions destroy the credibility of Goldman's research based upon Piaget's work with regard to his denial of children's capacity to handle such concepts before the age of 11 or 12. The research shows that pre-school children *are* capable of thinking in abstract terms.

It is interesting and important to note that, even when Piaget's views on a child's conceptual development are still accepted, the danger of omitting theology from the young child's RE is becoming more widely appreciated. For example, John Hull argues that 'there is a theology appropriate to the concrete thinker just as there is one available to the abstract thinker' (Hull 1991: 13).

Impact of chance forces
Lack of sound education in building up more mature religious concepts has left pupils a prey to chance forces, snatches of conversation and the effects of the implicit and nul curriculum. Many today are not encouraged at all in the development of imagination. Let us consider the poverty of understanding which a child growing up in a religiously deprived background might have of one of the most evocative concepts in religious language, that of 'heaven'. A chance hearing of the Lord's Prayer produces the following conversation:

Child: What's heaven?
Adult: Don't know – I suppose it's where you go when you die.
The child asks again: But where is it?
Reply: Up there, in space somewhere.
The child, better acquainted about science than about religion, then asks: In space?

Reply: Well these ideas got around before people knew about space.
Child then asks: Why do they believe in it?
The adult replies: Oh, come on. Stop day-dreaming. Tidy your things up.

It might have been even worse if one of these fairly common replies had been given: 'Because it gives people a nice cosy feeling that there's a home somewhere' or, 'Don't know. I think it's a bit stupid myself.'

What will be the effect on the child if there is no further discussion at all in that child's life of 'heaven'? Almost certainly the child will think of 'heaven' as a funny idea which people believe in for some nonsensical reason which does not fit in with a scientific way of looking at life. If not dismissive in this way it is likely to be considered unimportant and never thought about again.

At the same time a quite different attitude to life is being constantly reinforced which ignores such questions and focuses on what is useful or factual or enjoyable.

The responsibility of RE

RE needs to address this situation. For 'heaven' we can read any and all of the other religious concepts, including the crucial concept of 'God'. Crude anthropomorphism effectively closes the door to understanding of religion for most pupils. Furthermore, all the great world religions pronounce it false. Whether or not there is a God, none of the great religious traditions can be saddled with intentionally fostering such anthropomorphism, for it goes against the fundamental tenets of their faith. (See Tables 5.1 and 5.2, and Chapter 8 for further discussion on this.)

We are not therefore helping children to get on the wavelength of any of the religions by failing to address haphazardly acquired anthropomorphic ideas. This is like just allowing children to pick up a bottle of poison, and leaving it in their hands as though it is a matter of no consequence to us whether or not they drink it.

RE must endeavour to revive the natural awareness and sensitivity which most likely has been lost by middle junior school, and apply this recovered awareness to the religious vocabulary which pupils need to understand in order to make sense of religion. Otherwise, the views which they have about religion are no more valid or meaningful in themselves than those, for example, of a beginner mathematician on advanced calculus about which he/she knows nothing.

Table 5.1 **The concept of 'God' as found in most of the world religions**

How 'God' is understood at the deepest level in all religions, with the possible exception of certain forms of Buddhism:

GOD is ONE –	the difference between God and gods
GOD is SPIRIT –	the difference between physical and spiritual
GOD is REALITY –	not an idea or a product of human imagination
GOD is OMNIPRESENT –	the difference between a spatial 'here, there, everywhere', and being outside space altogether
GOD is ETERNAL –	the difference between time past, present, or future, and timelessness
GOD is INFINITE –	not limited and dependent on time and space
GOD is IMMORTAL –	not subject to death or deterioration
GOD is INCOMPREHENSIBLE –	beyond thought and reasoning about
GOD is INDESCRIBABLE –	beyond description in words or pictures
GOD is CREATOR –	not made, but making or causing to be made; responsible for this world of time and space
GOD is OMNIPOTENT –	not limited in power
GOD is ALL-KNOWING –	not ignorant or limited in knowledge or deluded
GOD is BEING –	not capable of ceasing to be
GOD is HOLY –	'separate' and not to be trifled with; concerned with justice and rightness
GOD is SUPREME –	greater than anything that we can possibly imagine or conceive
GOD is TRANSCENDENT –	above everything in the world
GOD is IMMANENT –	present in the created world as its basic energy, life, form
GOD is LIFE-GIVING –	not dependent on any other source for life
GOD is GOODNESS –	concerned with morality and right living
GOD is LOVE –	concerned with compassion and caring
GOD is TRUTH –	concerned with honesty, integrity and understanding

Table 5.2 **Concept of 'God' for under-8 year olds**

This is how Dora Ainsworth as an experienced primary school teacher and lecturer sums up what of the list in Table 5.1 is most easily understandable by the under-8 year olds.

1. That God is One not many and that God is known by many names.
2. That God is the creator and sustainer of all.
3. That God is love and desires our love, and our love for each other.
4. That God is spirit and that God is beyond description.
5. That religious people use language in a special way when they talk about. God – 'pointing towards' language.
6. That God is good and just, and wants us to be too in the way we behave.

What can RE do to encourage the imagination necessary for understanding religion?

The use of story

RE needs to introduce pupils to religious myth and story. These can incorporate religious truth in a far more effective way because they appeal directly to the imagination of the listener who can then recreate it anew.

An example of story is given in Chapter 8 on p. 116: that of The Little Fox. The story makes some very profound points about the role of ritual in religion, the development of conceptual understanding, the meaning of the word 'spiritual' and how it is related to religion. Yet the story says simply what it may take many pages to explain in words.

Further points about the story are:

1. that it can be appreciated even by young children;
2. that it is memorable;
3. that it holds the attention.

Little wonder therefore that all religions have used story as a prime means of communicating and of inspiring people.

We need to remember, however, that story by itself will not do. The inadequacies of a diet of bible stories in RE has long been appreciated. Telling and re-enacting stories and myths is part of RE but dangerously not enough. In presenting the story it is necessary to bear in mind the effect of the information-expectancy syndrome on pupil's attitudes – that is, the way in which people tend to look for 'facts' as what matters: this means that unless content is useful, novelty and sheer immediate interest or entertainment are what count.

The teaching of the parables of Jesus is a case in point. The complaint used to be, and still in some schools is, that they are done ad nauseam. 'Oh, we've done them', meaning that they know the story of the Good Samaritan. Yet if they have been done in this way it means they have not been done! There are Christians who would say that one can meditate a lifetime on them. We have only done them when we know we have not done them, because there is so much more to them; and the more we think about them the more they have to say.

Of course fresh approaches to teaching them are necessary. To give parables to very young children for example is likely to be unhelpful unless they are done in a particularly skilful way, because they might be just accepted as a story (Ainsworth 1968). So RE needs to attend to encouraging pupils consciously to get beyond just looking for information or entertainment and see that there is a quite different way of looking at things.

A further reason for caution with regard to RE through story is that knowing a story does not by itself provide sufficient safeguard against serious misunderstandings which can have far-reaching effects on people.

An example is the Adam and Eve story. No-one can doubt its power to evoke the imagination of millions upon millions of people through the ages and today. Yet it has also spawned some monstrous offspring which include such distortions as a dismissive attitude towards women, a view of work as punishment, a view of pain and hardship as revealing personal guilt, a view of the body and anything to do with it as inherently evil, a view of the earth as the property of homo sapiens who can choose what to do with it, a view of God as an insensitive, self-opinionated, unjust task-master concerned about protecting his own property and the slavish obedience of the human-beings he has created.

The following example illustrates the problems involved here.[8] An advisory teacher for English, taking part in a scheme of curriculum enrichment and extension for ten-year-olds, used the Adam and Eve story. He got some excellent work from the children and he made an important point with regard to the level of conceptual development which is possible with this age-group. He wrote:

My plan was to use familiar material in a watered down way. In the event there was no need for any dilution. Once I had started to work with the children, I did exactly what I would have done with older children – or adult learners. [He went on] I had learned that age, like notional key-stage of development and attainment, is unimportant in learning and creativity. . . . Willingness to experience is the basis of all good learning.

(p. 4)

But how was this material used? In reporting on the children's work he noted this:

If any society wanted to perpetuate notions of female fickleness and the importance of accepting the proprietorial bias of moral authority, then here is a tale for the purpose. In a modest attempt to amend the damage accumulated over centuries by this pernicious little fiction, I asked the children to give me the Other Version, particularly Eve's, but Adam's or God's as well if they preferred.

(p. 5)

He commented on the results:

Even God came out of the thing with a more credible characterization than offered in the original . . . I was delighted with the attribution of a motive more understandable and more worthy than in biblical and Miltonic tradition and was lost in admiration of the boldness that could characterize the Supreme Being.

(p. 6)

I have quoted this incident at length to show that teaching story is not enough. Misinterpretation is easy for children today growing up in an environment very different from those in which the stories were told originally.

Within religious traditions myth and story have received overtones through many other factors which are not available to modern children (a total lifestyle, worship, theological language, above all a community of people to whom it is real). Most children today are religiously naked – they have none of these 'clothes' with which to adorn their perceptions. It is like expecting them to see distant stars without the help of any binoculars or telescopes but just with their own native eyesight. Some stars can be seen that way if the conditions happen to be appropriate, but children will not get very far as astronomers unless their own resources are supplemented by those accumulated by the tradition of astronomy built up over the centuries. For astronomy read religion.

The responsibility of the RE teacher is clear. How well most dereligionized pupils can come to an understanding of the profound significance of such stories for religious people depends on teaching which is both informative and inspiring. Even so, such work is unlikely to be enough.

Work on symbolism

Some explicit work on symbolism is necessary, and great care is needed on how this is done. Work on the external aspects of religion, such as putting on special clothes and going into special buildings, is likely to be seen by children as quite literally what religion is about. Even the most up-to-date methods and generously multi-faith context, which includes visits to temple, mosque, gurdwara, synagogue or church, may not overcome this hurdle but rather reinforce for children the cultural and sociological explanation of religion.

Many of the resources available for RE are likely to have this effect. Often they are well-produced and informative. From this point of view, teachers should have no difficulty in finding suitable material. Yet there is a problem with many of them. They mostly do not adequately safeguard pupils against a casual, almost literalist, understanding of symbol.

There is normally, for example, little discussion of the difference between idolatry or superstition on the one hand, and authentic religious devotion on the other. Symbol seems to be thought of just as standing in place for the real thing because that is absent. The idea that symbol denotes presence within the means appropriate for time and space is hardly anywhere mentioned. A specifically religious term, 'sacramental', probably needs to be introduced at this point.

It is illuminating to note the difference between the average response to an icon and that of a member of one of the orthodox churches. For the former it is a work of art reflecting a particular symbolic way of describing certain believed truths. For the orthodox, however, it is not so much an aid to devotion as a way of communicating with God. The icon mediates a presence not an absence.

Admittedly this is a very hard point to get across. If the secularist assumption is operating it becomes almost impossible. This is because the assumption is that the significance of the icon is based upon the faith of the believer and so the possibility of a meeting between the believer and that Reality is discounted from the start. It is like in a story such as the ballet Giselle when Alberic goes to her tomb and is caught up in a vision of her. The secularist looking on will see the act of his taking the flowers to her grave as symbolic, in the sense of a way of expressing his grief, which is rewarded by an imaginary visit from her. Similarly, the act of lighting candles or passing round the *arti*-lamp in a religious ceremony will be seen in the same way. The possibility of there being a real lover, and a real response 'from the other side, as it were', is not even considered.

Unless, however, such a possibility is considered, the onlooker is not really appreciating what the ritual means to the religious person. This does not necessarily involve affirming it. I may believe it is possible that the dead Giselle really did communicate with Alberic, but that in fact she did not. But the difference needs to be grasped before I can venture an opinion usefully upon that.

In trying to teach such a distinction, it is helpful to discuss, as a kind of bridge or way in, such phenomena as ghost stories and other instances of paranormal experience. Fairy stories too, and at a more sophisticated level plays like Shakespeare's 'A Midsummer Night's Dream', can be helpful in raising the question of whether appearances are real or imaginary. The point is at least to raise the question.

Work on metaphor

Pupils are likely to be able to make more sense of symbolism if some work on metaphor is done from an early age. Here we need to encourage pupils to think and express themselves in vivid ways using word pictures. Contrasting proverbs with ponderous prose offers a way in: 'too many cooks spoil the broth' is a far more expressive way of saying: 'Over-maximization of the work force is counter-productive because it inhibits the realization of a satisfactory outcome.'

From such word-pictures we can move on to simile and metaphor, found especially in poetry. At a simple level children can appreciate this. Here is a poem by a ten-year-old girl who had never before written any poetry.[9] The class had done some work explicitly on metaphor, and the poem was a voluntary outcome of a visit to a churchyard. The accompanying notes, given when her teacher asked for them, indicate a sophisticated grasp of metaphor, and a high level of imagination.

Lavender Lily

Lily was a flower girl,
Her house was in the air,
Sweet lavender she picked gladly
Without a single care.
Her shop it was the streets;
After noon and after morn
Wearing her shoes, tattered and torn,
She walked to see her mother yew
Who once, in olden days, she knew.
Her bed was the moorland grass
On mountainside or in the pass.
Her fingers were the summer breeze,
Her voice like rustling in the trees.
Her face was pretty, like the swan,
Her sparkling eyes, a lake.
Her old white dress and purple shawl
She bought once from an ancient stall.
Her soul, God rest it, it has left –
People say 'it was for the best'.
They found her in the lavender field
With her flowers as her final shield.

Her conscious understanding of how she was using language is clear from the explanations she gives for the expressions she uses in the poem: (on line 2) 'She lived outside in the open, so the air was like her house'; (on line 5 'the streets were like a giant shop where she could pick and choose out of bins and gutters'; (on line 8) 'this means she was close to nature and she felt like the yew was her mother'.

From being able to recognize and use metaphor, we need to share with pupils how metaphor works. I.A. Richards has defined metaphor like this: 'In the simplest formulation, when we use a metaphor we have two thoughts of different things active together and supported by a single word, or phrase, whose meaning is a resultant of their interaction.'[10]

We can give simple examples such as, 'Lucy is a gem'. Here thoughts about Lucy and about gems are active together and cannot be given a satisfactory literal translation describing exactly the degree of similarity between Lucy and a gem. The metaphor of the gem here is like a filter or a screen through which Lucy can be seen in a fresh light, and as such the metaphor has the 'power to inform and enlighten' which a literal paraphrase would not have – it would fail 'to give the insight that the metaphor did' (Black 1971: 186f).

This applies also to the religious use of metaphor. When, for example, God is thought of as like light, the metaphor is meant to bring into play all kinds of overtones and ideas which can help the user to a greater understanding of the word God: light shares some characteristics which can be applied to God – but ones which cannot be neatly packaged up in literal words.

It is important to help pupils to appreciate that metaphors require interpretation within a background of shared ideas. It is very easy to pick up a meaning from a metaphor which was perhaps not the one intended. If God is likened to a king, as in Islam especially, it indicates that God is in control, that we can trust God, and so forth. But it is possible for people growing up in a totally different culture to see kingship in terms of tyranny, in which case they would receive the statement that God is like a king as meaning that God is tyrannical, even some kind of dictator, so that religion resembles a prison rather than paradise. Thus the same metaphor can lead to diametrically opposite understandings.

Within Judaism and Christianity, Psalm 23 for instance has spawned many misunderstandings. Likening God to a shepherd has made many people assume that the point of the metaphor was to emphasize the sheep-like quality of people – that they have no mind of their own, that they are there to be told what to do and treated like sheep. In fact in its original Hebrew setting the shepherd referred to a totally different picture – one who actually cared for and was perhaps even prepared to give his life for the sheep, protecting them from very real danger from which they could not be expected to protect themselves. None of the overtones of subordination and all the rest of it would have been present to the Hebrew.

Another very telling metaphor used of God – supremely so within Christianity – is the metaphor of the father. This has run into very heavy water in the twentieth century, and not only because of Freud's onslaught on religion in the name of wish-fulfilment, where he portrayed the idea that people create an imaginary father in the skies to give them comfort. Other factors have been the break-up of family life, the prevalence of one-parent families, very often only a mother, and the whole feminist movement which sees such language as sexist. Attempts to rewrite the Lord's Prayer and the whole of Christian theology are now being seriously considered.[11]

The problem here is the failure of very large numbers of people today, both religious and non-religious people, to appreciate the metaphorical nature of the language they are using. The term 'father' was never intended to be taken literally. The question of whether God is male or female is supremely bad theology. It is like saying that if Jim Bloggs is an ass it means he has got long ears and brays. In our society we would normally not interpret a phrase like that wrongly, because everyday usage confirms that when we say someone is an ass we mean they have been rather stupid. But in theology we commit enormous howlers. The point of the metaphor of father is to indicate the experience which religious people have of God as a loving creator. It has nothing whatever to do with gender.

Of course this does not mean that we should not be careful about the metaphors which we use. It is possible that if a metaphor ceases to mean what it used to mean in another society then we should abandon it. This is often seen with regard to metaphors like shepherd for example. Work with pupils can often translate these metaphors or similes into something more meaningful, like that in Carl Burke's book *God is for Real* (1967: 34) where the 23rd Psalm is given a quite different translation by one boy: 'The Lord is like my probation officer': the probation officer was the only person in his life who had ever shown any real love and care for him. I am not arguing therefore that metaphors should not change, but that it is impossible for us to change them organically unless we understand them in the first place. If 'father' today means for many people a non-existent person, a drunkard, someone unkind or hateful, or if it denotes for others an exclusion of women, then it needs to be appropriately translated in different terms.

Specific teaching on the concept of 'God'

What has already been said in discussing metaphors for 'God' indicates the need for some specific teaching on the kind of understanding of the word current within world religions.

The concept of God is as salient for any understanding of religion as is the concept of number for mathematics. It requires therefore time and some kind of structured development. The occasional discussion period, in which pupils express their current level of thinking about God, is no substitute for study in depth of how religious people understand 'God', why they do, and whether they are justified in so doing.

A lack of ability to think clearly about 'God' will adversely affect all other aspects of attempted RE. In all probability pupils will miss the point of the otherwise excellent work they may be doing on the phenomema of religion, its rites, customs, beliefs and moral values and so forth. All these gain their significance as 'religious' phenomena because of their underlying relationship to an understanding of 'God'. The only possible exception within the major world religions is Theravada Buddhism, but even here the concept of Nirvana is all-pervasive and has more features in common with an understanding of 'God' than with a Western secular atheist view. (See Chapter 8 for further discussion of this.)

Effective RE will help pupils develop specific skills concerning the concept of 'God'. Extensive time-allowance should be given to this. The temptation for teachers to cut off at this point and move on to something easier and less controversial is great, but the real value of RE lies in following the development through. Otherwise it is rather like spending several days journeying to a famous tourist site, but when we get there only allowing ourselves 20 minutes to see it. A possible way in might be the following.

Outline of a scheme of work on the concept of God
Aim: to help pupils forward in their thinking concerning the concept of God, and the question of whether or not God exists. No level of belief or un-belief in God is assumed; the purpose is clarification and enabling pupils to enter into the debate, at their own level, from a basis of developing knowledge and awareness of the complexity of thinking about God.

[1]
Is your idea of God anything like any of these?:

1. a celestial policeman;
2. an absentee landlord;
3. a magician;
4. a being greater than anything we can possibly think of;
5. an old man on a cloud;
6. light which gives life;
7. the conclusion of a mathematical theorem;
8. the chairman of a rather boring harp-playing assembly;
9. a presence who is loving and just;
10. a crutch for people who can't cope;
11. an all-powerful dictator;
12. a character in a fairy-story;
13. a power that is either evil or indifferent to suffering;
14. a heavenly Santa Claus;
15. a king who is just and holy;
16. electricity which is invisible and powerful, useful but dangerous;
17. a slot-machine whom you can approach with a coin and get out what you want;
18. the ground without which nothing in this world could exist.

[2]
How we think of 'God' affects what we think about other things too, for example especially whether or not 'God' exists. Can you match any of the following statements to the images of 'God' in the list above?:

1. 'I've never seen God, nor has anyone else.'
2. 'You can't prove God exists.'
3. 'God's O.K. for little children – Christmas carols and all that.'
4. 'Talk about God makes me sick – 'Thou shalt not . . .' etc.'
5. 'God's never answered *my* prayers.'

6. 'Miracles don't happen, so God doesn't exist.'
7. 'God made the world and loves everyone everywhere.'
8. 'I sure would hate to be in heaven!'
9. 'Going to church doesn't make people any better – just look at Mrs X down the road. If you want a kindness doing, don't ask her.'
10. 'Even if God exists, it doesn't matter anyway.'
11. 'It is the will of God, and we must trust Him.'
12. 'Religion is basic to life.'

Do you think that members of the different religions you have studied would be likely to agree with any of these? If so which? Do you think there would be important differences between the religions on this? Why/why not?

[3]
Collect some comments about religion. These could be from your family and friends, or from newspapers or television, or books in the library. Write them out and beside each one describe what picture of God is behind the comment. Where do you think people get their pictures of God from? Do you think some of them are ones which genuinely religious people would not adopt?

[4]
What do you think yourself – whether you believe in God or not? What is the picture of God you have? Perhaps you have several, in which case what are they? And do they contradict each other?

[5]
How do the various pictures of God you have been looking at, and also those which you have yourself, compare with the lists in Tables 5.1 and 5.2 which most of the great world religions would agree on? If there is a difference, why do you think there is?

Why do you think they think of God in these ways? Do you think their reasons are good ones? What reasons do you yourself have for your answers?

Fundamentally the successful development of children's capacity for imaginative thinking depends on their own development as persons as well as on particular thinking skills. The next two chapters will discuss these in turn.

Notes

1. H.G. Wells (1904), *The Country of the Blind*. See H.G. Well's *Selected Short Stories*, Penguin, 1958:123ff.

2. Quoted in the Introduction by Nicholas Lash to Cardinal Newman's *A Grammar of Assent* (1979 edn, p. 15) from his *Letters and diaries*, vol. 30: 159.
3. The importance of concepts is increasingly acknowledged today, e.g. Westhill College (1991). The Stapleford Project directed by Trevor and Margaret Cooling, (Religious and Moral Educational Press (RMEP) 1992) is an example of classroom material based on a conceptual approach. See article by M & T Cooling in *Resource* vol. 14, no. 3, Summer 1992: pp. 1–3.
4. Xenophanes, from his didactic poem on 'Nature'.
5. Voltaire, *Le sottisier,* (xxxii).
6. 'Anthropomorphism' refers to thinking about God in terms of a human-being. It is important to distinguish between a crude use, and an appropriate, mature use, of anthropomorphism. The former *identifies* God with a human being, the latter *likens* God to a person in some respects, i.e. here the user realizes that the language is metaphorical.
7. This was quoted in a health magazine by Deborah Hutton under the heading 'Transcendence'.
8. Peter Thomas, 1991, 'Pupils with Potential . . . the Iknield partnership' Newsletter 21 of the National Association for Curriculum Enrichment and Extension (Summer 1991), p.5f.
9. Julie Gage. This was given to me by her teacher, Elizabeth Ashton.
10. Quoted from I.A. Richards, 1936, *The Philosophy of Rhetoric*, Galaxy Books, New York by Black in Ramsey 1971, p. 180 on its application to religion, see e.g. Soskice J. M. 1985 *Metaphor and Religious Language*.
11. See Richard Holloway's collection of essays 1991 *Who Needs Feminism*? An example of current debate is Daphne Hampson's book, 1990, *Theology and Feminism* which is discussed by Denise Newton 1990 in 'Shattering the dream of a post-patriarchal Christianity: can not even feminists redeem Christianity?' *Journal of Beliefs and Values*, vol. 11, no. 2.

CHAPTER 6

In search of the spiritual: the experiential approach

The purpose of this chapter is to examine the question of how pupils can gain some inkling, through their own experience, of what religion is about, so that their imagination is stimulated to conceive of the *possibility* of the spiritual dimension being more than meaningless talk.

It is well-known that experience teaches far more effectively than talking about something. To understand what an ocean is, it is far more helpful to see one rather than just read about oceans, and if we experience it by swimming in it or crossing it by boat, we are likely to have a much more real understanding. So experience is important, but, apart from that in which we are purely passive recipients of what happens to us, we have to have the will and the courage to seek it.

The experiential approach to RE

> We cannot discover
> New oceans
> Unless we have courage
> To lose sight
> Of the shore

These lines from André Gide are quoted in *New Methods in RE: An Experiential Approach* (Hammond et al. 1990: 26) – an approach which is gaining ground in schools. It is a method of RE which focuses on pupils' own capacity to relate to themselves at a deeper level – to their own authentic feelings and insights. It sees the RE teacher's task as two-fold: to help pupils to learn first: to take seriously their own inner experience, thereby coming also to respect that of other people; and secondly, to appreciate the role of metaphor in interpreting experience (p. 17).

The approach originated in the findings of the Religious Experience Research Unit originally set up by Alister Hardy in 1969.[1] The data so far accumulated suggests that half or more of the adult population of this country believe that they have had some sort of direct religious experience. Nearly half of these people never attend a place of worship and quite often they are unwilling to use religious language at all because they do not want to be associated with a particular religious institution. An interesting additional finding which is stressed is that it appears that such people are more rather than less likely to exhibit qualities of psychological balance and social responsibility.[2] David Hay deduces what this means for RE:

> There will be some pupils who know from their own experience what the RE teacher is talking about. Some of these may formally belong to a religious group. Other members of the class, because of their upbringing, may accept intellectually the beliefs of their own religious community, but lack any confirmation from their experience. Yet others may lack both religious belief and any experience that might make them dubious of their secularism.
>
> (Hay 1990: 108)

There is a distinction here between personal religious experience and formal membership of a religious tradition. The former can be found both within and outside the externally religious. This in itself constitutes a major difficulty for RE: how do we enable pupils to appreciate this distinction? It is so easy to judge by externals. Chapter 7 will discuss this further.

Another major difficulty to which Hay draws attention is the effects of secularist conditioning in restricting the horizons of children and young people. He confirms the analysis of western society given in Chapter 2: 'The problem for most RE teachers is . . . that the minds of the pupils are tightly closed against the possibility that reality might plausibly be seen in any other way than that transmitted via the dominant culture.' He therefore sees effective RE as essentially helping to liberate all pupils 'from the taboos which inhibit them from exploring freely the experiential and cognitive options available' (Hay 1990: 109).

The experiential method (outlined in Hammond, Hay *et al.* 1990) sets out to give detailed help to the teacher on how this kind of work can be begun in schools. The intention is to correct a serious imbalance in education as a whole, not just in RE. The emphasis on the desirability of academic detachment – however rarely achieved in practice – has had the effect of disengaging pupils at a personal level from what they are studying. This has been presumed to be desirable, as the only way in which to guard against indoctrination and rampant subjectivism.

Today this detached attitude to learning is being questioned even in subjects like science where it would seem to be most at home. Its unsuitability therefore for gaining understanding of religion is becoming more widely appreciated. It tends to view religion as something external, only appropriate possibly for other people.

The experiential approach therefore tries to get pupils in communication with the depths in themselves so that they may have some idea of what that is like for other people, as well as helping them to be more truly 'present' in what they are studying. It is important to note that the intention is de-indoctrination. 'The teacher is not attempting to convert pupils to any particular belief, but to increase their insight into other ways of seeing' (Hay 1990: 109).

The strengths of the approach are clear: it gets away from being content-dominated and takes the teaching of skills seriously, especially skills of stilling, centredness and attentiveness. The purpose of the exercises is to affirm a person, and also to integrate experience – they are holistic in intention. They are also interesting, which is a major point because without interest there is no learning.

Weaknesses of the experiential approach

It has, however, been open to criticism. For example Adrian Thatcher (1991) takes issue with the emphasis on private individualism which talk of 'inwardness' tends to convey, seeing this as based on a radical distinction between what is objective and what is subjective – a distinction which, though very influential since the seventeenth century, is now regarded as mistaken.

In a reply Hay and Hammond (1992) assure readers that they are not guilty of dualism or rampant individualism. The experiential approach is seeking to supply a missing ingredient in so much education including RE, that of genuine involvement and learning to become aware of the depths in one's own experience. They point out also that they offer, 'a practical means of complementing (not replacing) the other parts of the religious education syllabus' (Hay 1992: 149).

What I think is more debatable is how successfully the method can in practice avoid the following criticisms.

First, the experiential approach to RE tends to be only lightly related to religion. It affirms the 'spiritual' dimension but fails to make clear links with the great religious traditions except with regard possibly to Buddhism and certain aspects of Hinduism. This is a serious weakness in an approach intended to aid understanding of religion.

Secondly, while it wishes pupils to experience freedom, in practice it is easy for the teacher to determine the structure. Techniques such as guided fantasy reveal the teacher's presuppositions which are not discussed, and these are put across in a way which can have a particularly binding effect upon the recipients. The comment by one teacher about the objections of her class to one of her guided fantasies is an honest acknowledgement of this problem. She wrote that without the challenge of some who were Christians of a particular persuasion, 'I would not have been aware of how deeply my own assumptions had constructed the fantasy that I had desired' (Kathy Raban in Hammond *et al.* 1990: 219).

There seems indeed to be an unacknowledged weighting in the direction of a particular religion. Another teacher told me, after attending in-service courses, that while the approach offers an exciting avenue to explore which pupils find rewarding and even mind-blowing, and many of the exercises are valuable as a means of self-awareness, she felt that pupils were being steered towards abandoning the mind as a means of knowing and just accepting the subjectivity of values which do not have to be justified. She sees the insights of Zen at work here, and commented that, if this is so, then it should be stated and some critique of Buddhism as a religion given.[3]

Thirdly, although its intention is to encourage depth it can end up as being rather superficial, and indeed possibly dangerous, in failing to be aware of the pitfalls into which meditation not properly understood can fall. Precisely because it is seeking to bring some awareness of spirituality to those mostly brought up in a spiritual desert, great care is needed to avoid conveying misleading impressions. The confusion between introspection and meditation can be very serious. The purpose is not to reinforce egoism but to refocus awareness of the self. Within Eastern traditions this is usually expressed in the language of self-transcendence, annihilating the ego. It has nothing to do with self-centredness in the sense of moral immaturity. It does not fall under the strictures of Thatcher's criticism referred to above. Within semitically-derived religions the emphasis is on self-surrender and sacrifice in the interests of love.

It is of crucial importance that this distinction between centredness and self-centredness is appreciated by pupils – between affirmation of oneself which implies, and leads to, affirmation of others also, and selfish self-absorption which leads eventually to an incapacity to see others as persons at all.

Fourthly and finally, the nature of the participation asked for is not made clear. The approach states:

Experiential learning uses the tools of phenomenology, in particular the device of bracketing out, or putting aside, our personal assumptions when attempting to understand the religious life of another person.

(Hammond *et al.* 1990: 198)

From one point of view we all know probably what is meant by this: the importance of not allowing one's own stance to block the way to understanding someone else's. There is no doubt that this is something to which constant attention needs to be drawn. I argue for this in Chapter 12 concerning the possibility of participation in school worship at different levels, one level being a conscious but temporary withholding of the critical faculties in order to get on the wavelength of a particular belief.

Yet pupils cannot get on the wavelength of the experience of others by bracketing out all aspects of their own. There is little chance of the 'professional' participator emerging with real understanding, for to find out the truth of religion it has to be wrestled with and lived, not just safely and probably patronizingly studied from a safe distance. How do we know that the experience that we presume that other people have in their religion is what we ourselves experience as we come apparently empty-handed to it? The level of sophistication required here is very great even for highly educated adults. For pupils in school, the problems are infinitely more complex still. It is in any case impossible to come empty-handed. Even in the midst of 'participating' we are constantly interpreting in the light of what we know and expect.

The need for a broader experiential approach

It is important that this potentially very valuable approach safeguards itself so far as possible against misinterpretation: in particular, that the content of religious belief does not really matter, that knowledge of religious tradition is unimportant, and that any opinions and beliefs are acceptable so long as they are sincerely held. For in the present climate of opinion this is what might be conveyed.

One way of ensuring that such misinterpretation does not occur is to adopt an approach to 'experience' which is not so tied to 'inwardness'. Experience is, after all, part of the whole way in which all education happens, including RE, and it should not be associated with something particularly special or precious. It needs to be seen as part of a continuum of experience from the most ordinary and humdrum to the most sublime and special.

What would such a broader experiential approach look like? It might have at least six strands:

1. Integrating what is studied in school with personal experience

It would encourage pupils to relate to their own uniqueness as a normal activity – not as something done in special sessions or requiring special structures or special input by someone like a teacher. This integrating process needs to go on all the time, whatever is happening or being studied. It is the most important use of the word 'experiential' in its application to education. Because each person is unique, and has experiences which no other person has ever had quite in that way or in that combination of circumstances, this learning cannot be structured by teacher or syllabus or advisers from without, except possibly in certain exceptional situations where a sustained one-to-one relationship is possible or required. All the teacher can do – but it is a most important and fulfilling role – is to <u>encourage</u>

self-reflection through appropriate teaching style (see Chapter 10 on this). Reflectiveness should be seen as natural and part of the normal rhythm of daily life.

Elizabeth Ashton, an experienced primary school teacher and now lecturer at Durham University, has found that work on particular symbols can energize children into relating effectively to their own experience (Ashton 1989). This helps them to produce work substantially more creative and thoughtful than what they have been able to do before. The poem, 'Lavender Lily', quoted in Chapter 5, is an example of this from one of her classes. It is an expression of the child's experience at several levels, especially an awareness of a love of nature. The poem reflects on themes such as poverty and death in a way seemingly detached, but yet at considerable depth indicating the writer has really been involved in what she was expressing.

Effective RE would take such reflection a stage further. It would discuss specifically religious views on the purpose of life and attitudes to death. It would also discuss how general experience may be potentially seen as religious experience. Words such as 'spiritual' would probably form part of the discussion.

2. Opening up possibilities for interpreting experience

It is important for RE to engage explicitly with those aspects of experience which open up for many people a religious frame of reference. Pupils can be helped to appreciate the link between the spiritual dimension and religion, and to do this in such a way that the outcome is not assumed. Pupils may respond to seeing this possibility in different ways.

The links between the spiritual dimension and religion are in fact close. Peter Berger spoke about 'signals of transcendence' which are given in and through our normal human experience (Berger 1969: 70–96). People can immerse themselves in the spiritual dimension without being religious at all. Yet if these signals are really thought about, they can lead people to an awareness of religion.

Berger noted five:

1. the sense of order;
2. the phenomenon of play;
3. the experience of hope;
4. the concept of damnation – a sense of cosmic injustice to be put right;
5. the fact of humour.

Such aspects of life are normally just taken for granted yet, if thought about, they are at odds with a materialistic understanding of the world; they point to something other – something more.

We can add many other signals of transcendence present within ordinary and everyday experience. They can include:

1. a sense of wonder at beauty, especially the beauty of nature;
2. artistic creativity;
3. the experience of personal rapport with other people;
4. altruism;
5. the fact of love.

Such signals of transcendence can often consciously give rise to an awareness of the need to use a different kind of vocabulary. A very striking example was told me not long since by someone who attended a dinner party in Moscow soon after Gagarin's space trip[4] – the Gagarin who had reported that he did not see God in space (see p. 57). Apparently Gagarin said that when he looked out of the right window of his spacecraft and glimpsed the earth for the first time, he had an experience or sense of – and then he used a word which the interpreter did not know the meaning of, so he had to go to another table and ask another interpreter to help. After considerable discussion they came out with the word 'numinous'. Gagarin had had to search into the past for a word which perhaps he had heard from his granny!

Whether or not such factors develop religious awareness depends on the degree to which people can see a relationship between them and religion and can tease out the implications.

3. Experience explored through the arts

A stepping-stone for many people is through the arts seen not just as providing means of expression but also as giving meaning and helping to structure experience. Here the central point is not to try to imitate arts education in RE, but to encourage links with what pupils do and experience in their arts education. In this way RE continues to do what it should without trespassing outside its domain unduly – it can focus on *religion*, while the arts retain their integrity and are not treated like 'visual aids' or 'follow-up work'. Also it promotes that holistic sense of the whole of life's experience being brought into harmony, including the discords.

The arts are especially important and effective in arousing spiritual awareness because they can speak directly at a feeling level, as well as being free from any slavish dependence on religious ideas which are often rejected out of hand by secularists. The arts therefore provide an invaluable way-in for many people. Veronica Williams, for example, has developed an interesting approach in connection with her work on art history. She has found that she can interest modern teenagers, and develop attitudes of stillness and attentiveness and reflectiveness, through detailed study of certain masterpieces.[5] Involvement in the visual arts is one way in for many young people today.

The same can be said about music which provides an immensely satisfying spiritual experience for many people for whom religion is totally dead. Religious masterpieces such as the Messiah continue to exercise a fascination which is much more than enjoyment of good tunes.

Arts education and its relationship to RE is an area being explored in some depth today, for example by the Department of Arts Education at Warwick University and at King Alfred's College, Winchester.[6]

4. Investigating what is meant by 'spiritual' experience

The word 'spiritual' is often used in connection with aesthetic experience. Unfortunately, however, there is a great deal of uncertainty as to what the word means. This is not just an academic matter – it affects practice, for example in the arts. The art critic, Peter Fuller, considers: 'One worrying feature of recent years has been the fashionable appropriation of the language of the 'spiritual' to defend work of a numbing vacuity' (Fuller 1990: 18). It is important therefore to try to achieve some clarity.

The HMIs who produced the Supplement to Curriculum 11–16 (DES 1977) had an intense debate on this very matter. They could not reach agreement and so in the end two definitions emerged in the document:

1. The spiritual area is concerned with the awareness a person has of those elements in existence and experience which may be defined in terms of inner feelings and beliefs; they affect the way people see themselves and throw light for them on the purpose and meaning of life itself. Often these feelings and beliefs lead people to claim to know God and to glimpse the transcendent; sometimes they represent that striving and longing for perfection which characterizes human beings but always they are concerned with matters at the heart and root of existence.
2. The spiritual area is concerned with everything in human knowledge or experience that is connected with or derives from a sense of God or of gods. Spiritual is a meaningless adjective for the atheist and of dubious use to the agnostic. Irrespective of personal belief or disbelief, an unaccountable number of people have believed and do believe in the spiritual aspects of human life, and therefore their actions, attitudes and interpretations of events have been influenced accordingly.

There are difficulties with both these statements. The latter is unacceptable because non-religious people do talk about the 'spiritual'. Furthermore, we cannot equate the spiritual with the religious. As Basil Yeaxley put it back in 1925: 'the spiritual has a wider character than the religious, just as the religious does not fall wholly within the spiritual' (Yeaxley 1925: 46). True religion may be said to add to the spiritual a conscious relationship to the Source of the spiritual. Yet it is possible to have a real relationship without such consciousness, just as it is possible to talk about God without being spiritual.

The first definition is also unsatisfactory despite its broader nature and the way in which it might be regarded as potentially containing the second definition. The problem is that although the beliefs and feelings are 'always concerned with matters at the heart and root of existence' – which does suggest or give opportunity for something which is not just subjective in interpretation – it tends to subsume the religious view of life under what we might call a humanist umbrella. 'Often these feelings and beliefs lead people *to claim* to know God.' The phrase itself suggests the uncertainty of what is claimed, and in any case directs attention away from the content to the fact that some people are claiming it – in other words the human element is the focus of attention.

More therefore needs to be said. Yet even this is highly controversial! For any attempt to define what is meant by spiritual is easily killed in infancy by pointing out how ridiculous such an attempt is: the spiritual automatically transcends all possible categories and definitions. Nevertheless, the word continues to be used a great deal, even by those who do not wish to pinpoint its meaning. Have we therefore exhausted all possibilities of being clearer as to what we are talking about?

Clarifying what is meant by 'spiritual'
Table 6.1 suggests a way of drawing attention to what the spiritual dimension is, without giving the misleading impression of its being some kind of object. It refers to three radically different kinds of human behaviour and attitudes, one of which expresses ordinary human nature, one the 'spiritual' dimension, and one the reverse of both: what may be called the 'demonic', whether that word is understood symbolically or not.

Of course I am not here arguing for a return to a three-tier model of reality seen in literalistic terms. 'Supernatural' has had all kinds of misleading innuendoes associated with it – such as a separation between this world and another higher one. The spiritual plane is for all the great religions inseparable from the physical and psychological ways in which it manifests itself and becomes known by us, but yet it is truly distinguishable. Its relationship with the molecular 'vehicles' which express it is a non-reciprocal one: its presence can explain theirs, but they cannot explain it.

Table 6.1 **The spiritual dimension**

Ordinary plane:	Spiritual plane:	Demonic plane:
It is part of human nature –	It is a qualitatively different attitude	The ordinary and spiritual capacities of people can become corrupt so as-
1. to give in order to receive, or to give as good as you get	1. to give without thought of receiving anything in return, not even thanks, or to give when it costs far more than the person receiving suspects and therefore appreciates	1. to give in order to manipulate, to make someone dependent, to show off, or to bribe
2. to see things from one's own point of view, to measure the importance of things as they are important *to me*, to be interested in what is of use or value or pleasure *to me*	2. to see things really and seriously from someone else's point of view, to be really interested in what is of use or value or giving pleasure *to them* – to get on their wavelength though it is not one's own	2. to be obsessively self-centred, or to use the knowledge which one has acquired to control others for one's own ends, or be willing to harm them if they stand in one's way
3. to get pleasure from being successful, from being praised, from being listened to with approval, from being acknowledged, from receiving applause	3. to delight in other people's success and status, especially when lacking it oneself, or even when the other's success is at the expense of one's own	3. to delight in doing other people down, in working for their failure, in enjoying their misfortunes, in working in fact to destroy them as people
4. to fear disease, poverty, disgrace, loneliness, imprisonment, death	4. to accept all these things philosophically – to regard them lightly as worth risking in order to achieve some greater purpose, to be uncomplaining, even to find joy through such experiences	4. to take a macabre delight in hurting oneself, in being masochistic

Spirituality concerns a quality of life which transcends the natural plane and resists what may be called the unnatural, evil, or demonic.

Spirituality is a genuinely different dimension to reality. To see it requires imagination, and yet it is not itself the product of imagination. Imagination is the faculty whereby we perceive it – or better, glimpse it – but imagination does not create it.

The examples given in Table 6.1 refer to the kind of experience well within the capacity potentially of everyone, and may be so much accepted as part of everyday life as to go unnoticed. For people to see these as consciously linked to 'spiritual' and religious experience, other qualitites would normally be present:

1. *Inclusiveness* – a sense of unity and seamlessness, awareness of the inter-relationship of everything
2. *Assurance* – concerning the way things are, the great matters of life and death, the reason we are here – an inner certainty not imposed from without or dependent on other people's approval, nor reflecting chance moods.
3. *Inspiration* – used in its sense of 'being-breathed-in-to' and 'allowing' power to work within us. As a friend of mine – who has only the most ephemeral links with any religious tradition – put it recently to me: 'We must learn to be *channels* not *engines*!'
4. *Acceptance of mystery* – taking it for granted that the spirit is beyond our total comprehension, that this dimension cannot easily be put into words, or expressed adequately in any art form. It is to be pointed towards, implied, and therefore intuited. People see it or they do not. It is as primary as that. It cannot be proved or deduced. But people who glimpse it know its power and supreme attractiveness.

These four qualities or characteristics are only a beginning in attempting to say what spirituality is about. It is a dimension which meets us everywhere if we will let it, or which will elude us everywhere if we will not. Its natural language is one of symbol and paradox, and yet it is also utterly rational.

5. Relating 'spiritual' to 'religious'

The seemingly flowery language which people often have to resort to when trying to talk about spiritual experience results from an inability to use religious language as a means of communication; even if known, it is so likely today to be misunderstood. RE should help pupils to appreciate that there is another language possible – one which perhaps makes more sense, but that is for each person to decide for him/herself.

How do religious people understand the term 'spiritual'? Evelyn Underhill, speaking as a Christian, defined the spiritual life as one in which 'God and his eternal order have, more and more, their undivided sway' (Underhill 1985: 25). Different religions would express this in different ways. Buddhists for example would probably speak of it as progress towards a state of enlightenment in which persons are liberated from all false forms and images. In most religious traditions the concept of 'God' is invoked as the name for that Mystery which is at the heart of religion (see Chapters 5 and 8).

All major religions offer a deepening understanding of spirituality because of the way they enable people to be consciously in the presence of that Mystery. True religion makes spiritual progress easier because it provides a vocabulary, a structure and a community, all of which can help people to attend to this dimension. Religion also furnishes many inspiring examples as well as yardsticks to chart progress and guard against the hijacking of high intentions by evil forces, however these are understood. In a similar way, talk of the spiritual can help to revitalize religion. It is the goal of authentic religion and the judge of pseudo-religion.

RE should give access to the great spiritual traditions – the vocabulary used, and the kind of symbolism. In so doing, any hint of attempted indoctrination, conditioning, manipulation, even influencing and persuading, is misplaced because this dimension can only be grasped in freedom, or it is not grasped at all. It has to be experienced through people being able to be honest with themselves and reaching towards integrity. For each person is unique and it is useless as well as mistaken to try to be someone else. A recent anthology on spirituality has a quotation by Martin Buber from Rabbi Zusya when he said a short while before his death, 'In the world to come I shall not be asked why were you not Moses? I shall be asked why were you not Zusya?' (Buber 1985: 5).

'Be yourself' is, interestingly enough, a piece of advice at home in secularized Western societies as much as in traditional religion. But it is vital that this is seen not as legitimizing self-centredness, introspection or social irresponsibility, but as a means to ever deeper exploration of life in its totality. One of the best ways to do this is to study in depth particular people who have claimed to have religious experience.

6. Study in depth of religious experience

A study of, for example, St Francis of Assisi and the Hindu mystic Sri Ramana, who founded a flourishing ashram in South India and died in 1950, could be illuminating. This could help to give substance to what is meant by the spiritual dimension, for both of them lived out the kind of character expressed in the middle column of Table 6.1. In addition, work on Sri Ramana can help to illuminate many of the 'inwardness' – exercises suggested by the experiential approach to RE, for he constantly advised devotees to meditate on the question 'Who am I?' The bonus with St Francis is in helping pupils to appreciate a depth in what it means to be a Christian which is so easily today seen at a superficial externalist level.

There are several striking similarities between the two, as Table 6.2 shows. Both had particular experience which was overwhelming in its impact upon them. Sri Ramana used to say that he had only one

Table 6.2 **Similarities between Sri Ramana and St Francis**

Sri Ramana	St Francis	Similarity
Father a lawyer	Father a merchant	Middle-class background
Left home without saying where he was going	Feud with father led to hearing before bishop	Unconventional attitude towards parents
Experience at Madurai when he was 16	Meeting with the leper Praying before the crucifix in San Damiano Hearing words from St. Matthew's gospel	Overwhelming experience that changed the course of their lives
Life of a *sannyasin*	Life of poverty	Astonishing single-mindedness in pursuing the ideal
Ashram at Tiruvanamallai	Order of friars	Neither of them set out to found a community, but it happened spontaneously
E.g. 'Birthday ode'	E.g. 'Perfect joy'	Both excellent teachers using colourful, homely language
Composed *bhajans* – devotional song	One of the first great poems in the Italian language: 'Canticle of Brother Sun'	Both poets
Devotees included professors	E.g. anecdote of his being able to resolve a difficult theological problem which defeated the scholars at Siena University	Not academic, but revered by academics as wise
Animals at ashram	E.g. wolf of Gubbio	Love of animals
Many came to him for advice	Anecdotes of his visit to Bologna, and to the Muslim Sultan	Peace-loving and active in trying to end feuds and fighting
Died of cancer without taking drugs of any kind	He became almost blind and died at the age of 44 from various diseases	Both endured great suffering with incredible stoicism

experience in his life; he spent the rest working it out. At the age of 16, alone in his uncle's house in Madurai, he describes how a sudden terror of death overtook him, and he found himself dramatizing the occurrence of death.

I lay with my limbs stretched out as stiff as though rigor mortis had set in, and imitated a corpse so as to give greater reality to the enquiry. 'Well then,' I said to myself, 'this body is dead. It will be carried stiff to the burning ground and there burnt and reduced to ashes. But with the death of this body am I dead? Is the body I? It is silent and inert but I feel the full force of my personality and even the voice of the 'I' within me, apart from it. So I am Spirit transcending the body.' All this was not dull thought; it flashed through me vividly as living truth which I perceived directly, almost without thought process. 'I' was something very real, the only real thing about my present state, and all the conscious activity connected with my body was centred on the 'I'. From that moment onwards the 'I' or Self focussed attention on itself by a powerful fascination. Fear of death had vanished once and for all.[7]

For St Francis there were a number of decisive moments, such as when he saw the leper. He dismounted from his horse and embraced the leper even though the thought of doing so was so repulsive to him. He wrote in his Testament not long before he died: 'While I was living in sin, it seemed a very bitter thing to look at lepers; but the Lord Himself led me among them, and I had compassion on them. And when I left them, the thing that had seemed so horrible to me was transformed into happiness of body and soul for me.'[8] Another experience was when he was praying before the crucifix in San Damiano and it seemed to him that it gave him the message, 'Build my church', which he immediately interpreted quite literally as, 'Save this church from crumbling into ruins'. And the third occasion was in another church outside Assisi when he heard the reading from St Matthew's gospel about absolute poverty, and he became convinced that that was the path he had to follow.[9]

The self-authenticating nature of their experiences meant that neither of them was able to doubt them, yet the similarities must not blind us to certain differences. The experiences were interpreted quite differently, even though they produced remarkable resemblances in character. This raises the interesting question of whether by having different expectations the experiences were in fact different. Usually religious people tend to see these as different, Sri Ramana's being an experience of enlightenment and awareness of the Oneness of being, whilst St Francis's conveyed a sense of communion with God – a sense of a Presence revealing itself.

Such study can deepen RE as well as promote spiritual awareness across the whole curriculum. All religions furnish many examples. A list of books and materials on Sri Ramana and St Francis is given below[10] and there are other references to Sri Ramana in Chapter 10 (pp. 152, 155–7) and to St Francis in Chapters 8, 10 and 12 (pp. 122, 147 and 189).

The need for reflection on experience

It is important in coming to understand religion to appreciate the role of experience in the founding and development of it. Beliefs are not conjured up out of nothing but are rather a response to experience. There is always a certain mismatch between belief and experience, because the latter is untidy; it comes to us without our asking for it, while the expression in words of our interpretation of experience tends to have a more clear-cut, fixed character about it. A doctrine such as the Christian belief in God as Trinity arose out of the way in which Christians experienced God as personal and in three quite distinct ways and yet as one.[11] Logically this may not seem to make sense, yet for Christians it is like paradox pointing beyond a neat literalism to that reality which has impinged itself on them. Paradox defies logic, yet not by dismissing it but by teasing us to think wider and deeper and extend our horizons and challenge our starting-points.

Awareness of the possible truth of paradox is a most helpful way in to appreciating the nature of religious language as it wrestles to express experience. The theologian, Donald Baillie, used to give the example of two quite different kinds of maps – one showing hemispheres and the other straight. Both are needed to convey a spherical world in two dimensions, for although they contradict each other at every point to some degree, yet together they correct and balance each other in attempting the impossible, i.e. to convey an accurate impression in two-dimensional terms of the spherical world.

Such problems in expressing the insight arising out of experience cause some people to ask: Why bother? Why not just accept experience – why try to understand it and encapsulate it in words which will necessarily have an imprisoning effect upon the insight? T.S. Eliot spoke of 'the intolerable wrestle with words and meanings'.[12] Why do with such hard work?

Basically, it is necessary to do so because interpretation and experience inevitably interact. This is so even if the interpretation given to an experience, or which stimulated the experience, is one not authentic to it, conditioned perhaps by the society of which the individual is a part. In order to ensure that the expression given to experience is as little of a mismatch as possible, it is necessary to develop the capacity for reflective thinking, and to this I now turn.

Notes

1. Now known as the Alister Hardy Research Centre. It is housed at Westminster College, Oxford.
2. Hammond et al. (1990) sets out visually some research findings on this on p. 16.
3. I gratefully acknowledge correspondence with Penny Thompson, a Liverpool secondary school teacher.
4. Conversation with Michael Graham-Jones at a conference held in 1991 at the Selly Oak Colleges, Birmingham by the Gospel and our Culture Project.

5. Veronica Williams: unpublished MA thesis in religious education (1988) Kings College, London. Examples of the approach can be found in a booklet on *Marriage* (Christian Education Movement, 1990: 32–50) – a book of materials drawn up as part of the *Project Revalues Four Five* of which she was the director. She is now Head of RE at King Alfred's College, Winchester.
6. See e.g. Dennis Starkings, 1993, *Religion and the Arts in Education: Dimensions of Spirituality*, also J. Hinnells, 1990, 'Religion and the arts' in King 1990 and J. Begbie, 1992, *The Gospel, the Arts and our Culture* in Montefiore, 1992. A classic is W. Kandinsky, 1977, *Concerning the Spiritual in Art* .
7. Described in his own words, and translated by Arthur Osborne, 1970 p.18f.
8. Translated by Leo Sherley-Price, 1959, *St Francis of Assisi*, Mowbrays, p. 200.
9. See, e.g., J.R.H. Moorman, 1963, *Saint Francis of Assisi,* 11 and 19.
10. For Sri Ramana see:
    Arthur Osborne, 1970, *Ramana Maharshi and the Path of Self-knowledge*; T.M.P. Mahadevan, 1977, *Ramana Maharshi – The Sage of Arunacala;* T.M.P. Mahadevan, 1976, *Ramana Maharshi and His Philosophy of Existence;* M. Subbaraya Kamath, 1973, *Sri Maharshi – A Short Life-sketch*
    For St Francis see:
    John R.H. Moorman, 1963, *Saint Francis of Assisi*; Leo Sherley-Price, 1959, *St Francis of Assisi*; Marion A. Habig (ed.), 1973, *St Francis of Assisi – Omnibus of Sources*; Wallet of materials on St Francis from the Farmington Institute.
11. For discussion of how creeds came into existence see for example: R.P.C. Hanson, 1984, *The Making of the Doctrine of the Trinity*; Frances Young, 1991, The Making of the Creeds.
12. T.S. Eliot, *Four Quartets*: 'East Coker II'.

CHAPTER 7

They can't all be right: developing reflective thinking about truth-claims

A major task for RE is to help pupils forward in their thinking. It is not for teachers to tell them what to believe or value, but it is for them to try to equip pupils in such a way that they can enter into the debate and develop a coherent and perceptive worldview for themselves. Another way of putting it is to say that RE has to offer feasible road-maps enabling pupils to chart their own way around the difficult country of religion with its complexity and ambiguity. This involves – whether we like it or not – teaching them how to think; the capacity for being scholars in the true sense of the word has to be shared with everyone instead of being for an elite of specially gifted, specially privileged pupils.

The time-honoured expectation that pupils have to be told what to believe by authority in the form of parents, teachers or the state, can no longer operate today. In the modern world the reasons for accepting any particular authority can be and are challenged. It is as impossible as it is undesirable to try to put the clock back and treat the majority of pupils as being necessarily philosophical and theological infants incapable of any more. Their level of sophistication in other areas of life has become much more marked. This must happen with regard to RE too.

The importance of developing reflective thinking

There are many other reasons for giving careful thought to developing children's capacity for reflective thinking:

1. such an emphasis in RE relates to the questions pupils actually ask. Even young children are interested in metaphysical questions. As one 8 year-old pupil explained: 'I'm quite good at thinking. I just need someone to start me up.' (Fisher 1990: 245) How far does RE start them up? The interest continues, even intensifies, during adolescence. The Head of Humanities in a large comprehensive school commented in my hearing, in a staff meeting about 3rd year general discussion groups on controversial issues, that 'in about half of such groups the question of God is brought in by

some kid or other' and that he felt 'put on the spot'. RE is one of the few opportunities in the school timetable where such questions can be pursued in some depth.

2. reflective thinking takes questions of truth – which won't go away – seriously. In a world of potentially conflicting beliefs it can thus help to extract the sting from many otherwise nasty situations of conflict and tension. Many wrong turnings in discussion and communication in general can be avoided, as unnecessary difficulties are pre-empted. For example, many Protestants used to criticize Roman Catholics on the grounds that they worship the Virgin Mary. Yet this was in fact a pseudo-problem because Catholics do not worship Mary, but honour her as mother of the Christ whom they do worship.

3. truth per se matters; beliefs and values based on a falsehood or mere prejudice are not only unstable but likely to cause much damage and hurt to the people holding them as well as to others who may become their victims. The twentieth century has seen many horrific examples of the power of wrong thinking, and this has often turned on matters of religion. Such an emphasis in RE can therefore help to guard against delusion and prejudice.

4. such work would help to protect pupils from indoctrination from whatever source, religious or secular. Only thus, in fact, can over-pressurizing of the young be avoided – by developing their capacity to be able to think effectively for themselves.

5. such work will also help pupils approach the diversity of religious beliefs in an open and non-dogmatic way without succumbing to the relativism which tends to regard different beliefs as just a matter of opinion. This will enable creative exploration of the well-worn comment 'but they can't all be right!' rather than saying there's no point in the question behind the statement.

Implications for RE

It is easy to understand, however, why teachers tend to run away from helping children to evaluate truth-claims. A minefield seems to open up: complexity, controversy, doubt, anxiety, anger, bitterness, bigotry, intolerance . . . all these are possible.

Yet by embarking on these difficult waters we are confronting what religion really is, not a safe cardboard version of it neatly packaged up for general retail. This is therefore preparing pupils for the real world; they will not have to unlearn, nor painfully make many avoidable mistakes, when forced by life's vagaries to make the journey across the waters (or the minefield) alone.

Also this is the point at which RE really comes radically alive, where it shows the excitement and challenge of which it is capable. By comparison the seemingly safe approach is anaemic and superficial – it does not really engage pupils. This does.

Pupils of all ages and abilities have deeply held opinions about the way things actually are, about reality, about truth. If teachers tap into this they plug into a powerhouse of emotional – and potentially intellectual – energy. As this also is the way to understanding religion, we must go forward at this point.

But we ought to make the journey as safe as possible – can we ensure that at least beneficial results are *more likely* to ensue than unfortunate results? By 'beneficial' I mean those summarized in Chapter 12 on page 176 which accord with the five-fold quality of respect outlined in Chapter 1 as basic to education as to civilized living. I think certain guiding principles can help and offer starting-points for reflective thinking.

Before turning to these – set out in two stages (see below, pp. 93–106) – we need to be clear what we mean by reflective thinking, and that pupils *can* do it.

Why 'reflective thinking'?

This term is useful to get away from certain stereotypes which tend to come into people's minds when 'thinking' is mentioned. Figure 7.1 lists some of these, together with the kind of thinking I have in mind.

First, it has a quality of first-handedness and authenticity about it – a person's own thinking not somebody else's. In an unusual analogy Coleridge described people as 'tanks' or 'springs' according to the way they borrow ideas from others: 'tanks' just take over ideas and store them like water; 'springs' adopt them, producing a stream of water and so making them their own.[1] The one can easily become stagnant, the other has ongoing vitality of its own.

Secondly, it is mindfully directed thinking, displaying a quality of attentiveness. Without this quality, nothing can be learned or understood. Yet it is important not to confuse attentiveness with the kind of frowning application traditional academic work has often encouraged. We have probably all experienced failing to see something and then later, as we do the washing-up or walk to the post, suddenly 'the penny drops', and we exclaim 'But of course . . . '. Insight is like that: the quality of attentiveness must not be spoilt by our getting in the way of it – by the wrong kind of effort or by anxiety and feelings of self-doubt.

Thirdly, thinking which is reflective is intimately linked with feelings, imagination and involvement in life, and is concerned about truth. Pure logic is only a small part of the thinking we habitually do, and can only be so because it is only appropriate for certain limited activities. In fact what we feel relates to what we think – the concepts

Figure 7.1 **What kind of thinkers do you want pupils to be?**

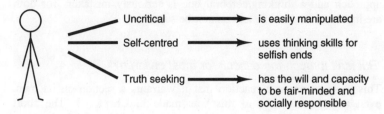

Uncritical	is easily manipulated
Self-centred	uses thinking skills for selfish ends
Truth seeking	has the will and capacity to be fair-minded and socially responsible

All people think. The question is **how** they think, and for what purpose.

Reflective thinking refers to truth-seeking.
Such obstacles as these

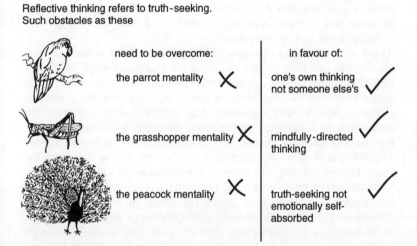

need to be overcome:	in favour of:
the parrot mentality ✗	one's own thinking not someone else's ✓
the grasshopper mentality ✗	mindfully-directed thinking ✓
the peacock mentality ✗	truth-seeking not emotionally self-absorbed ✓

we have, how we interpret situations, what we think ought to happen, and so on. And what we think relates to what we feel. Subjective reactions colour all we hear and see, and the words we use. Also there is a close connection between reason and emotion in other ways. The rational person *cares* about truth and is *disposed* to seek it.

Reflective thinking can perhaps be summarized by a quotation from the philosopher Basil Mitchell. He sees it as:

a matter of individuals attempting, incompletely, to make sense of the total environment in which they find themselves and to respond rightly to it. It is an activity which involves the whole person and calls for sympathetic imagination, sensitivity and constant self-criticism.

(Mitchell 1990: 210–11)

Any view of RE that sees a split between a feelings/affective approach and a thinking/cerebral one is seriously mistaken, for both are involved all the time and cannot be separated.

'But isn't it much too difficult for most children?'

This is so common a reaction that it warrants a section on its own, even though reference to this was made in Chapter 5. The short answer to this question is no: it is not something which demands special intellectual capacity. To do it one must be human, with feelings, experience, and some basic capability for getting on the wave-length of other people, as well as having a certain innate logical ability – the kind which enables a baby to learn unaided the mysteries of language. The capacity to make sophisticated discernment in thought-processes is within the grasp of almost everyone and constantly demonstrated in everyday life. It is this capacity to which RE must seek to relate, enabling transference of skills from the general to the religious sphere of enquiry.

If I want children to become philosophers in RE it is because they are already incipient philosophers, as for example Gareth Matthews (1980) has persuasively argued. Reflective thinking is not beyond the capacity of any but the most severely mentally retarded. How far children take it, and especially the language they use and the sophistication with which they employ concepts, will obviously vary enormously, but none should be excluded because of a teacher's prior decision that they are not capable. How far they progress depends on many factors, but they will not progress unless given a chance.

A scientist I know is amazed how often his eight year-old son can see immediately through a tangle of ideas in a problem – the directness and uncomplicatedness and openness of the child is a huge asset which many adults have lost. Wordsworth spoke of children 'trailing clouds of glory',[2] and their intuitive appreciation of Mystery may be one aspect of this which many adults have lost to their own deprivation and that of others.

An exaggerated and misplaced reliance on the research of Piaget and Goldman has encouraged teachers to have low expectations concerning children's abilities. Criticisms of that research have already been discussed in Chapter 5 (pp. 58–9). Here we can just note that limitations of expression and vocabulary can give the impression of naivety, just as sophistication in language can hide naivety in thought. A lively and optimistic search to find hidden depths and insights and questioning within pupils must replace negative attitudes towards children's capacity for thinking. In an illuminating interview on management, John Harvey-Jones made many comments as relevant to teaching as to management:[3]

One of the roles of management is to grow people's belief in themselves and raise their aspirations . . . They can do what they believe they can do but they sure as hell cannot do what their manager believes they cannot do. If you are told enough times that you are incapable, you begin to believe it and lose the self-confidence you need to do your job. . . . Most people are switched on by recognition.

(Harvey-Jones 1991 p. 80)

This applies profoundly to pupils' capacity for reflective thinking.

A structure for reflective thinking

For helping pupils towards greater sophistication in their thinking, the following suggestions may be helpful. Two stages are involved, the reason for which is neatly summarized in this quotation from C.S. Lewis:

The first qualification for judging any piece of workmanship from a corkscrew to a cathedral is to know what it is – what it was intended to do and how it is meant to be used. After that has been discovered the temperance reformer may decide that the corkscrew was made for a bad purpose, and the communist may think the same about the cathedral. But such questions come later. the first thing is to understand the object before you: as long as you think that the corkscrew was meant for opening tins or the cathedral for entertaining tourists you can say nothing to the purpose about them.[4]

STAGE 1: Being sure we understand what the belief under discussion really is

This is often much more complicated, especially with regard to religion, than many people think. Discernment is called for at at least seven levels before seriously trying to evaluate whether a belief is true or not. They can be thought of as seven tests to be applied. Trying these out helps to ensure that we actually understand what we are talking about and what the beliefs actually are. Table 7.1 lists these and examples discussed in the text, and suggests an exercise on them.

Communication test
This concerns the importance of understanding the words used and making sure that in an argument both sides mean the same by them. The problem of thinking we are attaching the same meaning to a word or action when we may not be can be appreciated humorously. Pupils can enjoy making up nonsense sentences like 'For goodness sake, put the table into the teapot!' or 'The house looked up and ran away.'
    Conversations such as this can help children see the point:

Table 7.1 **Levels of discernment necessary for understanding religion**

Level	Focus everyday example	Simple application	General religion	Applied to
1. COMMUNICATION	Meaning of words	'Giraffe' conversation (p. 95)	'Democracy' conversation (p. 95)	'I don't believe in God' 'I do' (p. 95)
2. ACCURACY	Facts and honesty	Doctor's prescription (p. 95)	Charles II anecdote (p. 95)	Protestant/Catholic attitude to Virgin Mary? (p. 89) Do Hindus worship many gods? (p. 95)
3. INTEGRITY	Sensing hypocrisy or other mis-match between belief and behaviour	Car-driver (p. 96)	'Listening' conversation (p. 96)	Vicar down the road; Terrorism (p. 96)
4. IMPORTANCE	Outer words actions and inner meaning	Shaking hands (p. 96)	'School uniform' conversation (p. 97)	Church-going for incense/music Muslim prayer-mat (p. 97)
5. DISTINCTIVENESS	Both/and	HO^2 = water hand/body (p. 97)		'Bible yes or no?' (p. 98)
6. CONTEXT	Historical sensitivity	'Stop talking' (p. 97)		'Let us pray' 'Jesus the Son of God' (p. 98)
7. AFFIRMATION	Creative relationship	'Football' (pp. 99–100)	'Anti-semitism' (p. 101)	'Meditation' (p. 100)

Exercise on these using an example from everyday life to illustrate each level

CHEESE * Match the sentences with the levels.

a. '*Cheese* and biscuits after the meal is a middle-class eating habit.

b. 'The *cheese* made an enormous noise and then flew off.'

c. 'The wedge-shaped chalk may look like *cheese* but it doesn't taste like it.'

d. 'I personally don't like *cheese*, but many people love it – try some for yourself.'

e. 'I hate *cheese*' (because the Gorgonzola mum eats smells horrible) 'I love *cheese*' (especially with toast for Saturday supper).

f. '*Cheese* is curdled butter.'

g. '*Cheese* is different from eggs and flour but in a souffle is not separate from them.'

*The kind of food analogy not under attack in Hull's *Mishmash* (1992)!

Penny: 'I love giraffes – I love stroking them on my lap – I'd love to have one for a pet.'
Daphne: 'I would be scared out of my wits to have a giraffe – it's a wild animal and far too big for our garden!'

The same kind of mistake – usually entirely hidden from the people with the opposing views – can easily creep in to discussion about more serious matters. Thus, for example:

A   'Democracy is the finest form of government.'
B   'It certainly is not.'

(*A* thinks of equality and liberty when the word 'democracy' is mentioned; *B* of football hooliganism and anarchic free-for-all.)
This is an example concerning religion:

Fiona: 'I don't believe in God – science has disproved all that stuff.'
Mark: 'I do believe in God – it makes sense to me as nothing else does.'

The disagreement here is at least partially one over the use of words. Fiona and Mark mean something quite different by the word 'God' such that they come to diametrically opposite conclusions.

Accuracy test
This concerns being fair with regard to what a belief actually claims. Accuracy matters in everyday life. For example, in a doctor's surgery:

Patient: '4 tablespoons, did you say?'
Doctor: 'Good God no, 4 teaspoons.'

A famous example of the importance of checking whether the so-called facts are right occurred on the occasion of Charles II founding the Royal Society in 1660. At the inaugural meeting he posed this question: 'Why does water not spill over a bowl filled to the brim when goldfish are added?' Several months later, after much mental sweating, someone thought to ask, was the King right? They did the simple experiment and of course found that he was not!
A religious example was given on page 89. Another example might be attitudes towards Hinduism. The question is often asked whether Hindus believe in many gods and goddesses. Most Hindus whom I have met would say that they do not, for they believe that at the heart of life is Oneness – Brahman – which manifests itself in an infinite number of forms. Veneration of the images is therefore for the devout Hindu worship of Brahman.

Integrity Test

It is important when evaluating a belief to weed out of consideration any form of pretence or hypocrisy associated with the people claiming to hold the belief. Here are two examples of mismatch between statement and behaviour. A car driver indicates that he is turning right but goes straight on with disastrous consequences, as my brother discovered to his cost recently! Advice to drivers is to act according to the direction in which the wheels of the car are pointing, not trusting the signal given.

Y talking to Z:

Y: 'Listening is so important.'

Half an hour later:

Z: 'I couldn't get a word in edgeways', muttered as he managed finally to get away.

What *Y* said may be right, even though Y fails to act by it.

The application of this distinction to religion is exceedingly important. Comments such as these are quite common: e.g. 'I'll have nothing to do with religion – that vicar down the road couldn't care a damn for anyone.' Or what about the newspaper headline: 'Religious mania behind terrorism?' It is easy to lump together under the heading of religion the political powermonger and the self-effacing saint, the ignorant victim of conditioning and superstition with the thoughtful and intelligent worshipper, the sensationalist religious leader with the painstaking scholar. Unless we sort this out there is no hope of reaching any intelligent or sensible evaluation of religion.

These phenomena are as different as chalk from cheese. To eat chalk is as foolish as to try to write on a blackboard with cheese! Yet thousands of people do in effect do this when they reject religion because of the hypocrisy, superstition and dogmatism of some of its advocates, and when they accept religion because of their own taste for status, a safe life, or being hypnotized by the magnetism of some charismatic figure.

Importance test

Equally important for understanding of religion is the ability to distinguish between what is peripheral and what is central. The relative ease with which external forms and behaviour can be observed, and the degree of sensitivity required for penetrating their inner significance make this a special 'trap for the unwary'.

It is best to begin with some everyday examples which might include: 'They shook hands.' What did they mean by this? Did they agree? Were they just being polite? Were they deceiving each other?

Head to visitor: 'The purpose of school uniform is so that pupils have a pride in belonging to the school.'
Later the visitor gets in conversation with a pupil.

Visitor: 'Why do you wear school uniform?'
Pupil: 'Because I'd get into trouble if I didn't.'
Visitor: 'So it doesn't make you feel as though you belong.'
Pupil: 'Bloody hell no – I hate wearing it.'

Applied to religion, people often say things like this: 'I can't stand all the incense, candles and ceremony, and above all the sermons, so I'm having nothing to do with religion'; 'I go to church because I love the music'.

Scores of examples can be given from all the great religions, for this touches on the relationship of external words and actions to religious belief. This quotation from the *Muslim News* shows how important the distinction is, and what misinterpretation is possible if pupils are not helped sufficiently to see it:

In Islam, only the Qur'an is considered 'holy'. A teacher for example may hold up a prayer mat to signify a 'holy' object. The distinction between the mat being just an object upon which prayer is performed on and not the object of worship may cause problems.[5]

(See Chapter 8 for further discussion on this as applied to religion.)

Distinctiveness test
It may seem an arid and dull activity to analyse and make distinctions. Wordsworth can be quoted:

> Our meddling intellect
> Mis-shapes the beauteous form of things
> We murder to dissect[6]

Yet his friend Coleridge could see a middle path – distinguishing, not in order to divide or separate, but in order to discern or understand.[7] An obvious example is the relationship of a part to a whole. The hand can be distinguished from the body, yet it belongs to it in such a way that it cannot operate as a hand unless attached to the body – except in fantasy as in Ted Hughes' story of The Iron Man. Similarly, things can be inseparable even as they are distinguishable, as water = H_2O.

The difficulty which many people have in seeing this where religion is concerned is because of an either/or mentality. There are of course many cases where there is a necessary either/or in that if something is inherently contradictory, then choice has to be made. If I am writing on this side of the paper I cannot at the same moment be writing on the other side. Either the car engine is on or it is not. Either there is some cake left or there is not. Either there is money in the purse or there is not, etc.

But there is often a strong temptation to see things as either/or when they are in fact both/and. A graphic example was given me when on my first day of lecturing in a college of education a student came up and earnestly asked me: 'Do you believe the Bible – yes or no?' I was presented with a choice between just two positions when in fact there are many more possible ones.

Context test

This test highlights the necessity to understand the original context of a belief and make sure that something is not being wrenched out of that to a setting where it does not apply.

The question of context is extremely important. The same remark can cause very different reactions in different settings. 'Stop talking' can be seen as plain common sense if everyone is talking at once, but if it comes from an over-talkative mother with a shy child it can have serious consequences on the child's character. Similarly, in a court where a witness is being browbeaten under cross-examination, or in a meeting where someone hogs the discussion and refuses to listen to an important point which is being made, it may be important that the injunction is resisted.

These are terribly obvious points, but we tend to forget them when dealing with complex and highly controversial matters which matter emotionally to us. Applied to religion here are two statements which can be received in totally different ways according to the context.

a) The phrase, 'Let us pray'. If this comes in a school assembly where there are many agnostics or atheists possibly present it can provoke the reaction, 'How dare they try to make us Christian'. But for an ordinary church service this can be regarded as absolutely matter of fact. If it occurs at the beginning of a committee meeting where something is going to be pushed through and the agenda manipulated it can provoke the reaction, '. . . hypocrites'. If it is said in the context of a vicar with a bereaved family who are deeply religious it can mean, 'Yes indeed, this will really help us'. If it is said in a situation of trouble or danger at sea or at war it can be received, even by people who are not religious, as 'Perhaps there is something in it. It's worth a try'.

b) A second example is the statement: Jesus was the son of God. It is interesting to compare the reactions of people from different religions to this statement. Most Hindus will be happy to say, 'Yes everyone is'. Muslims, however, are likely to say, 'No this is blasphemous. God is not a person who can have a son.' The agnostic and the Buddhist might say, 'So Christians believe, but other people do not', while the Christian within the context of worship might say, 'Yes, his life revealed God in a special way'.

This is the same statement which brings into play a totally different set of reactions in each case owing to the different perspectives. But in order to be understood it needs to be seen within its original context of faith in one God who can only be spoken about by using metaphorical language.

Affirmation test
This concerns the capacity to discern how far the content of a belief is positive as opposed to negative, and how far this promotes engagement with people rather than indifference to them or denial of them as persons.

The word 'affirmation' can be used in two quite different ways: as affirming a statement and as affirming people. These are related, however, if the first is a matter of central belief to a person, as it often is with religion – what they spend a great deal of time and effort on, what makes them tick. A negative judgement passed on such a belief has repercussions on the person, however indirect these may be.

Table 7.2 **Affirmation test**

Remark	How positive or negative the remark is about football	How positive or negative the remark is in affirming people who play or watch football
	+ –	
(a) Football's a fine game	<1> 2 3 4 5 6	1
(b) Football's a fine game, though I don't happen to like it	1 <2> 3 4 5 6	1
(c) Football can be enjoyable, even though it often isn't	1 2 <3> 4 5 6	2
(d) Football's boring, even though sometimes it is a good game	1 2 3 <4> 5 6	5
(e) I think football's a poor game	1 2 3 4 <5> 6	6
(f) Football's a waste of time	1 2 3 4 5 <6>	6

Table 7.2 gives an example which most people would find relatively straightforward. The content of the opinion in each case would have a spin-off effect on people who happen to love football and give a lot of time to watching, playing or training for it. The effect of our comments is likely to be intensified towards either (1) or (6). Thus it is clear that

(a) affirms the footballer;

(b) also affirms the footballer because the speaker has made it clear that it is a personal reaction of liking or disliking which has nothing to do with appreciation of football's being a good game;

(c) is affirming also because although criticism of the game is stated, its positive value comes first, and in any case the keen footballer is likely to be the first to agree that the level of enjoyment varies according to different games of football;

(d) however veers towards dismissal of football and therefore dismissal of what is meaningful to the footballer, because although it acknowledges that sometimes it is a good game the emphasis is on the negative side;

(e) is not affirming because even though the hurt to the footballer is cushioned by making it clear that this is a personal opinion, a very negative judgement is in fact articulated;

(f) has the straight effect of dismissing the footballer as well as football because it implies that anyone who spends time on football is stupid.

The importance of affirmation With regard to football it perhaps does not matter very much – people who like playing it or watching it are not likely to be seriously affected by our negative comments; they will just think that *we* are stupid and go on playing and watching as before. But substitute something like modern art, or even more so religion, and the repercussions of positive or negative statements on the people who do it are likely to be considerably greater. Applied to the theme of meditation, for example, such as is practised within Buddhism and many forms of Hinduism especially, but which is also present within other major religious traditions, a range of possible opinions is possible:

1. meditation is extremely helpful;
2. meditation is extremely helpful for many people, even though it is not for me;
3. meditation can be helpful, even though it often is not;
4. meditation is unlikely to be helpful, even though there are exceptions;
5. I think meditation is a waste of time;
6. there's nothing in meditation.

What will be the likely effects of such judgements on someone for whom practising meditation has become an important part of life, perhaps helping them to cope with difficulties and gain a sense of freedom and peace? If we care about other people – and if we want so far as possible to affirm other people – we shall walk warily before dismissing out of hand, discourteously or clumsily, what is deeply meaningful to them.

Yet authentic conversation and involvement must allow for a full range of likes and dislikes to be expressed, and also for criticism as well as acknowledgement, but we need to do this in such a way that we do as little damage as possible to other people as people. Therefore, we should be very wary indeed of (e) and (f) types of statements unless we are sure that there is something really negative that has to be exposed and which, even if it hurts people in the process, is nevertheless necessary.

The non-affirmation of what is negative An example might be the following. Here are six statements about a belief which is wholly negative in itself and in its implications:

1. anti-semitism is justified;
2. anti-semitism may be justified, but some Jews are all right;
3. anti-semitism is sometimes justified, though often it is not;
4. anti-semitism is not justified, though sometimes there may be a case for it;
5. I think anti-semitism is evil;
6. anti-semitism is evil.

Statement (6) is the one to which most civilized people would subscribe. It is judgemental and not affirming of, for example, Nazis. Yet it does not falsify the principle of affirmation for which I am arguing. First, a distinction can and should be made between judging a belief or behaviour, and judging a person – we can affirm a person as a person without condoning his/her beliefs or behaviour. We can, for example, account for the latter, even if we dislike it, by means of finding various reasons for that behaviour such as upbringing, unfortunate company, or unpleasant experiences. There are many instances of victims of Nazi aggression who have been able to do just this – to forgive despite terrible hurt.

Secondly, although the belief we are denying poses as an affirmation grammatically or verbally, yet its content refers to a non-recognition of people, a negative judgement in this case of mammoth proportions on a whole people. A mathematical analogy might help us to see what is involved here: to affirm a real affirmation is positive, but to affirm something which is itself negative is to end up with a negative in the same way – no better than what we are criticizing. For a minus and a plus make another minus. But if we oppose the negative point we make possible something positive, for two minuses make a plus.

STAGE 2: Evaluating the truth of a belief

This kind of thinking is leading on from the question of analysis to that of evaluation. The issue here is not only Where *do* I locate my response?, but Where *ought* I to locate it in order not to be misguided, or plain wrong, or reveal my ignorance or blindness? There is a need for criteria which relate to the basis upon which we evaluate anything. And these we need to share with pupils. Thus, about beliefs and values in science education, Michael Poole writes:

> In science education and in other areas of the curriculum more help needs to be given to students to enable them to discern where beliefs and values are located, how to spot where they follow from the subject matter or were imported at the beginning, what are the available options among them and what are appropriate criteria for testing their truth-claims and adjudicating between the ones on offer.
>
> (Poole 1990c: 72)

A range of questions
Evaluating truth-claims: do the beliefs correspond to reality – are they right rather than wrong?

In order to decide whether something is sound or not, we can ask a number of questions. For example, with regard to the belief in the existence of God we can ask:

1. is it logically satisfying or is there anything contradictory or inconsistent in believing in the existence of God?
2. can it offer an adequate, and perhaps more than adequate explanation of the phenomenon of existence than a denial of the existence of God can?
3. is it inclusive of as many aspects of experience as possible, or is it exclusive, ignoring or dismissing many other aspects? – Is it welcoming potentially to all insights?
4. does it have the support of major well-tried traditions, or does it stand out on a limb as possibly idiosyncratic?
5. can it be seen as sustainable in people's lives and through the centuries. Can it pass the test of time?
6. does it accord with a majority sentiment in most cultures and situations, or is it very much a minority opinion?
7. can it provide a powerful motivation for practical outcome leading to a workable way of life?
8. is the outcome likely to be beneficial – producing creative consequences?
9. does it allow for the possibility of greater understanding or fresh insight? Does it lead to – even require – greater openness, or does it close the mind up?
10. is its thrust positive and not negative, referring to what is and not to what is not?

This is quite a battery of questions. The criteria they imply are

Figure 7.2 **Criteria for evaluating beliefs**

Symbol for test	Name of test or criteria	Focal-point of concern	To ensure that a belief is:
→→ →→ →→	STRICT LOGIC	RATIONALITY	non-contradictory
(puzzle pieces)	EXPLAINABILITY	ORDER	non-fragmented
(spiral)	COMPREHENSIVENESS	WHOLENESS	non-prejudiced
(graduation cap)	RELEVANT AUTHORITY	ROOTEDNESS IN TRADITION	non-idiosyncratic
←→	SUSTAINABILITY	CONTINUITY (TEST OF TIME)	non-ephemeral
(dots →)	CONSENSUS	NORMALITY	non-elitist
(crane)	WORKABILITY	PRACTICALITY	non-'ivory tower'
(smiley)	BENEFICIAL CONSEQUENCES	RESULTS	non-destructive
(sun)	POSITIVITY	HARMONY	non-negative
(waves)	OPENNESS	ONGOINGNESS OF EXPLORATION	non-rigid or dogmatic
(arrows converging)	CUMULATIVE EVIDENCE	DECISION-MAKING	non-dilettante

summarized in Fig. 7.2. Some of them have already been used in this book. In Chapter 3, for example, the first and the third, strict logic and comprehensiveness, were applied four times, (pp. 27–9, 30–1, 32–3, 35) and the second, explainability, once (p. 27–8) and the eighth, beneficial consequences, once (p. 31).

It is in weighing these up one against another – in balancing them and seeing them altogether cumulatively – that these criteria may become effective.

The use of the criteria
It is important to guard against certain misunderstandings however.

First, by themselves none of these criteria is foolproof, for example reliance on authority can be abused – called in when not necessary or appropriate. An example has already been given in the anecdote of Charles II on page 95. Authority can be mistaken and it can cover up ignorance with prestige and prevent people from thinking for themselves. Again the criterion of sustainability is inadequate by itself. An article in *The Times* carried the heading 'Yuppies oust the hippies of yesteryear'.[8] This offers a good example of a test developed by Newman who called it 'Chronic vigour'.[9] This is not, however, to be understood as 'whatever is old is good'. Mistakes and ignorance can be handed on from one generation to another, habit can blind, and tradition can bind.

Secondly, the criteria become stronger as they interact with each other like interlocking links. The following quotation from Basil Mitchell can illustrate this. Here the three criteria of (*a) explainability, (*b) comprehensiveness and (*c) positivity intertwine, as I indicate by means of the asterisks:

The problem for the atheist is to provide a convincing account (*a) of religious experience, and with it of the entire (*b) religious history of mankind, which will do justice (*c) to its character and effects. Such an account has to be a purely naturalistic one (*a); it has to deny (*c) that these experiences are what they purport to be, namely, instances of human awareness (*b) of the supernatural. And it is important to notice that the onus is upon the atheist to show the reason why (*a) the experience is not (*c) to be trusted. Of course *no* experience is self-authenticating, but it is reasonable to accept claims made on the basis of experience (*b and c) unless sufficient reason is produced (*a) for not doing so.

(Mitchell 1990: 208)

Thirdly, it is often helpful to consider the opposite – as Mitchell does here. The difficulty of expressing what we think adequately in matters concerned with assumptions and beliefs means that it is often easier to say what we do not agree with than what we do. For example, in applying the first criterion – logicality – belief in God is held by religious people to be more than a matter of logic. So to ask whether it is logical can be misunderstood. Yet most would want to agree that such belief ought not to be contradictory in any way (while bearing in mind the distinction between paradox and contradiction referred to at the end of Chapter 6).

Applying the criteria to a negative belief
In a similar way, the negative alternative to the belief in the existence of God – its denial – can be usefully subjected to the criteria. Because this is so crucial a matter for consideration in RE, I discuss this example in some detail. We can ask:

1. Is it really any more rational to deny rather than affirm – am I, for example, sure that I mean by God what a religious person does, because if I do not then my dismissal of God's existence rests on a logical non sequitur.

2. Can I offer any more satisfactory explanation of the mystery of existence? Big bang, or chance, or evolution cannot provide any answer of any kind to this overall why? question.

3. Do I acknowledge the power and ubiquity of religious faith? Which of the alternatives on offer do I choose and why? Are any of these fool-proof, and if not might I be wrong after all and religious experience right when taken at face value?

4. Have I actually understood how the saints and scholars of the great religions have understood 'God' and why they consider that God exists? Otherwise my opinion may be based on ignorance.

5. Have I underestimated the importance of sustainability? How do I know that the alternatives to belief in God, like Marxism and Humanism, are sustainable in the same way?

6. Is my dismissal of God something which on the total screen of human existence is rather a freak?

7. Can non-religious worldviews offer as much, or as adequate, inspiration as belief in God for actual living and initiative in carrying practical projects through?

8. Are non-religious undertakings necessarily more beneficial than those based on belief in God? If the charge of hypocrisy can be raised against the latter, is it not also possible to raise it against the former?

9. Is the evidence on which I base my denial of God actually non-experience, in which case how can I be sure that this is not caused by my own limitations in accessing what in reality exists?

10. Does dismissal of God's existence make for greater openness and enquiry, or does it have the effect of closing the door on trying to understand what is strange or threatening to itself which might be, for example, the claims of other religions?

The value of the criteria

I do not claim any more for these criteria than that they raise at least the possibility of a belief being affirmable. How far anyone is convinced by them depends in the last resort on the themes of the last two chapters – on imagination and experience. The artistic eye, for example, will see what the pedestrian and clinically-minded eye does not. Van Gogh could not possibly demonstrate the validity of his vision to someone who lacks that inner visual sense by which his greatness as an artist is perceived. Instead that sense has to be nurtured by more direct experience over a long period of time. This is why a child who grows up in an atmosphere where artistic beauty is in evidence and talked about and striven after has an enormous advantage over the child from a background of visual ugliness in which people are innocent of any artistic discernment.

For art, substitute science, languages, history and all the other curriculum areas including religion. Inner awareness is essential. What school-work can do, however, is help to arouse the desire for understanding. It can establish certain foundations, give pupils some strategy by means of which to proceed. It can especially help to remove unnecessary stumbling-blocks to the way forward for any given person. For example, no amount of arguing by itself will convince anyone of the truth of Genesis, 2–3, but knowledge of the possibility of interpreting it in different ways – which include the symbolic – can help people to think again about an easy dismissal of it. This can help to prevent the kind of simplistic denunciation of it which was given in the example quoted on page 62–3 in Chapter 5.

If we do not ask these questions, can we be sure we have not abandoned the search at too early a point, so that we are like the police officer who judges too soon that the death in a detective story was a suicide and not a murder? Talk of ongoingness, openness to evidence, exploration, needs to be taken seriously. The problem is that many people tend to decide far too soon concerning religion that there is nothing there to search for – nothing important to be bothered about. This is very far from the attitude which almost all religions agree is essential for understanding and which is encapsulated in the parable of the pearl of great price. Maybe only to those of such a mind will religion or its truth be perceivable. As I was writing this, the post brought some advertising blurb: 'Are you tuned in to the Win a Fortune Show?' Maybe that is the point: without being tuned in how can we know whether there is anything there or not? It is important to wrestle with questions of how far a belief corresponds to reality or is illusory. This is part of making sense of the world and of our experience in it.

Applying the criteria encourages such wrestling. These are all challengeable but nevertheless not negligible. Their cumulative force can serve to point out weaknesses, both in the content of a belief and in its expression in words, in a way which we can helpfully discuss with other people. Our awareness of the area under discussion, and our capacity for exercising choice, will increase through the effort of applying them, and balancing them against each other.[10]

Notes

1. Coleridge in a letter of 1811 referred to in Owen Barfield, 1971, *What Coleridge Thought* : p. 6.
2. Wordsworth, *Intimations of Immortality*. See *The Penguin Book of English Verse*, edited by John Hayward. 1956: 264.
3. John Harvey-Jones in *Management Week*, May 1991, no.4: p. 77–80.

4. C.S. Lewis from opening of Preface to *Paradise Lost*.
5. *The Muslim News*, 21 December 1990, p. 4 under the heading 'Finding a text to teach RE' by Tayieba Shah and Ahmed Hassan.
6. Wordsworth, 'The Tables Turned'.
7. See Barfield, 1971: 18f.
8. Letter from Kathmandu by Christopher Thomas, *The Times*, 24 February 1990.
9. Newman from Chapter 5, *Essay on the Development of Christian Doctrine*, one of the seven tests or 'notes' for weighing the trustworthiness of tradition, referred to in Nichols, 1990: 51f.
10. Important philosophical questions lie behind much of what is written in this chapter. I cannot here discuss the issues involved in any depth, but would direct attention to the following:
    S.C. Brown, 1979, *Philosophical Disputes in the Social Sciences* Part IV; C. Gunton, 1992, Knowledge and culture: towards an epistomology of the concrete, in Montefiore, 1992; J. Hick, 1990, *Philosophy of Religion*; M. Hollis and S. Lukes, (ed.) 1982, *Rationality and Relativism;* B. Mitchell, *1990, How to Play Theological Ping Pong;* R. Trigg, 1989, *Reality at Risk: a Defence of Realism in Philosophy and the Sciences;* K. Ward, 1990, 'The study of truth and dialogue in religion', in King, 1990.

There is considerable interest today in helping pupils learn skills of thinking, e.g. R. Fisher, 1990, Teaching Children to Think; M. Lipman, A.M. Sharp and F.S. Oscanyan, 1980, *Philosophy in the Classroom*.
M.J. Coles and W.D. Robinson (ed.) 1989, *Teaching Thinking* has chapters reviewing Lipman's Philosophy for Children Programme, Richard Paul's Critical Thinking movement, Feuerstein's Instrumental Enrichment programme, the Somerset Thinking Course, and the Oxfordshire Skills Programme.
There are a few books for the classroom, e.g. W. Raeper and L. Smith, 1991, *A Beginners' Guide to Ideas* for sixth-formers and R. Kirkwood, 1990, *Looking for Proof of God* for younger pupils.

CHAPTER 8

Beyond facts: the coming together of religions

Criticism of the phenomenological approach to RE was given in Chapter 4, particularly on the grounds that in practice it tends to lose touch with much of the religion it sets out to understand and include. Yet it remains important to take on board the intentions behind that approach: the global vision, the search for harmony, and the emphasis upon fairness to all religions, has never more been needed in the world than today. A deeper analysis of religion is therefore needed – one which can affirm, instead of being rather dismissive of, the intuitions behind the confessional approach which has the merit of taking religious claims to truth seriously. But the confessional approach in its turn needs to be deepened and extended to become worthy in expression of the ideals of religious people.

This chapter gives some idea of the scope possible for a world religions course which is open, affirming and critical. It assumes a high regard by teachers and pupils for the themes of the last three chapters – imagination, experience and thinking. The sensitivity needed in this area calls for an emphasis on certain points before the more controversial ones are attempted.

Introductory points on approaching truth-claims in multi-faith RE

1. Share with pupils the educational task. This involves in particular cultivating certain attitudes and skills associated with education in general (see Chapter 1, pp. 2, 4, 6–10).
2. Emphasize the difficulty of saying anything at all with regard to religion which may not be received by someone in a misleading way. Controversy is unavoidable. What is needed are ways of expressing controversy courteously. Even very young children are aware that people think differently, and as they get older they need a model of how to discuss differences honestly without papering over the cracks.
3. Underline that the purpose is not quickly to arrive at understanding, but to embark upon a lifetime's exploration. All religions stress the need for preparation in depth for any understanding of their religion.
4. Put forward the idea that 'answers' are like hypotheses in science

which have to be tested and tried out and replaced by better ones if necessary, but the testing has to be appropriate to the subject-matter. Scientific method will not do. We cannot literally weigh religious truth-claims or look at them through a microscope. Instead we need to reflect on them, ponder and wonder, find out all we can about them, learn to appreciate some of the time-honoured ways of approaching them such as meditation and prayer, and be prepared to think about these matters in all sorts of different situations and moods. Otherwise, whether we eventually accept or reject any particular religious belief, it may not be on the basis of understanding but of mis-understanding that we choose.

5. Emphasize throughout how important it is to appreciate the 'pointing towards' quality of religious language, gesture, behaviour and ritual. It is crucial not to take everything in either a literal sense or in a humanistic, reinterpretative sense. (The meaning of symbol in religion can be undermined not just by literalism, but by evacuating the content of the symbol, making it 'just symbolism'.) Questions of meaning open up vistas which can be exciting to explore.

6. Always stress what can be seen to cohere and fit together before attending to what does not fit. It is rather like doing a jigsaw puzzle where one might never get started if insisting first on finding the exact home for this one particular piece before trying with the rest. We cannot expect to arrive at consensus easily – there are a lot of things which may not seem to fit at all – but we can at least *want* to find out what is in common before worrying about what appears to contradict.

Sharing these points with pupils will help to build up the appropriate attitudes and skills in a relatively safe way, as well as increasing understanding of the great world religions.

Something of this should be attempted with all children, including those who are quite young, using appropriate examples and language. To delay the attempt to begin to understand religion in these ways is to risk making it very difficult for people ever to understand.

Applying the principle of critical affirmation to world religions

The kind of descriptive approach already widespread in schools – and for which there is plenty of published material available – needs from an early stage to be supplemented in an important way. The following series of 7 diagrams gives some suggestions on a possible order. The six world religions specified under the GCSE National Criteria are included (DES, 1985, 4.3.1), but there is scope for others such as the

Bahai faith, as well as for work on distinct traditions within each religion. Depending on the age and aptitude of pupils, as well as on local circumstances, work on just two or three religions may be appropriate.

The point of the approach is to apply an attitude of critical affirmation to the different traditions enabling them to be studied and discussed in a way which is affirming of members of the traditions without succumbing to naivety or blandness.

What major world religions hold in common

Figure 8.1, using the shape of a circle containing equal segments, gives an example of what religions have in common: they all teach very high ethical standards and ideals which are seen as intimately related to the metaphysical reality behind the world – a reality which in most religions is called 'God'. Morality, for religious people, is not something invented by people to keep community life sweet; it is for them an obligation arising out of the nature of the way things are.

*Figure 8.1 **The Golden Rule: an example of what major world religions hold in common***

BUDDHISM
'Hurt not others
with that which
pains yourself'
(*Samyutta Nikaya
V. 353*)

CHRISTIANITY
'Always treat others
as you would like
them to treat you'
(*Matthew 7 12*)

HINDUISM
'Do not to others what if
done to you would
cause you pain'
(*Mahabharata,
Anusasana Parva
113.8*)

SIKHISM
'As thou deemest thyself,
so deem others'
(*Kabir*)

JUDAISM
'What is hateful to you,
do not do to your
fellow man'
(*Talmud: Shabbat
31a*)

ISLAM
'No one of you is a
believer until he loves
for his brother what
he loves for himself'
(*Forty Hadith of
an-Nawawi 13*)

Morality may not be the same as religion – although in many of the great religions this distinction is not clearly perceived – but sincerity in pursuing religion is normally expected to carry with it sincerity in pursuing a high moral code. The reverse also holds, that failure to live morally betrays and invalidates religious devotion unless there is genuine penitence.

A clear example of the degree of common ground is what has been called the Golden Rule in the different religions. This is developed in almost all religions into a requirement to love even enemies. The degree of emphasis given in each religion may vary considerably – some may not give it the prominence which another does. But yet it should not be regarded as a quirk development, but as part of that to which the other more familiar aspects of the religion are pointing. Many other themes concerned with moral education could be given.

Pointing towards the Mystery at the heart of reality

Figure 8.2 **Pointing towards the Mystery at the heart of reality**

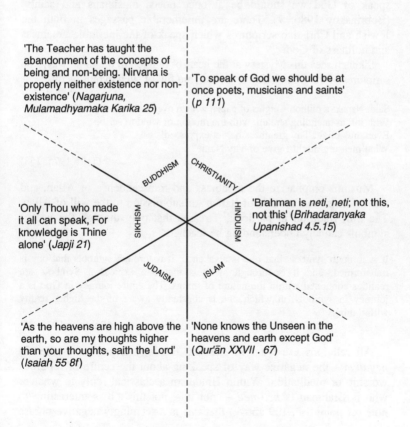

'The Teacher has taught the abandonment of the concepts of being and non-being. Nirvana is properly neither existence nor non-existence' (*Nagarjuna, Mulamadhyamaka Karika 25*)

'To speak of God we should be at once poets, musicians and saints' (*p 111*)

'Only Thou who made it all can speak, For knowledge is Thine alone' (*Japji 21*)

'Brahman is *neti, neti*; not this, not this' (*Brihadaranyaka Upanishad 4.5.15*)

BUDDHISM CHRISTIANITY SIKHISM HINDUISM JUDAISM ISLAM

'As the heavens are high above the earth, so are my thoughts higher than your thoughts, saith the Lord' (*Isaiah 55 8f*)

'None knows the Unseen in the heavens and earth except God' (*Qur'ān XXVII . 67*)

Figure 8.2, starting at the centre of a circle and pointing out towards an indefinitely increasing circle, relates to the way in which all religions point towards Mystery. This is so fundamental a point that I will develop this in some detail. As already discussed on page 55, Mystery has nothing to do with a 'who-dun-it'. There is a profound difference between the kind of problem-solving which encourages us to use reason in order to reach a solution and the awareness of Mystery which leads to feelings of wonder and awe and worship in the light of what is being contemplated. This is how a modern scientist, John Cole, has put it: Mysteries 'are not the product of thought, but of experience. We can think about them, but not explain them, only know them. We must never attempt to reduce Mysteries to problems.' He then summarizes what Mystery means to religious people of many faiths as 'an intense awareness of the Presence abiding with and within themselves and the world', and he then quotes from Hindu and Muslim as well as Christian sources (Cole 1988: 13).

This has profound implications for the way in which religions talk about God. As a Russian Orthodox Christian has expressed it: 'To speak of God we should be at once poets, musicians and saints' (Bobrinskoy 1986: 7). There are innumerable passages in both the Jewish and Christian scriptures which speak of the ineffable greatness and holiness of God.

Sikhism sees this Mystery at the heart of religion in the same way. The scriptures of the Sikh faith, the Granth, are full of such hymns as this:

Saith Nanak: a million weights of paper, written over with learning and devotion,
With ink in unending stream, with the motion of wind to scribe-
Even thus might Thy greatness be not expressed!
What measure might I give of Thy Name?

(Talib 1975: 158)

Muslims emphasize the greatness and transcendence of Allah, and this informs their attitude of 'Islam' or submission to the will of Allah. The Sufi tradition in particular stresses that only through the use of symbols can any understanding be reached:

It is through symbols that one is awakened; it is through symbols that one is transformed; and it is through symbols that one expresses. Symbols are realities contained within the nature of things. The entire journey in God is a journey in symbols, in which one is constantly aware of the higher reality within things.

(Bakhtiar 1976: 25)

All religions use what in classical theology is known as the *via negativa* – the negative way of speaking about the centre of religious worship or meditation. Within Hinduism a classical reply to what or who is Brahman is *neti-neti* – 'not this, not this'. It is interesting to note (cf point 5 p. 109 above) that this is a seemingly negative phrase which is actually affirming something positive. The phrase does not indicate that Brahman does not exist, or that we know nothing about Brahman, but that we know that Brahman is so far beyond our understanding that anything we say will be misleading and therefore we must content ourselves with saying *neti-neti*. Christians too use the *via negativa*. They speak of God as immortal, invisible, infinite, incomprehensible, ineffable, and so forth. In trying to understand Hinduism, Christianity or any other religion, as well as in seeking to affirm Hindus, and Christians, and members of other religions, it is essential to practise this level of discernment. (See especially pp. 99–101.)

This approach is most obviously to the fore in Buddhism which emphasizes the necessity for getting beyond concepts by the use of words like *anatta*, *anicca*, and *nirvana*. Indeed most Buddhists are unhappy even to refer to 'God' at all. The point is worth making that historically it was out of a background of theological wrangling by Brahmin priests over the nature of 'Brahman' that the young prince, Gautama, rebelled exasperated and went on to seek – and to find – enlightenment elsewhere thus becoming the Buddha. Knowledge concerning that enlightenment was what he passed on to his disciples, and this – the positive content of the Four Noble Truths and the teaching of the Middle Way – is what has made Buddhism live down the ages and still today.

Yet reluctance to use the word 'God' does not mean that Buddhists deny the reality of Mystery with a capital M. For they believe in 'Nirvana' as not literally referring to nothingness but to the enlightenment attendant upon the laying aside of barriers to it. It is greater than any concepts we can have to such a degree that they hold that any concept at all prevents our seeing it.

The word 'God' in all the theistic religions refers to that Mystery which is at once transcendent and immanent. It does not refer to naive anthropomorphism, to childish notions of a kind of finite Person resident somewhere. The language of person which is applied to God is metaphorical, as discussed in Chapter 5.

Religions as sociological entities are not meant to be more than stepping-stones to an appreciation of the profound Mystery at the heart of reality.

Outward forms of expression and inner meaning

Figure 8.3 offers a way of bringing the phenomenological perspective on one religion into relationship with other religions. What they each have in common is the use of various signs and symbols concerning both behaviour and belief. The diagram has one segment filled in;

Figure 8.3   Outward forms of expression and inner meaning

Round the edge are some of the practices of the religions.
Their purpose is to lead beyond themselves.

One example is given, that of Sikhism.

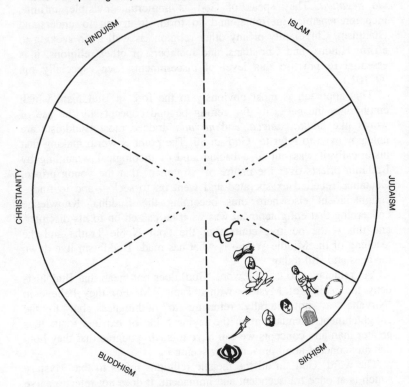

Fill in the segments to show objects or buildings or ritual near the rim, then
values and attitudes, then religious concepts – all of which need to be
understood as pointing beyond themselves.

pupils could fill in the others themselves, working either in groups or
individually.

The arrangement of the signs and symbols is designed to encourage
a deepening awareness of their 'pointing-towards' character; the
deeper we penetrate behind the scenes as it were of the various words
and actions, the closer can they be seen to become because all alike
are pointing towards that Mystery which is beyond straightforward
conceptual understanding.

The outward characteristics of religions have an inner meaning
which brings them from their very separate and distinct starting-points
towards an appreciation of the Mystery at the heart of religion where

paradoxically the distinctions merge. This does not eradicate the distinctiveness of each religion's approach. The unique insights of each are not lost, for in order to have a less inadequate appreciation of what is at the heart of reality we need to affirm all insights.

If all this seems somewhat esoteric, the Jain parable of the Blind men and the elephant, which is given in Chapter 13, could be made into a similar diagram, and other examples then worked through such as 'getting to know about' a work of art, an event, a person, a culture. In each the same point can be made, that different people can see different facets of something or someone which may all be *part* of the *whole* which is beyond our complete understanding.

Rituals, creeds and so forth are important, for they can help people to reach a state of awareness of what is beyond understanding. By the same token, teaching them is important, but only if it is constantly related to their purpose within religions. For they are not the goal, but a means to something else, and any understanding of the religion concerned must acknowledge this. Thus if the first purpose of a particular religion is to help people to a sense of the presence of God and express a response to God, then the study of the ritual which helps them towards this goal must constantly draw attention to this significance. A short section on the teaching of ritual may be helpful.

Teaching about ritual
The warning concerning how we teach about ritual is necessary. It is easy to make this colourful and fascinating, with varied activities. But what will pupils take away with them? Will they equate being religious with performing ritual? Will they see this as largely superstitious – the invocation of a kind of magic? Will they assume that people engage in this ritual because they have always done so and have been conditioned into it? Will the details of the ritual mean anything to them? Will the experience of studying the ritual bear any creative relationship to their own lives?

In order for work on ritual to become really educational, it would be necessary to share with pupils what the functions of ritual are. Thus, for example, it enables expression of religious conviction in more than intellectual terms: the appeal to the senses, the performance of actions and so forth. These become vehicles by which an idea is conveyed with immediacy – the power of the symbol for evoking an emotional and emotive response. Another important feature is that it helps to overcome distractability so that people can focus attentively in prayer or meditation. Dissipation of energy through lack of concentration is one of the chief sources of non-awareness.

The difference between routine and ritual needs to be discussed. Superstition occurs when the distinction between the outer action or words and the inner meaning or purpose is forgotten. This is a great temptation facing the religious believer. But failure to appreciate the force of this distinction can also shipwreck attempts by observers to understand religion – to read correctly what is going on as a person performs a religious ritual or speaks religious words (see Chapter 10 where an assessment task on this is suggested).

A story which can help pupils to discuss the role of ritual, and the way in which other people can misconstrue it, is that of the little fox in the Legends of Moses.

Moses finds a shepherd in the desert. He spends the day with the shepherd and helps him milk his ewes, and at the end of the day he sees that the shepherd puts the best milk he has in a wooden bowl, which he places on a flat stone some distance away. So Moses asks him what it is for, and the shepherd replies, 'This is God's milk.' Moses is puzzled and asks him what he means. The shepherd says, 'I always take the best milk I possess, and I bring it as an offering to God.' Moses, who is far more sophisticated than the shepherd with his naive faith, asks, 'And does God drink it?' 'Yes', replies the shepherd, 'He does.' Then Moses feels compelled to enlighten the poor shepherd and he explains that God, being pure spirit, does not drink milk. Yet the shepherd is sure that he does, and so they have a short argument, which ends with Moses telling the shepherd to hide behind the bushes to find out whether in fact God does come to drink the milk. Moses then goes out to pray in the desert. The shepherd hides, the night comes, and in the moonlight the shepherd sees a little fox that comes trotting from the desert, looks right, looks left and heads straight towards the milk, which he laps up, and disappears into the desert again. The next morning Moses finds the shepherd quite depressed and downcast. 'What's the matter?' he asks. The shepherd says, 'You were right, God is pure spirit and he doesn't want my milk.' Moses is surprised. He says, 'You should be happy. You know more about God than you did before.' 'Yes, I do,' says the shepherd, 'but the only thing I could do to express my love for Him has been taken away from me.' Moses sees the point. He retires into the desert and prays hard. In the night in a vision, God speaks to him and says, 'Moses, you were wrong. It is true that I am pure spirit. Nevertheless I always accepted with gratitude the milk which the shepherd offered me, as the expression of his love, but since, being pure spirit, I do not need the milk, I shared it with this little fox, who is very fond of milk.'

(quoted in Anthony of Sourozh 1986: 150f)

Discussion of this story occurs in Chapter 5. It is interesting here to note that it is paralleled by one from Islam of how

Allah sent the angel Gabriel to search for a pious man in a certain place. Gabriel saw a man praying before an idol, lying prostrate. He reported back to Allah that he could find only an idol worshipper. He was asked to go and look again. This time he heard the idol speak, saying: 'I forgive you your sins, go in peace.' He returned and told Allah the curious story, and Allah replied: 'That was not really the idol speaking my word, that was me!'

This story was told by a Muslim in the course of some Christian/Muslim conversations held in Birmingham recently. Andrew Wingate comments: 'Where this comes from I do not know, but it is a very surprising story for a Muslim to tell, considering the normal attitude to idol-worship' (Wingate 1988: 28). This little incident shows the way in which ideas can cross barriers, and is itself an indication of the transcendence of religions.

Points of convergence

Figure 8.4 refers to the way in which, whilst all religions emphasize many particular understandings, ideas, beliefs, and practices not found in other religions yet many of these are not contradictory to those

Figure 8.4 **Points of convergence**

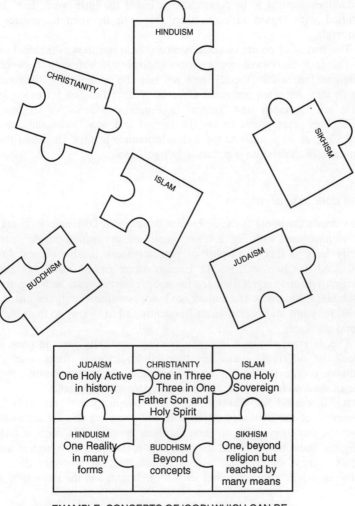

EXAMPLE: CONCEPTS OF 'GOD' WHICH CAN BE
SEEN AS COMPLEMENTARY NOT CONTRADICTORY

found in other traditions: they are different not contradictory. Mostly indeed such 'insights' are also present in other traditions but not stressed to the same degree. Sometimes this is because they are actually taken for granted.

By affirming these non-contradictory emphases, members of different religions can move closer together without fearing loss of integrity. Many themes can be explored in this way, like pieces of a jigsaw coming together. The diagram gives as an example the concept of God. Some may object that there are important differences in the way religions see this concept. I quote such a comment in Chapter 11, p. 162–3 and I agree there are, but there is more common ground than a superficial look might suggest.[1] Once again, the parable of the blind men and the elephant could be used to illustrate this point. Their deductions seemed to be contradictory, but if the little word 'like' is inserted with regard to each, then they can be seen as possibly converging.

The reality of points of convergence should not, however, blind us to the fact that there are enormous divisions, not only between religions but within them. They are not the monolithic structures which they are often presented as being. Within Judaism for example there are Orthodox and Reform or Progressive Jews, or as Jews themselves often prefer to say Traditional and non-Traditional Jews (see Chapter 9, p. 129–30 for further reference to this). In Islam the Sunnah-Shi'ah division is particularly significant.

The dark side of religion

This draws attention to the ambiguity of religion. Differences do not, as we have seen with Fig. 8.4, necessarily mean conflict, but they can easily lead to this if a spirit of possessiveness is also present (as discussed in Chapter 3, p. 34). Human nature can so easily become competitive and aggressive, fearful and defensive; and then bigotry, intolerance, bitterness and enmity are born, as unfortunately the history of *all* religions shows. Religions frequently fail to live up to their high moral standards.

The diagram shows a way of depicting how religions can present two quite different – and this time contradictory – faces: one of radiance and perfection, for which light is an appropriate symbol, and one of shadow for which darkness is an appropriate symbol.

As discussed in Chapter 2, many people today are acutely conscious of the dark side of religion, and some see this failure as so colossal that they wish to have nothing more to do with it. All religions show how difficult the path is to embodying their high moral ideals – they acknowledge a high failure rate, the majority do not come anywhere near achieving what they should, and the more saintly

Figure 8.5 **The dark side of religion**

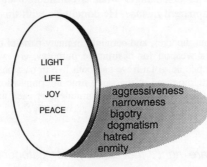

Which impression of religion do you mostly have?

Would it be fair to say that one side represents
true religion, the other is a degenerate form of it?

Which appears to be the most commonly held
view of religion in our society and among children
and young people?

or holy within the religions see this the most clearly. The fulminations
of the Hebrew prophets such as Amos, Hosea and Jeremiah against the
betrayal of religion are an example.[2]

The story is told of Guru Nanak that even as a boy he argued that
the ancient Hindu ceremony of tying on the sacred thread did not
prevent men from acting wrongly. Centuries earlier the Bhagavad Gita
had noted the same difficulty: 'Self-conceited, haughty, full of pride
and arrogance of wealth, they do acts of religious worship in name
alone.'[3]

Yet, just so – indeed, because humans are fallible, the history of all
religions has its dark side. The holy war can be terrible in its course
and consequence, and is open to distortion and misuse for a variety of
purposes.

The distinction between human fallibility and the goal of the
religious quest is constantly referred to in all religions. Sigmund
Sternberg, as chairman of the International Council of Christians and
Jews, considers that:

Many recent religious revivals experienced in particular by Jewish, Christian
and Muslim communities . . . have assumed frightening forms of intolerance,
exclusiveness, racism and fanaticism as well as nationalism, using religion as a
weapon in defence of particular causes.

He then refers to the conference held in 1991 with some 300 theologians, historians, educators and lay leaders from 25 countries who endeavoured to disentangle what is considered legitimate use of religion from its apparent misuse. He concludes with this paragraph:

If religion throughout the ages, and certainly in many parts of the world today, has been used as a weapon for destructive purposes, are we not called to demonstrate that as people of faith we can both live in passionate commitment to our respective tradition and at the same time in compassionate respect for each other and to affirm that the faith commitment of each one is only truly realized when we live in that mutual respect accordingly?[4]

'We know we are right': the capacity for categorical assertion within religions

Figure 8.6 relates to one aspect which is often associated with the dark side of religion: the insistence within all religions that 'we know we are right'. Normally there is present a great deal of assurance and this finds expression usually in ways which are not too finely sensitive to the assurances of others. Each religion and religious tradition has been subject to geographical, historical and sociological factors which have influenced its vocabulary and the thought-forms enshrined within that vocabulary, and which have become unknowingly exclusive of the insights of others.

One of the things which religions have in common, as John Taylor, the then Bishop of Winchester, noted, is 'the capacity for categorical assertion': 'It is the nature of religious experience to put into the believers' hands a key which is absolute and irreducible. But when one considers the different things claimed as the key, comparisons crumble' (Taylor 1978: 9).

The really important task facing all religions is whether these particular categorical assertions can be unpacked in such a way as to reveal a piece of the jigsaw which fits with others. Or is each to remain stubbornly not a piece of a jigsaw puzzle, but in its own watertight compartment, as shown in this diagram?

The problem here is not just possessiveness and failure to live up to the high ethical ideals proclaimed by a religion. It is also confusion between a proper assurance based on experience and the insight deriving from it, and the dogmatism which so easily follows but is distinct from it, and which insists that what we happen to know is the *only* thing that matters – what others have discovered or had revealed to them is unimportant. This attitude can be unintentionally fostered through sheer repetition, through authoritarian methods of expression, and by reason of the default factor (i.e. what is *not* taught). These can be as much responsible as actual content of teaching for the development of dogmatism.

Figure 8.6 'We know we are right': the capacity for categorical assertion within religions

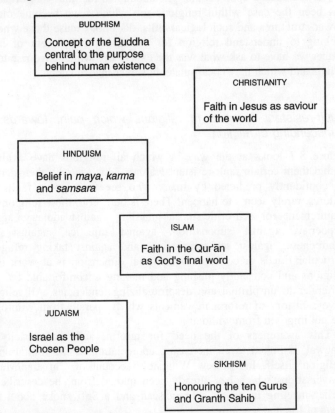

Yet as Keith Ward, writing as a Christian, notes: 'I can say "Jesus shows me what God is like, and makes the love of God available to me" without having to add, "Jesus is better than any other spiritual teacher, saint or prophet; so all other ways are inferior to mine" ' (Ward 1991: 69). But it is a great temptation for people to say the latter, especially if they are ignorant of what others believe. And it is this spirit of competitiveness which can cause a link to be forged between the 'categorical assertions' of religions and the dark side of religion.

John Taylor has something extremely important to say about these potential sources of offence: 'We may learn to reformulate these irreducible convictions in the light of our dialogue. But we know that the reformulation may never reduce or dilute the content of experience which it interprets' (Taylor 1978: 12).

The reference to experience leads us back to Chapter 6, for the beliefs of all religions arise out of experience and are misinterpreted at a very fundamental level by outsiders who see them as merely forms of words imposed upon people. The undoubted fact that very often this has been the case within religions too which have become merely power-structures and sociological units, does not excuse those who are seeking to understand religion for dismissing beliefs out of hand. Rather we have to ask what was the experience which gave rise to the beliefs and which they encapsulate, however inadequately.[5]

Fault-resistant features in religions which point towards the transcending of religion

Figure 8.7 looks at the way in which all religions have available within them certain fault-resistant features which is why their demise, so confidently predicted by many who see their grave faults and failures, rarely seems to happen! There is built in to these religions the requirement for self-criticism, a guarding against idolatry, against hypocrisy, against superstition, against injustice, against self-centredness, against self-satisfaction, and against taking refuge in particular rituals or concepts. A spiritual dimension is at work in all religions and constantly pushing and making uncomfortable the easy surrender to unspiritual and despiritualizing tendencies. All religions have a history of reform movements which operate from within and are not imposed from without.

This awareness of the need for reform, and the capacity for renewal, is linked to an increasing appreciation of the limitations of 'religion' itself. In Andrew Wingate's account of Christian/Muslim conversations which has already been quoted from, he describes an earlier meeting in which a Franciscan and a Sufi spoke about their ways of life and teaching.

A Franciscan brother from the college is now part of the group and, wearing his habit, he held all of us spellbound with a simple but profound account of the calling of St Francis, his life and teaching, and of his own response to this. The message seemed to speak quite beyond the bounds of one religion. We then heard an exposition of what being a Sufi was about from Nazir's own brother – and he suggested that this was no more and no less than what being a truly spiritual Muslim was about.

(Wingate 1988: 40)

Again what the Sufi said leapt across barriers between religions. There is a sense which is appreciated in almost all the religions that religion is itself unsatisfactory and has to be left behind. Such awareness is considerably to the fore today where people appreciate the need for a global concern – the need to relate in a non-violent, just, perceptive and generous way to the traditions of others.

It is worth noting that the word 'religion' either does not naturally

Figure 8.7 *Fault-resistant features in religions which point towards the transcending of religion*

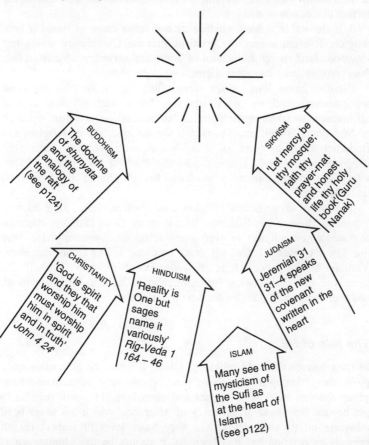

feature in some religions, or is regarded by many religious people with considerable disapproval. For sociological grouping of religions has encouraged an attitude of defining each over against others. We need to consider the possible question with pupils, especially as so many are de-religionized anyway, of whether religion, in order to be true to itself, needs to transcend the 'religions'? If the latter are regarded as territory to be defended, as rallying cries for confrontation with others, perhaps we ought to be asking whether they need to be so territorial?

Many passsages in the Jewish scriptures refer to the way in which religious observance itself can become an enormous obstacle and has constantly to be overcome. Thus Jeremiah speaks of a 'new covenant being written in the heart'.[6] And Jesus, in his conversation with the Samaritan woman who asked him where true worship happened, answered that 'God is spirit and they who worship him must worship him in spirit and truth,' for 'the time will come when neither here nor in Jerusalem will men worship'.[7] (See Chapter 11, pp. 170–3 for further discussion of this.)

It is debatable indeed whether or not Jesus came to found a new religion. It often seems to Christians that the Christianity which has wrapped itself round the person of Jesus has served to obscure rather than communicate its raison d'être.

Hindus have long since seen that we have to transcend separateness. And for Buddhists this forms part of their central affirmation, to arrive at the point of 'emptiness' – the central doctrine of Mahayana Buddhism (*Shunyata*). On the question of religion, the Buddhist tends to think of it as a raft with which to cross the tempestuous seas of existence, and the Buddha once asked, 'What would you say to someone who carried his raft around with him when he had arrived?'

The need to transcend religion has nowhere been more clearly expressed than within Sikhism. Was it really Guru Nanak's intention to found a *new* religion, or even a new religious community? It is true that just six months before his death he chose Lehna as his successor. Various stories about him, however, confirm how strongly he perceived that the outward forms of religion have to be internalized, and therefore could perhaps become redundant.

The role of RE

In its approach to world religions, school RE may be able to be truly pioneering, blazing a trail whereby seemingly very different and rival groupings can meet with respect and even love. This will help us to get beyond the phase of advocacy of 'tolerance' which has never been adequate on its own. Only at a very basic level of respect for all persons as persons has this been so. It cannot be the ultimate value because it manifestly ignores so many other values such as those of justice, as well as ignoring the truth-claims which religions inevitably have to take seriously.[8]

Chapter 12 on school worship will take up this point, and discuss the possibility of overcoming the unfortunate dichotomy between Christian or multi-faith at the practical point of assemblies.

I want to finish this chapter with a quotation which brings together the idea of loyalty to a particular tradition and openness to change. It is a vision which in a simple way the RE we do in schools can offer to pupils.

It is a sense of this mystery which is without price, particularly in times of rapid change, whatever one's particular religious inheritance. It provides the resources with which to face the implications of change for one's own religious tradition without fear, but with exhilaration. The Christian disciple experienced this, though exiled on Patmos, and was compelled to articulate its renewing power: 'Behold, I make all things new.' Out of the contemporary turmoil of Hindu tradition Rabindranath Tagore wrote of the same mysterious sources of renewal:

> I thought that my voyage had come to its end
> at the last limit of my power – that the
> path before me was closed, that provisions
> were exhausted and the time come to take
> shelter in a silent obscurity.

> But I find that thy will knows no end in me.
> And when old words die out on the tongue,
> new melodies break forth from the heart;
> and where the old tracks are lost,
> new country is revealed with its wonders.

(Brown 1980: 152f)

Notes

1. A scholarly but accessible book examining the concept of God as it appears in world religions is Keith Ward's 1989 *Images of Eternity*. What is important is that such points of convergence are held in balance with the awareness of the Mystery which transcends all our categories of thought (Fig. 8.2). Maurice Wiles, in his *Christian Theology and Inter-religious Dialogue* 1992 notes that all theology – talk about God – is 'perspectival' – comes from a particular perspective – , 'parabolic' – uses language in symbolic or metaphorical ways – , and 'provisional' – can never imagine it has said the last word (Wiles 1992: 64f).

2. E.g. Amos 5: 21–24, Hosea 8: 11–13 and Jeremiah 7: 1–15.

3. Bhagavad Gita, 16, 17.

4. Sigmund Sternberg, 1991, Use and misuse of religion, in *The Times*, 1.8.91.

5. See discussion in Chapter 6 on creeds pp. 85–6. Wiles (1992) makes the point that Christian faith should not lead to a rigid attitude towards doctrine because 'absoluteness of commitment is to Christ as symbol of the God who is ultimate mystery'(p.74). Thus 'full commitment and openness to change are not incompatible' (p. 81).

6. Jeremiah 31: 31–34.

7. John 4: 24,21.

8. The problems in the way of inter-faith dialogue must not be underestimated, but considerable strides have been taken by many members of different religions. On the impulse behind inter-faith dialogue, Rudolf Otto, writing about a proposed Inter Religious League in 1931, noted that the members of the different religions who wanted to form it 'realize the peculiar and difficult problem caused by the differences that religion creates among people. Yet it is a religious conviction which impels them to seek contact with men and women of other faiths . . .' (*The Hibbert Journal*, vol. 29, 1931: 587–94). I am grateful to Robin Minney for drawing my attention to this article.

Here is a short booklist: On the general relationship between religions see, e.g. M. Barnes, 1989, *Religions in Conversation*; K. Cracknell, 1986, *Towards a New Relationship – Christians and People of Other Faith*; G. D'Costa (ed.), 1988, *Faith Meets Faith – Interfaith Views on Interfaith*; B. Griffiths, 1982, *The Marriage of East and West*; B. Griffiths, 1989, *A New Vision of Reality: Western Science, Eastern Mysticism and Christian Faith*; R. Hooker, 1989, *Themes in Hinduism and Christianity*; R. Hooker and J. Sargant (eds.) 1991, *Belonging to Britain – Christian Perspectives on a Plural Society*.

There is some in-depth study of possible reconciliation of truth-claims in different religions: e.g. R. Corless and P.F. Knitter, 1990, *Buddhist Emptiness and Christian Trinity*; G. D'Costa, 1990, *Christian Uniqueness Reconsidered – the Myth of a Pluralistic Theology of Religions*; W. Teasdale, 1987, *Towards a Christian Vedanta*; F. Whaling, 1986, *Christian Theology and World Religions*.

General books on world religions include: N. Smart, 1989, *The World's Religions: Old Traditions and Modern Transformations*; H. Smith, 1991, *The World's Religions*, and John R. Hinnells (ed.) 1984, *A Handbook of Living Religions*.

CHAPTER 9

Approaching the teaching of the Bible

The Bible used to be the staple diet of religious education. Today the pendulum tends to have swung to the opposite extreme so that many pupils leave school knowing very little about it at all (an example was given in Chapter 2, p. 22). Those who choose to do GCSE will almost certainly have an opportunity, if they wish, to study the gospels, but only a small proportion of pupils do public examination work in RE, so what happens to all the rest?

All pupils may be considered entitled to be introduced to the skills of biblical interpretation, for some understanding of the Bible really is necessary for the understanding of Judaism and Christianity. The Bible is reverenced within both in which liberal as well as orthodox traditions give it a unique place in worship. It has also played a remarkable role in the spread of both religions throughout the world, both historically and today.

Just as in Chapter 7 the need to share thinking skills with all was emphasized because we cannot today expect people to rely on authority, so it is essential to share skills of biblical interpretation with all. To fail to do so is to leave pupils dependent on whatever variety of opinion on the status of the Bible and its content happens to come their way. This amounts to an abdication of responsibility on the part of RE teachers.

The highly controversial nature of the Bible

A certain reluctance, however, to grasp what is in fact a difficult nettle is also understandable. The Bible is not easy material; it can quite easily appear alien to people today, it is highly controversial, and it is very easy to offend somebody in the process of doing any work on it. Nevertheless its very difficulties make it important that it be tackled in schools.

Small or large B, and the attitudes behind the dispute

We can perhaps begin by referring to the dispute over the spelling of the word. Should it have a capital B or not? There is no easy answer to this because with a small B it suggests that the Bible is like any other book, and with a capital B it suggests that it is something more special. It has to be spelt one way or the other, so that a decision is unavoidable. I have chosen to spell it with a capital letter because the Qur'an, the Granth and the Upanishads, for example, are so spelt, and the Bible is equally regarded as scripture by Jews and Christians.

Emphasizing that the Bible should be studied 'like any other book' became almost a catch-phrase among scholars in the early part of this century. They were reacting against what was felt to be an over-pious approach to the Bible: in its extreme form the latter has been likened to 'bibliolatry', a term coined from the word idolatry to describe what can happen when the Bible is put at the centre of religion instead of the worship of God.

The non-pious approach appears to be ideally suited to the study of religion in schools. But there are drawbacks. If it is the case that the world's scriptures are not just 'like any other book' – and who has decided and on what grounds that they are or are not? – then the methodology is flawed from the start. Furthermore, even *if* this is not the case, *if* the purpose of study is to understand religion, then we are not helped to do that by approaching scriptures in a way very different from how religious believers themselves do. A Muslim regards the Qur'an as a Sikh regards the Adi Granth, namely, as a book that is unique.

I remember being impressed by a conversation in India with someone involved in teaching the Upanishads to Indian students, both Hindu and Christian.[1] The students were tending to find the work heavy-going, but she found that their degree of understanding was transformed when she adopted a quite different approach, one more in line with that of a Hindu guru. This involved a moment of silence at the beginning of a lesson, and then the recitation of a mantra, followed by the passage for study being intoned. She said that the atmosphere thus established, instead of being one of arrogant interrogation, became one of expectant enquiry. To my comment that this did not meet Western ideas of openness and opportunity for criticism of the text, she replied that, so far from preventing criticism, it actually enabled it to be far more to the point. She said that in fact they had far more searching discussion than would have been the case had an interrogative style been followed. And she countered my comment further by asking whether an interrogative style was as open as it gave the appearance of being: does it not preclude from the start the possibility of any real understanding and openness to spiritual insight?

Many religious people indeed claim that the only way that scripture can reveal its secrets is to those who approach it with humility. Among Christians a style of participatory Bible study is much in evidence today. One recent book outlining such an approach begins with this story from East Africa.

A simple woman always walked around with a bulky Bible. Never would she part from it. Soon the villagers began to tease her: 'Why always the Bible? There are so many books you could read!' Yet the woman kept on living with her Bible, neither disturbed nor angered by all the teasing. Finally, one day she knelt down in the midst of those who laughed at her. Holding the Bible high above her head, she said with a big smile: 'Yes of course there are many books which I could read. But there is only one book which reads me!'[2]

This story may give the impression of an uncritical attitude to the Bible. It need not be that however, because interpretation is inevitably involved in the hearing. And this is where controversy comes in at another level.

What constitutes the Bible?

Christians have normally had no trouble referring to the biblical testaments as 'the Old' and 'the New' Testaments, but Jewish people do not accept the latter as the Bible, and they take offence, justifiably, at being relegated to the domain of the *Old* Testament. This is how Christians talk, but not how Jews talk. Much more care therefore is needed in discussing the Bible. The legacy in RE of Christian-controlled Bible work in schools has not yet run its course, and unintentional Christian triumphalism should be avoided.

This does not mean banning the use of terms like the Old Testament, because from the point of view of Christians that is how they have related positively and creatively to the Jewish heritage out of which Christianity grew.[3] Instead of repudiating this Jewish heritage or ignoring it they embraced it, and in the process have enabled its insights to become known far beyond the actual extent of Judaism. They interpreted it in the light of their faith in Jesus as the fulfilment of the Jewish religion.

Range of possible approaches to interpretation

There are no easy answers therefore even to seemingly simple questions of what do we call the scriptures. Teachers need to be sensitive to the issues involved and share awareness of these problems with pupils so that they are invited into the ongoing debate. In particular this should include sharing the range of possible approaches to the Bible which religious people themselves show: from extreme conservatism to extreme radicalism. Thus within Judaism there are three main groups usually known as Orthodox, Conservative and Reform. They have different attitudes to worship, to customs and so forth, and these are related to a different approach to scripture. The Orthodox believe in a strict and traditional kind of approach, while both Conservative and Reform Jews consider that the tradition needs to develop and change to bring it into line with the modern world; they believe that in this way the timeless truth of the tradition can be appreciated today. Reform Jews tend to be more radical in the level of modern interpretation they advocate. There is a continuum between these three positions just as in views among Christians on their Bible. Table 9.1 summarizes these positions. A worksheet suggesting how this kind of work might be introduced is given on p. 135–6 of this chapter.

Table 9.1 **Spectrum of Jewish opinion with regard to the Bible**

Possible questions concerning the Bible	Orthodox	Liberal Conservative	Reform
Authorship: Did God give the Bible?	'God spoke'	'God spoke and man interpreted what he said'	'Man believed that God spoke'
Authority: Must the Bible be accepted literally?	'You must accept what God has said, not pick and choose as though you know more than God'	'You must be open to God's truth and ready to see it, and then work out what it means and how it should be understood'	'You must read carefully what people have believed to be God's truth and accept what reason and common sense tell you'
Reliability: Is the Bible true?	'It is true'	'It is true but the way it is understood may vary according to the different perspectives of people'	'What is called true is relative; it may have been true for them but is not necessarily so for people today'

Note: If used in teaching all this could be within a big circle with the words: All Jews believe the Bible has a great deal of metaphor and symbolic language in it. The idea of a spectrum of opinion could be conveyed through colour coding.

Different attitudes to the concept of revelation

Attitudes towards scripture reflect different attitudes towards revelation. The concept is important within most religions in varying degrees. Scripture does not fulfil quite the same function for each. Its status in Indian-derived religions for example is variable, normally important, and sometimes fundamental, but usually it wears the character of inspirational material associated with the handing-down of a great tradition – its uniqueness concerns its ability to infuse worshippers today with the same quality of spiritual seeking for enlightenment as that which motivated the great seers and gurus.

Jewish, Christian and Muslim scriptures on the other hand, while they also perform such a function for believers, have another precise role – that of witness to the fundamental belief that God has in a special and unique way influenced the course of human history. Revelation in these religions is linked to history, and their scriptures are historical source material concerning that revelation. This remains so even if this aspect of scripture is mostly overlooked in the light of the overwhelming impact of a deeper belief. In some ways, as Cantwell Smith has argued: 'Torah is to Jews what Qur'an is to Muslims and what Christ is to Christians' (see Levering 1989: 18).

The Bible as historical source material

An important aspect of the controversy surrounding interpretation of the Bible, in both Jewish and Christian circles, is its status as historical source material and how far it should be subject to historical investigation. Some emphasize the symbolic rather than the literal meaning of Biblical narrative, tending to downgrade the importance of the historical question, 'what actually happened?'. One teacher put it like this:

In 1951 a 7-year old demanded in class whether I really believed that a star led the magi to Jesus. A few days before Christmas 1991 the same question was put to a bishop on Any Questions and he didn't say no. . . . It is typical of our society that intelligent and successful people prefer, or rather insist, that their religion remain childish; that it was a child who found the Christmas story ludicrous in 1951.[4]

The assumption here is that the historical question is both irrelevant and damaging. Such exasperation is reflected in much recent RE which has tended to over-react to earlier emphases by stressing the greater importance of contemporary living Judaism and Christianity. The historical side of this is usually acknowledged, but in passing as it were. Often it is spoken of as 'story'. Thus, for example, the Teachers' Manual of the Westhill Project states that: 'The story of Jesus . . . is central for all Christians' (Read *et al.* 1986: 7). The word 'story' may seem to be an impeccable and non-judgemental word to use, but it tends to carry associations for people similar to the word 'myth'. Much used by scholars, 'myth' is often misunderstood by the general public as indicating something which primitive people believed in, but which we have outgrown. 'Story' too tends to be seen by many as something either appropriate for children, or to do with fiction. Of course it can be true to life and show insight into human behaviour, just as the novel or fairy-tale can, but it is not to be taken seriously as history.

This can quite easily be the impression which is conveyed by the

Westhill Project's reference to story just quoted – however unintentionally – because it is not counterbalanced by particular attention to New Testament evidence. The lack of this encourages one to think that the word 'story' may quite reasonably be picked up by children as meaning 'made up'. The list of the stories given on the same page confirms this – Jesus' birth in a stable and the visit by the shepherds is listed alongside the crucifixion and the resurrection. There appears to be no awareness of the extreme confusion that such a listing can give. The stories surrounding the birth of Christ are thought by many Christians to be just stories and certainly not on the same level of historical reliability as the account of the crucifixion and of the resurrection.

Thus overuse of the word story in connection with biblical material can convey the impression that the Gospels for example are not history. But an immediate retort from some people would be, 'But the gospels *are* story – they are certainly not history.' Yet this comment raises all the questions. Who says they are not history, and why? The gospels were certainly written in the form of history – purporting to be history.

The historical question in fact will not go away. This is especially so with regard to Christianity. Even very radically-minded Christians still assume a basic core of historical affirmation concerning Jesus – so long as they still wish to be called Christians at all. So it is essential to focus on this question if we want pupils to understand Christianity today. It matters very much who he was, what he actually taught and so forth. To say it does not matter is to reinterpret Christianity in a way that loses touch with almost all Christians of all ages.

It is also failing therefore to prepare pupils for the real world not to help them understand the controversy over such matters engendered among religious people. The disagreement, for example, between evangelical and radical is felt by Christians to be extremely important, and it is equally important that pupils appreciate what is at stake.

Unless we open up the possibility for pupils of their own authentic exploration of Biblical material as historical source material, as well as a source of religious and spiritual inspiration, we cannot be said to be playing fair with them in helping them to understand either Judaism or Christianity.

The importance of work in the classroom on the Bible

Work on the Bible in RE needs, therefore, to have a reasonable time allowance given it. I am certainly not arguing for a lion's share of the time, because the opening up of the subject beyond its Bible teaching role has been extremely important and valuable. But I am arguing for a serious amount of attention to be given to conveying skills of interpretation, and this requires some ongoing work. It is not possible or desirable to do this only very occasionally or in the odd lesson every now and then.

Teachers who associate the Bible with an old-fashioned approach to RE tend to be resistant to any sustained work on it. Yet its presumed irrelevance for pupils relates to how it is presented. Furthermore, the objection raised by Goldman in the 1960s, that it is beyond children's capacity to understand, has been seriously challenged (see Chapter 5.) Certainly children will never develop the appropriate skills and concepts if they are never given the chance of so doing.

It is particularly important that such work be done in primary as well as secondary schools because, if it is not, stereotypes develop in children's minds which it is very, very difficult later to replace. This is turning Goldman on his head as it were. His anxiety about Biblical work in the primary classroom was that children would learn things which later they had to unlearn. I agree that this is a serious consideration, but it applies if Biblical work is *not* done.

The teaching of Easter may be taken as an example. The impression is easily conveyed to young children that this is about new life in spring, and Easter eggs, yet fundamentally it concerns Christian belief in the resurrection of Jesus. This appears to be very unpalatable content in today's world, and well-nigh incomprehensible to the vast majority of pupils in schools. The educational requirement therefore is to help them to gain access to the idea, and to the evidence supporting it, so that they have some basis upon which to evaluate the Christianity which is based upon it.

Nor is it enough to tell pupils what Christians believe, thus by-passing the question of historicity – for, as discussed above, Christians do not see it as just an imaginary story. Again the narrative-style of teaching is inappropriate, whether announcing that 'The tomb was empty because Jesus had risen from the dead', or that 'No-one knows whether the tomb was empty and it doesn't matter anyway. It's the meaning which the idea had for Christians which counts.' Both would be equally indoctrinatory.

We need to share with pupils knowledge of the actual text and basic skills of interpretation, so that they have some chance of becoming detectives themselves and reflecting on the material, and not being at the mercy of the interpretations which other people give them. Such work can be exciting and challenging, and can exemplify an educational as compared with an indoctrinatory approach to RE.

Purpose of work on the Bible in RE

This can be summarized as basically threefold:

1. to help pupils to appreciate what a religious response to the Bible involves and how it can support faith in a basic way. For both

Jews and Christians, the Bible is regarded with reverence and
plays a significant part in public worship and private devotion;
2.   to give some knowledge of the techniques of historical and
literary analysis as applied to biblical material, by enabling pupils
to practise these techniques in a simple way themselves, and in so
doing become better informed;
3.   to enable pupils to think theologically in relation to the text, in
order to discover whether or not religious faith is reasonable, and
to stimulate their own authentic thinking about it.

A possible approach in the classroom

Opening questionnaire

This can provide a helpful starting-point with pupils, and the responses
furnish much material for subsequent work.

Which of the following statements about the Bible would you think
to be correct and which incorrect? Give reasons for your answer. The
Bible is:

1.   great literature;
2.   the inspired Word of God;
3.   a collection of fairy-stories;
4.   always right because dictated by God;
5.   useless and irrelevant to the modern world;
6.   the historical documents for the study of Judaism and Christianity;
7.   scientifically naive;
8.   a holy book which should not be criticized;
9.   a collection of material for prayers and meditation;
10. a 'pack of lies';
11. a text-book on morals;
12. the account of God's revelation to people;
13. always correct in its literal meaning;
14. inconsistent and contradictory;
15. not one book but consisting of many writings written over a long
period of time;
16. a medium of revelation.

Discussion of these points could include how far they contradict
each other, or whether some are compatible. Are some of them views
which can be shared by both religious and non-religious people? What
kind of answers might Jews and Christians themselves give? On what
grounds might they base their convictions?

In order to evaluate these views pupils need to look at some
Biblical material themselves. Work could be done on the different

kinds of material that are found in the Bible: myth, history, laws, prophecy, poetry, letters, parables, proverbs and so forth. The point can be made that they require to be read and interpreted in quite different ways: to read a poem as though it were a law code is manifestly stupid. There is plenty of material published to help with this kind of introductory work.

It would then be helpful to share problems of interpretation with regard to material which can be read in different ways, notably as straightforward historical material or as symbolism. An example from the book of Exodus could be given.

Worksheet on the giving of the law

When He had finished speaking with Moses on Mount Sinai, the Lord gave him the two tablets of the Testimony, stone tablets written with the finger of God.

(Exodus 31: 18)

This passage refers to the account of Moses going alone up the mountain to think and pray and receive God's commandments which were written on the writing materials available there – on pieces of stone. These tablets were evidence of what had been given to Moses; most translations in English describe them as 'testimony'.

1. Write out the verse, and underline the words or phrases (at least three) which are anthropomorphic (which means speaking of God 'as though he is a man' from two Greek words 'anthropos' = man, human-being, and 'morphe' = form, shape).

2. Recently, people have talked of computers in an anthropomorphic way. 'You must learn how to talk to a computer, and the next generation of computers will be able to talk back.' Do you think this is a good thing? Are there some dangers in speaking about a machine as though it were a human-being?

3. Whether or not you believe in God, do you think it is helpful to speak about God in an anthropomorphic way? Are there some dangers?

4. All Jewish scholars, whether they are Orthodox, Conservative or Reform, believe that God is spirit. God is not a human being, and language which suggests this is metaphorical. What does 'metaphor' mean? And why is it important to understand that this biblical passage is using metaphorical language?

5. This is a comment by a Jewish rabbi. Do you agree with him? In the light of it, do you want to add to, or alter, your answers to questions 3 and 4?

Many modern people have trouble with the idea that God speaks. On a simple level it implies that God has lungs, a voice box, and a mouth, which doesn't make much sense. It hardly seems what the Bible meant. Even trying to think of 'the voice of God', without a body behind it, is difficult. Americans like to think of God's 'voice' as a rich baritone, suggesting that women aren't created as much in God's image as men are. Does God's 'voice' speak Hebrew as some people think? It all sounds too little for the Great God of the whole universe.[5]

6. Although Orthodox, Conservative and Reform Jews would agree that expressions such as 'God spoke' and 'God gave' are metaphors, there is an important difference in how they interpret the metaphors, in what is being described in this way.

To the question 'Did God give the Torah to Moses?' they would give different answers. Study these answers and say in your own words where they disagree.

An *Orthodox* Jew might say, 'God gave the Torah in that Moses wrote down exactly what God told him to write, Moses was only a scribe, a vehicle of communication.

A *Conservative* Jew might say 'God gave the Torah in that God was like a teacher giving a lesson to Moses which Moses had to try to understand and then communicate to others.

A *Reform* Jew might say 'God gave the Torah in the sense that Moses wrote it but God inspired him.'

The worksheet draws attention to the importance of sharing the problem of biblical interpretation with pupils. This applies equally to teaching concerning Christianity. Thus within Christian interpretation of Jesus there is in fact room for wide divergence, yet it always homes in on the Palestinian Jewish figure who taught and healed people in Galilee and was crucified in Jerusalem and who convinced his followers of his resurrection from the dead. Certain skills and techniques for assessing the historical evidence concerning this figure can be taught. Here is an example: the language test.

Worksheet on the language of the gospels

The ordinary language which people spoke in Galilee in the first century AD was *Aramaic,* so this is the language which Jesus would have spoken. The Gospels were written in Greek which was the common language of the Eastern part of the Roman Empire.

[A]
1. Make a list of the Aramaic words in these verses, together with what they mean;

Mark 5;41, Mark 7;34, *Mark 14;36 Mark 15;34

(*This should be looked up in the Authorized or the New English Bible.)

2. Can you think of any reason why there should be Aramaic words in a Gospel written in Greek?

[B]

1. Perhaps you have tried translating from one language into another and appreciate how difficult it is to give exactly the same meaning. Some passages of the Gospel are in rather clumsy or peculiar Greek, and some passages are difficult to understand. If scholars find that when these passages are translated into Aramaic, they do read well and make sense, what does this suggest?

2. Here is an example: 'Forgive us our trespasses, as we forgive those who trespass against us'.

Where do these words occur? The Greek word for 'trespass' is *opheilema* which refers only to a *financial* debt. This does not make much sense in the Lord's Prayer. In Aramaic, however, there is a word *hōbā* which refers to either a financial or a *religious/moral* debt. Why does this suggest that the Lord's Prayer was not first spoken in Greek but in Aramaic?

3. Here is another. Some of the ancient manuscripts for Luke 14;5 have this saying of Jesus:

If one of you has a son or an ox and it falls into a well, will he hesitate to haul it up on the Sabbath day?

This is rather an odd sentence. But what do you notice about the words in Aramaic?

son = bera; ox = ber`a; well = bēra

Aramaic was fond of 'alliteration'. Look up the meaning of that word in the dictionary. Can you think of any reason why this is likely to be a sentence spoken by Jesus, rather than made up by someone else much later on?

[C]

In Aramaic people often said the same thing twice, once in a more negative way, and once in a positive way.

1. Write out the sayings of Jesus recorded in Mark 2;27, 10;27, and 13;31 with the more negative aspect on one line and the positive underneath.

2. Why might Jesus often have spoken like this?

The need for openness

Such tests offer considerations – evidence to be taken into account.

They do not give conclusive proof, and so the range of interpretations among Christians is as wide as that among Jews. This should be pointed out with regard, for example, to the question posed by the seven-year old as to whether the star really led the wise men to Jesus (see also p. 131). As part of work comparing the Christmas narratives found in Matthew and Luke (Matthew 1:18–2:23 with Luke 1:5, 1:26–38, 2:1–20, 2:39–40), information about the likely meaning of the term 'wise men', about Herod the Great, about the prophecy quoted by Suetonius, about certain astronomical data, and so forth, could ensure that pupils have sufficient input to avoid a simplistic acceptance of one particular point of view, whether of credulity or of scepticism. Care must be taken *not* to give the impression that most Christians believe, or do not believe, that the stories of the shepherds and the wise men are historically true. It *is* controversial, and it is indoctrinatory to give the impression that it is not. The possibility of coming to different conclusions must be kept alive for pupils.

Opinions on such a matter as the story of the wise men may seem not too important, but that is not the case with regard to the variety of views possible concerning, for example, the Resurrection of Jesus which is of central importance for the understanding of Christianity. A consideration of the historical evidence concerning this supposed event can illustrate some of the historical acumen which RE needs to share with pupils.

Views about the Resurrection of Jesus – background material for discussion

Reference has already been made to the impressions pupils easily gain concerning this. Mostly they reinforce the conditioning of society which tends to consider Christians who believe in the resurrection of Jesus as deluded – they are like children who still believe in Santa Claus. It is important to discuss with pupils the reasoning behind such doubt, as well as the various Christian views on the Resurrection. Public controversy on this matter, associated especially with the Bishop of Durham (in 1984), has drawn attention to the importance of this question.

Secularists tend to argue on two grounds:

1. It *could not* have happened – scientific laws forbid it – there's no more to life than this molecular world so obviously this is pure myth;
2. It *did not* happen – the historical evidence supporting it is not strong enough to prove so unusual an occurrence.

The first objection relates to the science/religion debate discussed in

Chapters 3 and 13 (see especially the bibliography on p. 202 n. 1). The important point here is that science purports to investigate what is in fact in the physical world. It ought not to decide beforehand on a priori grounds what the facts are. If the resurrection did actually happen it was indeed unusual – a miracle – but this is exactly what it is claimed to be – unusual and a miracle.

The second objection requires more extensive discussion here, for it is crucial to any handling of biblical material and can serve as an example. Norman Anderson in his book, *A Lawyer Among the Theologians* (1973), argues that no-one could question the actuality of this event unless indoctrinated with false suppositions.[6]

If we wish to disagree with his view that the evidence supporting the resurrection of Jesus is strong, we should at least know what the evidence is and be aware of certain historical considerations. These include, for example, the following points among others:

1. The accounts in the Gospels provide primary source material which should only be set aside for sound historical reasons. A secularist assumption that such an event could not have happened is not itself historical evidence but a particular mind-set.
2. The existence of Christianity owes its origin to this supposed event. All the evidence from the various parts of the New Testament including the earliest (the letters of Paul which happen to have survived) as well as the fact of Christianity and its beliefs and rituals, point to this conviction about the resurrection of Jesus as being central. The remarkable change in the disciples who had nothing to gain by being his followers – and much to lose, for it led to martyrdom for many – can be appreciated even by very young children.
3. If this event is doubted then stronger evidence for an alternative account should be given. Yet the variety of alternative explanations for the rise of Christianity, as well as for the existence of the resurrection narratives in the Gospels, argues for greater caution concerning scepticism about the accounts they give. As one scholar has put it recently, Jesus has been described as a political revolutionary, a magician, a Galilean charismatic, a Galilean rabbi, a Proto Pharisee, an Essene and an eschatological prophet. 'The plurality is enough to underline the problem. Even under the discipline of attempting to see Jesus against his own most proper Jewish background, it seems we can have as many pictures as there are scholars! (Crossan 1991: xxviii).
4. A particularly interesting point is the way in which alternative explanations for Jesus' resurrection tend to have even less evidence supporting them. They fall a long way short of any kind of proof. This does not seem to worry the scholars concerned, because they so often assume that if you can doubt something you

should; it is enough for these alternative interpretations of Christianity to suggest another possibility. Paul *could* have invented the resurrection; Christianity *could* have originated in the cult of the sacred mushroom, etc. How strong the evidence really is does not matter – to doubt is scholarly, to affirm is credulity. Yet the doubt is itself an affirmation, for example among other things of a secularist view of history. Furthermore, history is about what happened, not about the million possibilities which could have happened.

5. The objection that the resurrection is unusual and unrepeatable and therefore did not happen cannot stand, because Christians who have believed in it have never assumed it was anything else, and in any case history is made up of unique occurrences. History seeks to unlock what happened in the past, and should not have a fixed idea of what that must have been like. The whole point of the great search for objectivity lies precisely here: that the historian may endeavour to let the evidence speak for itself.

6. But is not doubt appropriate when there are discrepancies between the accounts in the different Gospels? Yet mistakes and inconsistencies by themselves do not necessarily indicate unreliability except in small details; they might indeed suggest authenticity in a way which carefully coordinated accounts may not.

7. But what about the question of bias? One thing which all scholars agree upon is that the Gospels were written by Christians with the purpose of putting Jesus in a good light. Yet such bias does not indicate the unreliability of everything a person says or writes, for it may be a justified bias – preference in the light of knowledge. A favourable reference given by a person who likes the candidate for a job is not automatically disqualified! Nor does the absence of bias necessarily, or even usually, indicate knowledge, for involvement with persons or events at some level is an essential means of acquiring knowledge.

The question of the historical evidence for the resurrection of Jesus is therefore something which should be looked at carefully in the classroom and not assumed to be non-existent. This is perfectly consistent with open teaching – indeed, it is a means by which pupils can come to their own authentic but informed opinions on such matters. It is also consistent with teaching which is relevant to pupils and twentieth century concerns. For interpretation of biblical passages underlies directly or indirectly current understanding of both the words 'Jewish' and 'Christian'.[7]

Notes

1. Dr Sara Grant at the Crista Prema Seva ashram in Puna, January 1978.
2. Quoted from Hans-Ruedi Weber 'Experiments with Bible study' in a preparatory document in a seminar 12 March 1992 in Durham led by Liz Varley on 'Participatory Bible study – is it a good thing?' See also Walter Wink, 1990, *Transforming Bible Study*.
3. See, e.g. W. Moberly, 1992, 'Old Testament' and 'New Testament'. The propriety of the terms for Christian theology, in *Theology*, vol. XCV, no. 763.
4. TRUST, newsletter of SCM Press Trust, no. 6 March 1992 p.3 – a letter from P.W. Thorpe.
5. From Eugene B. Borowitz, 1979, *Understanding Judaism*, p.15. This is a valuable book written for young people and giving Reform, Conservative and Orthodox perspectives on a series of key issues.
6. See also Ross Clifford, 1991, *Leading Lawyers Look at the Resurrection*. Refer also to Richard Harries, 1987, *Christ is Risen* and J. Wenham, 1992, *The Easter Enigma*.
7. A note on books. Andrew Walker (ed.), 1988, Part 2 of *Different Gospels*, has very useful discussion of different Christian attitudes to Biblical interpretation.

For scholarly discussion of an issue such as the relationship of Christianity to Judaism see E.P. Sanders, 1992, *Judaism – Practice and Belief 63 BCE – 66 CE* and J. Dunn, 1991, *The Partings of the Ways: Between Christianity and Judaism and their Significance for the Character of Christianity*. A book such as James H. Charlesworth, 1991, *Jesus within Judaism*, is more for the general reader. Very useful is D. Cohn-Sherbok, 1991, *A Dictionary of Judaism and Christianity*.

On the relationship of the Bible to scriptures in other religions, see for example *World scripture: a Comparative Anthology of Sacred Texts*, 1991, ch. 4 on 'Sacred words and sacred texts' in M. Barnes, 1991, *God East and West*, and M. Levering, 1989, *Rethinking Scripture: Essays from a Comparative Perspective*.

For historical evidence concerning Jesus, see E. Ives, 1992, 'The Gospel and history' in Montefiore, 1992. Scholarly books include J. Jeremias, 1971, *New Testament Theology:* vol. 1; J.D. Crossan, 1991, *The Historical Jesus: the Life of a Mediterranean Jewish Peasant*; M. Kelsey, 1991, *Myth, History and Faith*.

Books for use in schools include Carstein Thiede, 1991, *Jesus – Life or Legend?* and K.R. Chappell, 1991, *Investigating Jesus*.

For general introduction to the Bible see, for example, John Barton, 1991, *What is the Bible?*; Terence Copley, 1991, *About the Bible*; R. Abba, 1983, *The Nature and Authority of the Bible*.

CHAPTER 10

Can RE be assessed?

Assessment is an unavoidable part of the education scene, whether we view this with pleasure or irritation. The emphasis of the Education Reform Act on it, and the proposals regarding it which are emerging for the core and foundation subjects, have brought to the surface in a renewed way for many people the dangers of assessment. At the same time the excellence and forward-thinking nature of much of the Task Group on Assessment and Testing (TGAT) under the chairmanship of Professor Black has justified a more optimistic view. It is in fact possible that assessment really can serve education and help all pupils forward in their own personal development as learners. Obviously, it is in the interests of all concerned, especially teachers and pupils, that this be so.

Welcome emphases from the thinking on assessment developed by TGAT and other groups such as SEAC (Schools Examination and Assessment Council) include the following:

1. that teachers should *not* teach to test but see that assessment bears an organic relationship to what is being taught, – that it actually aids teaching;
2. that a variety of methods, including oral and practical as well as written, should be used which enable different aspects of the whole pupil to be evaluated;
3. that this involves teachers in freeing themselves from whole class teaching per se as the main style of their work with pupils, and taking account of various forms of group and individual learning situations.

The 1988 Act does not include RE under the assessment requirements which are restricted to core and foundation subjects. Nevertheless, the educational thinking behind those requirements is powerfully affecting the RE scene, and there are a number of important initiatives in different parts of the country which are trying to work out suitable assessment procedures for RE.[1] It is likely that eventually local Agreed Syllabuses will make such assessment schemes a mandatory part of their syllabus.

Is it desirable to assess in RE?

It is still a matter of debate as to how desirable it is to assess in RE at all. On the one hand there is the point made by Pring in 1984:

'There is something paradoxical in holding the view that personal, social and moral development is the most important aspect of education whilst at the same time arguing that there are no criteria either for selecting what is significant in this development or for assessing what counts as having developed successfully.

(Pring 1984: 153)

Nevertheless as Susan Hewitt, writing in the *TES* in 1988, put it: 'Assessment is, of course, always the problem. It is so much easier to test facts; how do you evaluate 'religious' development? What is it for heaven's sake?'

Table 10.1 outlines the spectrum of views possible. Can you add to it?

Table 10.1 **Why assess? Spectrum of views possible**

Assess because it is educationally desirable	Don't assess because it is anti-educational
Because it will give status to RE	Because it will risk reducing RE to what is easily measurable
Because teachers, governors and parents will know what is being achieved in RE	Because all assessment, except of a mechanistic kind, risks being unfair – subjectivity cannot be eliminated
Because it will promote professional efficiency, giving clarity to hard-pressed, often non-specialist, teachers	Because it is time-consuming, and yet another burden for hard-pressed teachers
Because it encourages pupil motivation	Because it encourages the wrong kind of motivation and discourages learning out of interest, and appreciation of the importance and value of learning
Because learning is developmental and goes through definite stages	Because classifying pupils at pre-decided stages of attainment is inhibiting to them, especially those of low ability, and those particularly gifted
Because it can promote curriculum change	Because it can encourage teachers to adopt curriculum change in a superficial way
Because it can help to give pupils self-esteem as they can acquire a sense of progression	Because it promotes competitiveness and comparison between pupils (and staff and schools) despite the desire to avoid this, and can underline a deep sense of failure for very many

Mary James, as deputy director of PRAISE,[2] has indicated the hope that RE should fulfil a role alongside all other subjects of encouraging a wide base for assessment and recording. She asks,

What place is there for an explicitly affective dimension that encompasses non-cognitive aspects of spiritual and moral development? Where is the place for youngsters to express and record a growing sense of mystery, deepening values, an awakening sense of commitment, if these are things that they regard as important to their wholeness as individuals? . . . Without wishing to advocate the kind of religious education that is properly the role of the church, mosque, synagogue, temple or home, is there still a role for the RE teacher in helping pupils to recognize and express their own religious experience, as well as helping them to understand the experiences of others?[3]

Mary James closed her paper by noting that the principles upon which the Records of Achievement movement, piloted by a number of local education authorities in the 1980s, was based are underpinned by values such as justice, fairness, equality, consideration for others' interests, respect for persons, and self-determination. The links with RE should be obvious.

There is a strong case therefore for educative assessment understood as something fairly low-key, but nevertheless professionally done and requiring *some* commitment, both by teachers and pupils. Table 10.2 sets out suitable aims and objectives. They are based on the three requirements of the National Criteria for Public Examinations: Knowledge, Understanding and Evaluation. They add a fourth which is widely understood amongst educationalists as essential to the other three – that of personal participation.

Features of educative assessment could include the following:

Project work
This is primarily self-chosen work at individual or group level which can be presented in a variety of ways, not just written. This kind of work encourages good motivation, and gives the teacher more opportunity for conversation with pupils. Projects enable the presentation both of knowledge and understanding as well as evaluation – they can, and should be, the expression of a personal opinion backed up by evidence showing a grasp of 'factual material'.

The giving of a 'seen' paper
This refers to an examination paper which is given to pupils a long time before they sit it, so that they can study towards answering specific questions, and then be required on a given date to answer the questions under examination conditions. (See below for details on such 'seen' papers on pp. 151, 153–4.)

Table 10.2 **Religious education aims and assessment objectives**

Aims	Assessment objectives
	Examinations should therefore:
1. *Knowledge*: the learning of basic 'factual' information about religion	1. provide a test of how far basic 'factual' material has been grasped
2. *Understanding*: awareness of the way in which religious beliefs are expressed, both verbally and in other ways	2. allow pupils to show how far they understand religious language and other means of expression
3. *Evaluation*: a) the development of skills for discernment both between what is central and what is peripheral, and between what is genuine, lived belief and what is superficial and second-hand, hypocritical or unthinking repetition of words. Such skills include both logical thinking and qualitites of empathy and sensitivity.	3. a) enable pupils to use the skills of discernment which they have built up
b) the appreciation of the controversial nature of religion and the need to make informed judgements about it.	b) encourage pupils to express their own opinion based on evidence of real reflectiveness
4. *Personal involvement*: appreciation, motivation or participation – a genuine engagement with the subject by awakening interest and awareness of its importance	4. give opportunity for pupils to express work in some depth on an aspect which particularly interests them

These four strands need to be plaited together as a single purpose

An unseen examination paper
'Unseen' refers to the standard examination procedure presenting candidates with a paper previously unknown to them to be answered within a particular time limit. It is important that unseen papers be less a test of memory and more an opportunity for pupils to express understanding and skills of evaluation.

Units of work
These can be both criteria-related and process-based. Mary James reported that there was strong agreement among pilot projects that assessment needs to be made in positive terms against criteria which are clearly laid down, the results of which can be described in words. Number grades or rating scales were not favoured. This approach favours the development of units of work with explicit objectives which could subsequently be assessed. A process approach, however, is equally possible, as some drama and arts teachers found, whereby

achievements were analysed after involvement in more open-ended classroom experience. Mary James noted that, 'possibly this is an approach that would find favour with RE teachers also although one can envisage a combination of both'.[4]

Work set during the normal course of teaching can combine engagement with central and fundamental issues with relative ease of assessing pupils' levels of understanding. The Appendix to this chapter gives an example.

Conversation with pupils individually and also in small groups
Oral work is important, especially for pupils who are more limited in written skills. It is, however, valuable in its own right as a way of helping teachers to assess the whole pupil.

The educational value of talking with and listening to pupils on their own or in small groups is clear from comments given by teachers taking part in the OCEA (Oxford Certificate of Educational Achievement) project:

OCEA opens up the possibility of real education concerned at least as much with the quality of the journey as with the ultimate destination.

OCEA has improved the relationship between me and every single one of the children.[5]

Many teachers found the one-to-one work quite challenging and demanding, but also exciting and rewarding. Such assessment further emphasizes the need for flexible grouping situations in the classroom in order that teachers can have time to get to know the pupils better.

Pupil self-assessment
OCEA is part of the Records of Achievement project which has brought to the fore, in a way which almost certainly will persist, the importance of pupils themselves taking a part in the assessment process. Pupil profiling of this kind necessarily involves sharing with pupils something of the purpose of education. This was a point mentioned at the end of Chapter 1. They can be involved in their own ongoing self-assessment through such means as completing forms. Suggestions for a possible layout for one of these are set out in Figure 10.1. This sees assessment in the shape of a ladder indicating the idea of development, and of competing with oneself and not with other people. The pupil's own experience and insight make the ladder as the pupil gives comments on each topic or unit of work, thus expressing in visual terms how understanding is being built up.

Pupils can also indicate what they see as their level of achievement on each side of the ladder, the one asking, How do I respond? and the other, What do I know? The three narrow columns on each side can be shaded in, the amounts varying according to the degree of

Figure 10.1 **Pupil self-assessment form**

PERSONAL DEVELOPMENT FOCUS:	CONTENT FOCUS:
SKILLS AND ATTITUDES	CONCEPTS AND KNOWLEDGE
How I respond	What I know

T H I N K I N G	F E E L I N G	B E H A V I N G		H O M E T R A D I T I O N	L I F E I N G E N E R A L	R E L I G I O U S U N D E R S T A N D I N G
			We visited a parish church and a mosque. They were quite different but a nice feeling in both. I still think religion is a bit funny. I suppose people do it because they've been brought up to it.			
			We had a student and she was ever so nice. We did a theme on light with her and she made it really interesting finishing up with an assembly we prepared ourselves. Why can't all of school be like this.			
			I didn't see the point of what we were doing and got rather bored. I don't think I learned anything.			
			It was Christmas so we all did the same thing. I liked it because when I said that Jesus is like Santa Claus or something my teacher got everybody saying what they thought and he put ideas on the board and we had ever such a good talk about it - it went on for the whole lesson and I got quite cross but then I liked what Ahmed said. He is not a Christian but he said "Jesus is special. So even if the Wise Men and the Shepherds are all made up, they are just a way of saying Jesus is special". I don't know why this made sense but perhaps it's because I do think deep down that Christmas is a bit special even though it all seems like a fairy story.			
			We could choose what to do this half-term so I chose attitudes to animals. I am horrified by how some people are nasty to them. Also others just see them as a means to making money. I love the story of St Francis. Not all religious people are like that - sacrificing animals should be abolished. I am going to collect for the RSPCA			

INSIGHT MAKES THE LADDER

understanding which the pupil considers he or she has gained. Alternatively, colour-coding could be used (for example, the idea of traffic lights: red denoting the need for more work and practice, amber that progress is being made, and green that a measure of success can be recorded). Such colour-coding is interesting for pupils to do and also makes it very easy for teachers as well as pupils quickly to see how pupils are evaluating themselves.

The uprights on either side of the ladder represent the two focal points of education: personal development which consists of skills and attitudes, and content of learning dealing with concepts and knowledge. Each of these uprights can be thought of as comprising three stands, distinct yet not separate. People think, feel and act – human development includes the mind, the emotions and the will; reflection, attitudes and behaviour. Pupils must be encouraged to value each of these aspects as necessarily involved in being human. The content focus can also be thought of from the point of view of RE as in three parts: life in general, religious understanding, and the home tradition. This perhaps needs explaining a little.

Whatever topics are covered in RE, elements in them will be of wide general significance as well as being specifically religious material. In this sense what has been called 'implicit RE' is unavoidable. (It is equally inadequate on its own as the criticism of the Highest Common Factor (HCF) model of RE discussed in Chapter 4 shows.) Concepts and knowledge will therefore extend both pupils' understanding of life in general as well as their appreciation of religion. But the addition of 'home tradition' acknowledges the supreme importance for each individual pupil of the familiar background, the form of nurture which he or she is receiving. It is vital for effective RE that this is not left out in the cold, laid to one side or marginalized, but treated to the serious attention which it deserves. Only the pupil concerned can do this. Each pupil must be the expert here in seeking to relate what is being learnt in school to that out-of-school learning which governs so much what and how the rest is assimilated. Putting this as a distinct strand does not mean that it is separate, but that pupils need to be encouraged consciously to relate to their own unique backgrounds in a spirit of growing critical affirmation.

The Pupil Self-assessment Form should have a second half allowing for comment from the teacher and from the parents.

The implications for the RE teacher of National Curriculum styles of assessment are considerable. A variety of assessment methods, together with the importance of pupils being involved in assessment, means that the teacher's role moves a long way from simply being the supplier of information or initiator of discussion. The teacher has to be 'adviser, consultant, critic and assessor' (Harris 1989: 11) and this applies in the primary school as well. The emphasis needs to be on pupil self-education, and the teacher as enabler of pupils' learning.

Steps for teachers

Knowledge of requirements

Some specific points can be made here.

1. Find out as much as possible about the assessment procedures which you need to work with. Check that you know what is required by the local Agreed Syllabus, the local Standing Advisory Council on Religious Education (SACRE), the school in which you work, and the external Examining Group relevant to your pupils. It is a good idea to reduce these requirements to note form on one or two sheets of A4. There will be much overlap almost certainly, but some tensions may emerge also which you will need to take account of and resolve in some way, perhaps by seeking outside help.
2. Check you understand fully the marking or grading system to be used for assessing, and how it is to be monitored and moderated, together with the timing of the various sections with regard to the age of pupils, and how the results are to be recorded, for whom and by whom.
3. Seek help if anything is unclear from the head teacher or assessment coordinator or local RE adviser or from the professional organizations listed at the end of this book.

Meeting requirements in an educational and creative way

Think out your attitude to these requirements. It is important that you cover them all with your pupils, otherwise they will be the losers (as well as you). You need, however, to be as creative as possible in fulfilling them, rather than getting bogged down under their weight. If aspects of content are specified, it is usually possible to find something which you can feel really happy about teaching, and other aspects could be made available for individual or group choice.

Skills specified can usually be developed through a whole range of material which can suit you and your classes. Concepts specified need to be inter-related, and this can spark very creative work as well as giving opportunity to work on associated areas which are not specified. Attitudes specified are unlikely to be ones inappropriate to the subject, though they may well need supplementing and you would be free to do this.

It is important that you try to make the work of assessment as integral and meaningful a part of your teaching as you can, so that it is not out on a limb or even operating against what you are hoping to achieve in RE.

Ensuring the minimum is covered
Make a timetable of likely pupil time needed for fulfilling the
requirements – remember that considerable opportunity for choice is
normally built in to the requirements. It does not mean doing everything,
but the really safe minimum must be done and allowed for. It only creates
an anxiety situation if this kind of thinking ahead is not done.

Pupil choice
Think out how much pupil negotiation and choice can be built in,
because this will greatly aid motivation to work well and enjoy the
learning. It is crucial that pupils do not learn so as to do well in
assessment, but that they do well in assessment because they enjoy
learning. All the time the pupil must be the centre of attention.
    This involves 'stretching' all pupils to achieve what they can, and
build up an image of themselves which is self-affirming as well as
self-critical. This relates closely to an emphasis upon normative rather
than summative assessment, even though the latter will clearly have to
play a part. 'Summative' refers to assessment for purposes of
recording what has been achieved: it is concerned with doing the
'sums' as it were at the end; 'normative' assessment, however, looks
to the future: its focus is on how knowledge of where we are now can
help us to move forward. Pupils, other staff, parents, governors, and
the general public including future employers, tend to be more
interested in what is summative, but teachers need to be far more
concerned with formative assessment.

Links with other subjects
Relate assessment in RE to what is happening in other subjects. The
post-ERA situation makes this easier because of the national
assessment procedures. For the primary school teacher this relating to
other subjects is obvious, but for the secondary school RE specialist it
is equally important to know what kinds of assessment the pupils are
experiencing or being involved in elsewhere.
    Because the skills and attitudes required for RE are mostly not
different from those needed for many other subjects, there can be a
considerable carrying-over of ideas and techniques from one to
another subject. Staff discussions can be very helpful in preventing RE
from being isolated for special treatment, and it will help pupils if
there is some continuity between how they are assessed in other areas
of the curriculum and what happens in RE.

Careful organization
One study has estimated that the new GCSE has increased teachers'
workload by about five hours each week. Even if this may be an
extreme case, all new forms of assessment do tend to make more work
if the teacher is not careful. Organization is therefore extremely

important and it is well worth taking trouble to set things up right in the beginning (Lawton 1989: 86).

A particular aspect of such organizational skills is likely to be the ability to analyse and record which parts of the Attainment Targets are being assessed by a particular task, question or topic. Because nothing is nationally agreed on this for RE, it is a matter for each teacher working according to what is locally required, but I give an example in Figure 10.2. The attainment targets given there are those envisaged by the Forms of Assessment in Religious Education (FARE) Project which are six in number:

1. awareness of mystery;
2. questions of meaning;
3. values and commitments;
4. religious belief;
5. religious practice;
6. religious language.

These are related to the work on metaphor argued for in Chapter 5. (pp 65–8) and to work on Sri Ramana discussed in Chapter 6 (pp 83–5).

It is important that the analysing and reporting does not get too complicated so that it runs away with itself. It should be kept as simple as possible, and a good rule of thumb is to try to share as much of it as you can with pupils so that they can learn how to fill in such charts themselves.

Forming questions
Try to ensure that all formal work or questions you set, so far as possible, a) require reflective thinking, b) are open-ended, and c) avoid jargon or difficult language. The type of questions or tasks set affects the kind of response, superficial or more meaningful, which pupils are likely to give. The Appendix at the end of this chapter discusses this further and gives examples of possible assessment questions.

Using 'seen' examinations
Try to use the strategy of 'seen' examinations, and think out the content well ahead for maximum educational value.

It allows for simplicity of structure and economy in the effort of assessment. The 'seen' examination, even in the more limited form of a single lesson, is feasible. The possibility of the school adopting such a policy is, however, something well worth discussing with other members of staff.

The advantages are considerable:

1. It provides a definite focal point for assessment which gives

Figure 10.2   Recording relationship of attainment targets to topics

ATTAINMENT TARGETS / TOPICS STUDIED	AWARENESS OF MYSTERY	QUESTIONS OF MEANING	VALUES AND COMMITMENT	RELIGIOUS BELIEF	RELIGIOUS PRACTICES	RELIGIOUS LANGUAGE
METAPHOR	focus on language as 'pointing' towards mystery encourages pupils to reflect	the nature of X raises question of purpose of life etc.		concept of 'God' especially as found in Judaism, Christianity and Islam		focus on the nature of religious language, and application to religious texts – getting beyond literalism
SRI RAMANA	central to Sri Ramana's experience therefore invites reflection	his story focuses on the purpose of life and the reality of life after death	his subsequent life shows his simplicity, courage, kindness, love of animals etc.	various aspects of Hinduism	meditation temple-worship learning from a guru	*karma, maya, samsara, advaita atman Brahman*
THE LITTLE FOX	discussion of the meaning of 'spiritual' related to various 'signals of transcendence' in pupils' own experience		discussion of the values and commitments of Moses and the shepherd. What did Moses lack?	developing understanding of concept of 'God' seen as 'spiritual'	helping pupils to see the difference between what religious practice can look like to an observer, and its possible inner meaning	the word 'spiritual'

Note: It is not important that each topic covers each AT, but an overall balance should be achieved. Filling in such a form as this can help to see clarity to both teachers and pupils – this can help to take away the burden of feeling one has got to be assessing all the time, and enable teachers to concentrate on educating pupils rather than on preparing them for being tested.

2. It minimizes anxiety and fear on the part of pupils and yet ensures that a pupil's work is his/her own. It is therefore a helpful supplement to the more varied forms of assessment which are ongoing.
3. It can help to prepare pupils for sitting public examinations.
4. It provides opportunity for work in depth and with a degree of flexibility to allow for individual response and at individual speeds of working, so that assessment can be seen as an integral part of education.
5. It gives the opportunity to set more challenging questions, and to require a higher standard of response. In this way, it can meet the demand for 'standards' at the same time as pupils can gain some sense of fulfilment in what they have achieved so far. In my own experiments with this form of assessment I have found that the level of achievement has been far higher. I have felt, and pupils have also felt, that it can enable them to do justice to themselves better.

It would be important to give the paper well before the examination date, perhaps as much as two terms, otherwise the educational value of the scheme is largely lost. A raid on the library and rushed preparation could increase anxiety and a mark-grabbing attitude. The success of the 'seen' examination depends on its allowing time for pupils to produce something authentic and well understood.

It is also important that the questions posed on the paper are stimulating and thought-provoking and take the commitment aspect of RE seriously. The holding of opinions should be encouraged provided that the pupil can put forward evidence in support. It must be insisted that pupils will be penalized not for holding an opinion with which the examiner happens to disagree, but only for the superficiality or absence of reasons given for the opinion.

A vital part of 'seen' examinations is sharing educational theory with pupils. The following notes might be given them.

Notes for pupils

1. In a 'seen' examination there are no 'model' answers. Its purpose is to encourage you to think in some depth about the complex themes involved in RE. This means

(a) finding out about particular themes;

(b) expressing your level of understanding about the material you have discovered and;

(c) thinking about it as deeply as possible.

For (a) you need to make as detailed a study as possible of each theme, getting material from various sources as appropriate. Lists of what is essential and what might be helpful for each question will be given you. If you read up more widely and give evidence of this you will be given credit for it. For (b) you need to make sure that you really understand the material. Look things up in other sources if you do not, and ask for help. For (c) you need to develop opinions about it which you can alter or change if fresh evidence comes to light.

2. You will not be marked on the basis of what opinions you hold, but on how relevant, and also how accurate are the reasons with which you support your opinion. It is worth noting that it is important to put views which you disagree with in as clear and favourable a light as possible. This not only shows qualities of empathy, but also strengthens your own case if you can answer the criticism of it.

3. English style as such will not be judged, but if the meaning of what you write is not clear, you cannot be given credit for it. It is particularly important not to use jargon – special terms which you do not really understand. You must try to express clearly what you genuinely think.

4. On the whole only give short quotations from the materials which you have studied. It is particularly important that all the work is your own, so anything which is copied from others must be openly acknowledged as such. Otherwise you will be heavily penalized for copying.

5. You will not be assessed on including this point or that point, or on the number of quotations, but rather on the degree of understanding indicated by the total way in which you present your answer. Understanding is shown by how you put the answer together, as well as by the wording you decide on for each phrase, together with your awareness of the complexity of the issues involved.

6. You will be allowed to take short notes in to the examination room, but they must be handed in at the end. They should contain only appropriate quotations with acknowledgement of their source which can be checked, or an outline plan containing only odd words or short phrases.

Appendix

Assessment within a unit of work

All tasks set can in fact be appropriate for assessment, and ones which are specifically given with assessment in mind ought also to be authentically contributing to pupil learning. Here is an example from work on pilgrimage: a worksheet on Understanding Ritual, using a picture of a woman worshipper on the banks of the Ganges at Varanasi.[6] (See also Chapter 13 pp. 200–02.)

A woman, dressed in a colourful sari, with necklace and bangles and flowers in her hair, and the mark of *tilaka* on her forehead, is performing a simple ritual on the edge of the Ganges. As evening draws near she places garlands of flowers and little clay oilwick lamps on the water which she then lights. She is presenting these as offerings to the river as to a deity. The Ganges is often called the River of Heaven, and contact with it is believed to wash away sin and to give liberation from rebirth.

Study the picture carefully. Here are some possible reasons why she is performing this act.

1. because this is what people do when they come to Varanasi;
2. because she is superstitious and thinks that, if she does not do this, something bad will happen;
3. because doing it helps her to concentrate upon Brahman;
4. because she is trying to show her husband and friends how pious she is;
5. because she is posing for a photograph;
6. because her mother and grandmother did it and so she does, for that is how she has been brought up;
7. because she believes it is an act of loving devotion to God;
8. because she is trying to pretend life is not as harsh and ugly as it really is.

Only two of these reasons are genuine religious ones. Which are they?

2. Here is a list of other reasons why people may perform religious acts: hypocrisy, conditioning, fear, escapism, sociability, as a hobby. Arrange the other reasons given above under these headings. Can you think of any other reasons?

3. Would you say the woman in the picture is being genuinely religious? Give reasons for your answer.

Essay-style questions

Questions for essay-type work need to be worded with care so that they encourage reflective thinking in an open manner. If for example work on Sri Ramana and the experience recorded in Chapter 6 (pp 84–5) were being assessed, we could ask a question such as this:

• Describe the conversion and subsequent life of Sri Ramana.

This could easily be answered in a purely descriptive way – a test of memory and ability to organize material and express it clearly. Any specifically religious understanding need not come in at all. The question could however be put more like this:

• Explain the difference made to Sri Ramana by the experience which he had when he was sixteen. How did he make sense of it? What concepts did he draw on?

The response this time is likely to be an improvement, in that skills of empathy and sensitivity are implied as necessary, and the focus of the question is on what it meant religiously to him. The Hindu concepts with the help of which he interpreted his experience would need to be discussed, and the way that this was done could give a good indication of the level of pupil understanding.

A third type of question could be applied to the material:

• Do you feel that you can understand Sri Ramana's experience and the way he reacted to it? Please explain your reasons.

This articulates the need for evaluation by the pupil – for personal involvement in the learning process. Sri Ramana and his experience is not now just a thing out there to be learned – which it could be according to the first question; nor is it something to be viewed in as academically detached a way as possible – which is the impression which could be given by the second question. Instead it becomes something living to which the pupil is asked to relate. It is important to note that the question remains an open one – it does not assume a particular response from the pupil. Pupil integrity is left intact.

The question could however be asked in another way:

• Show how the life of Sri Ramana can inspire us and help us to develop a more profound attitude towards death.

This also requires a personal response, but it does so by assuming that the pupil should answer in a particular direction. This is not an open question therefore and it could be regarded as indoctrinatory.

The question could however be phrased in another way which is open, but which still directs attention to the ultimate question which lies behind the last question:

• Discuss the helpfulness or otherwise of Sri Ramana's experience in penetrating the mystery of death.

This question includes an assessment of how far the pupil has knowledge and understanding of Sri Ramana's experience, even though it does not in so many words ask for it. It will, however, be very clear from the discussion which the pupil gives how far the work on Sri Ramana has been understood or has been misinterpreted. The question also makes explicit the choice which is open to the pupil, and it does so not in an either/or way, but suggesting that things may not be so clear-cut. This kind of question is, therefore, the one which we should be educating pupils towards, even if often it is necessary to ask simpler questions first.

Notes

1. At least four major groups have been set up: Association of Religious Education Advisers and Inspectors (AREAI) on 'Religious education for ages 5 to 16–18' 1989; Westhill College's 'Attainment in RE: a handbook for teachers' 1989; The FARE Project, completed 1992: the final report 'Forms of assessment in religious education' Exeter University School of Education. See the article by Stephen Bigger, 1991 Assessing religious education? in Journal of Beliefs and Values, vol. 12, no.1: 1–5; Religious Education Council (REC): *RE, Attainment and National Curriculum*, REC, 1991.
2. PRAISE (Pilot Records of Achievement in Schools' Evaluation) involving the Open University and Bristol University, has reported (1991) on the nine pilot schemes, involving 22 LEAs and over 250 schools, set up following the DES statement of policy in 1984 on Records of Achievement.
3. 'Principles for profiling and recording pupils' achievement: their implications for religious education' (p.9f). A paper given by Mary James at a seminar on 'Assessing religious education', supported by Keswick Hall Trustees and held at Homerton College, Cambridge on 9–11 April 1989.
4. Mary James, ibid p. 13.
5. In the Newsletter of the Oxford Certificate of Educational Achievement, OCEA in December, 1985, pp.1 and 3.
6. The picture is from a leaflet on Varanasi from the Indian Government Tourist office in London.

CHAPTER 11

What to do about school worship?

If assessment is a bugbear for many teachers, school worship is even more a danger zone for many headteachers who, with governors, carry responsibility for seeing that the provisions of the 1988 Education Reform Act are fulfilled. It directly also concerns RE teachers, both because they are often expected to be involved in running assemblies, and because what happens in them can influence attitudes to RE in general and specific work in RE.

Yet school worship need not be an anxiety area. There is plenty of latitude within the legislation for schools and RE teachers to fill it out in ways meaningful and interesting to themselves and their pupils. It is important to note that schools remain in control with regard to the how, when and what of the assemblies, in the same way as for assessment requirements where the teacher who delivers the goods in the classroom actually is the kingpin, and retains a large measure of freedom if he or she so chooses to exercise it. School worship should indeed be seen as an asset for RE, provided that both are seen in properly educational terms. There are many ways in which the RE teacher can encourage an approach conducive to such RE.

This may surprise some who think that school worship would constitute no problem for confessional RE, but that it *does* present a problem for reflective exploratory styles of RE such as argued for in this book. The division between education and worship is still assumed by many people, both religious and non-religious. The idea dies hard that education is open while worship is closed, that education promotes a critical approach whilst worship encourages a passive receptive attitude, that education is exploratory and wide-ranging whilst worship is narrow-minded and dogmatic.

So how can I argue that in fact education and worship can belong together, and even, if pupils are to achieve in RE what they are capable of, that exposure to the worship aspect of religion is in fact necessary?

As with RE and the way in which both the 'R' and the 'E' are understood, so with worship it all depends on how the requirement is viewed, and this in turn depends upon the meaning given to 'worship'. To this I will return after looking at what the 1988 Education Act requires.

The 1988 legislation

'All pupils in attendance at a maintained school shall on each school day take part in an act of collective worship.' Section 6 (1). I will comment on various aspects of the wording of this.

Collective worship

Translated into educational terms this means holding assemblies which give pupils and staff opportunity for worship. It is to be carefully distinguished from what is known as *corporate* worship which takes place within faith-communities, in which there is 'a *body* of believers bound together by their shared commitment'.[1] By contrast the school is a *collection* of individuals representing diversity of beliefs. What they do when they come together for such worship is therefore subject to wide variation.

It is important indeed to acknowledge that whether or not it is worship for any one person depends on their own free choice. The 1988 legislation did not make this clear enough. It tended to suggest that school worship could be required per se; it tended to give the impression that people were going to have to worship. Yet worship has to be freely engaged in otherwise it is a mere travesty of the real thing.

This was actually acknowledged by Baroness Cox – one of the chief 'Christian confessionalists' associated with the debates around the 1988 Education Act.[2] She notes that taking part in the act of collective worship is not making worship compulsory because no-one can do that. It means rather that opportunity for worship is given. It is a pity that the legislators were not more careful in their wording.

It *is*, however, the responsibility of schools to open up avenues or vistas for pupils to explore. Two analogies come to mind: attending a concert gives people the opportunity to have a musical experience, but it does not ensure it, for the response remains individual and free; providing mathematics lessons opens up for pupils the possibility of their becoming mathematically literate, but it cannot guarantee it.

Taking part

Pupils should *take part* in such assemblies as an educational activity to help them find out about religion, whether or not it can also be worship for them. Such taking part involves developing qualities of openness, empathy, imaginative thinking and the capacity for being still. Such qualities are educationally required within every area of the curriculum so there should be no discontinuity between the assemblies and what forms the rest of the school experience.

As I have developed elsewhere,[3] participation can take place also at two other levels besides that of educational enquiry: that of finding the assembly inspiring in a general way, and that of worship. See Fig.

11.1. Which it is for any given pupil remains known to each person in privacy – this is part of the great value of such assemblies that, first, time is given for reflectiveness and, secondly, that there is no necessity to communicate one's reactions – one can think things out for oneself without outside pressure. In this way such assemblies can perform a valuable anti-indoctrinatory function, helping pupils to achieve some real independence of thought.

Each school day
This emphasizes the importance of its not just being an occasional or one-off occasion. Such, for example, can be visits to religious places of worship, and such are RE units of work on worship. These are important, but they do not fulfil the same function as enabling pupils in a more normal situation to get on the wavelength of this dimension of religion. For this, rhythm and continuity and the absence of too much novelty are helpful because otherwise distraction can prevent attentiveness.

All pupils
This is important because otherwise some will be educationally deprived. In a predominantly secular society full of bustle and change pupils badly need times for quietness and reflectiveness, and opportunities to get on the wavelength of a different dimension to life. Voluntary assemblies leave pupils tied by their upbringing to particular forms or none at all, and even where choice is openly extended to pupils, a combination of secularism and peer-group pressure is likely to ensure that the choice is nominal only. Very few like to be associated with a God squad!

Content of assemblies
'In the case of a county school the collective worship required shall be wholly or mainly of a broadly Christian character' (Section 7).
    The Act specifies that the assemblies should be 'broadly Christian in character'. There has been much discussion over what this involves. Some have seen the requirement as a backward-looking nostalgic attempt to retreat into a parochial nationalism instead of welcoming the new pluralist flavour of society. Others see it as a vindication of the efforts of many to halt the marginalizing of Christianity which they consider has happened in many schools.
    Others see this as a very fair compromise showing political and educational astuteness. The presence of the word 'Christian' is based on an argument which almost all concede: the undoubted impact of Christianity on the kind of society which has developed in the West, and the appropriateness of children who grow up in this society understanding something of Christianity. The word 'broadly' added to 'Christian' acknowledges the reality of diversity of views and the need

of any national educational policy to cater for as wide a clientele as possible. A phrase like this is sufficiently vague as to leave great freedom for interpretation in different ways. It can include, for example, material which reflects Christian values without explicitly mentioning the word 'Christian', and Christian values are mostly understood today in a general sense such as 'caring' and 'co-operation' which most people, religious or not, find acceptable. Broadly Christian can also include anything which may be said to help pupils forward in their spiritual development – something which the 1988 legislation again refers to right at the beginning. This might include, for example, use of silence – and even young children can learn to appreciate this – listening to music, or evoking a situation of awe and wonder. All these give opportunity to awaken a spiritual attitude without any compulsion or any need to be explicitly 'Christian' about it.

Paradoxically the legislation seems to exclude only what is specifically denominational in Christianity, for it goes on to specify what it means by 'broadly Christian' as being 'without being distinctive of any particular Christian denomination'.[4]

School assemblies are not to be regarded as mini-church services, but this does not rule out the possibility of different types of Christian worship distinctive of denominations being shared with pupils in an educational way. In order to do so it is necessary to appreciate the levels of participation referred to in Fig. 11.1.

Exceptions allowed for
As John Hull and others have pointed out many times (e.g. Hull 1989), the 1988 ERA is important in officially acknowledging, for the first time in legislation, the presence of other major religious traditions in this country and requiring that cognizance be taken of them. The Act also includes the rights of parents to apply to the SACRE for permission to hold assemblies which are not 'broadly Christian in character' but specific to another faith.[5] It is probably fair therefore to see the 1988 legislation not as harking-back to a past when Christianity dominated, whether this be viewed with delight or with concern, but to see it as genuinely reflecting a changed situation. It gives permission for major changes, if local circumstances permit, in the content of assemblies. For effective responsibility rests with each local authority. The legislation, as we have already seen with regard to assessment, has recoiled from any attempt to prescribe a national system of RE, as local needs are so insistent and must be accommodated.

Delving deeper, however, a major criticism of the legislation which I see is that it assumes that worship must come under the umbrella of one or other religious tradition – however broadly this is understood – that all worship must be either Christian or Jewish or Muslim, and so on. It is this 'package' aspect of the worship which is the real bone of contention dividing people into separate camps. This is why the withdrawal clause had to be retained. It would become redundant if the thoroughly educational approach to 'worship' was appreciated and insisted upon. The disadvantages of separate faith-groups, besides practical difficulties, include the possibility of their being divisive and reinforcing existing barriers of belief. I want therefore to look again at the possiblity of inter-faith assemblies which can effectively bypass the Christian versus multi-faith polarization.

Inter-faith assemblies

Developments in inter-faith dialogue in the past few decades have indicated that there is much that can be done in discovering a common core of belief, attitude and feeling within the major world religions.[6] All the diagrams in Chapter 8 referred to common insight and/or a common task facing all religions.

Are they possible?

Yet the whole area of inter-faith worship is fraught with difficulty and no-one should approach it in a simplistic way. There is far more to it than simply choosing a reading from one religion, a prayer from another, and possibly a visual-aid from another. Ill-assorted assemblies can convey an impression of superficiality and be highly offensive to members of the faiths concerned. Of dubious educational value, they can become a subtle form of indoctrination – indoctrination into the beliefs and values associated with the particular type of pluralism which regards toleration as the highest virtue, on the grounds that all religions are basically saying the same thing. According to this view the fundamental one-ness of intention within all religions is taken as axiomatic, and diversity of forms of expression can become a source of celebration and not of either anxiety or controversy. Yet this is an inadequate view of religion as argued in Chapters 4 and 8 and elsewhere in this book. The effect of mixing faiths together in this way will be to compromise and confuse pupils.

The protests of many members of different religions at different aspects of the facile medley approach calls for caution. A paragraph from a booklet by David Bookless, written for Christians, many of whom are worried by the idea of possibly compromising the integrity of their own faith by taking part in inter-faith worship, effectively summarizes as well as possible in a short space the kind of attitudes to be reckoned with from different religions.

As well as different ideas of God and worship, the other faiths have very different attitudes to 'interfaith worship'. Most Orthodox Jews would reject it completely as *avodah zarah* (strange worship). Many Muslims would likewise reject it, although some would find serial acts (ie where worship of different faiths is presented in turn) and private prayer more acceptable. Sikhs generally have less problems, believing God to be at work in each faith, but some missionary Sikhs would reject pluralist approaches to the truth of all faiths. Undoubtedly the traditions within which 'interfaith worship' makes most sense are Hinduism and Buddhism, both of which tend to see different faiths as expressions of one reality. However, in all of these faiths there are exceptions to the above, and the more mystical and liberal parts of each faith (Liberal Judaism, Sufi Islam) find it easier to worship together.

(Bookless 1991: 15)

He goes on to underline, however, that there is a range of approaches within each religion – none is monolithic, so that too much should not be made of rigid generalizations.

A way forward

Bookless draws up three principles which I would apply to the school situation in this way:

1. Interfaith opportunities for worship should be *explicitly* discussed so that confusions and misunderstandings do not result.
2. There should be no attempt to gloss over the differences and difficulties – they should be acknowledged so that pupils realise they are entering an area of contemporary openness and discussion.
3. What is done in assemblies must be supported by and arise out of the kind of approach inherent in the RE they are receiving where opportunities for frank and honest discussion of religions is encouraged on the basis of critical affirmation.

This argues for a kind of assembly which focuses on general themes of deep religious significance, to which various religious traditions can contribute insights. The approach might be termed 'trans-religious' in that it does not evade the religions but allows them to point beyond themselves.

Such assemblies would be pioneering as discussed in Chapter 8. Suitable themes could include the following. A series of assemblies on each would be possible.

1. awareness of Mystery;
2. the use of symbolism in religion;
3. truth through metaphor;
4. problems of idolatry, superstition and hypocrisy;
5. the role of ritual in religion;
6. the inspiration of saints and holy people;

7. religious attitudes to the environment and to green issues;
8. religion and personal development;
9. religion and spirituality.

All these themes can help to illuminate all religious traditions. And yet they can do so in a way which is not in any sense imperialistic for any one religious tradition. (See pp. 170–3 for further discussion of two of these themes by way of example.)

Such assemblies would not step outside the 1988 legal requirement that they be 'broadly Christian' provided that the considerable common core which exists between religions is appreciated. Within such a framework distinctiveness can be acknowledged, understood and reflected upon. Figure 11.1 offers a discussion chart concerning such a possibility.

Attention needs to be paid not just to the lowest common denominator – the flat line in common – but to the apex of the common triangle – the highest common factor: the awareness of Mystery. For this is open and encouraging to an exploration of all the other triangles, including their apexes which consist of material highly distinctive of particular religious groupings.

Such a structure can provide a basis on which to build beyond religions, and schools have perhaps a pioneer task here. This *could* be a key-point at which schools could innovate and lead society instead of being led by society. It shows the way towards the possibility of worship-enabling assemblies which make sense religiously to people of different faiths without their having to resort to the cumbersome and possibly contentious procedures for opting out of the 'broadly Christian' requirement.

But what is worship?

Despite all this, doubt still remains in the minds of many whether the word 'worship' is appropriate within an educational context; does it not torpedo any educational validity for such assemblies? In a letter to *The Times*, 10 April 1989, John Wilson pointed out that in such assemblies 'students are offered the act of worship to experience and criticize, not to swallow whole'. Edwin Cox, in commenting on this in *The Times*, 20 April 1989, asked, 'If all are attending to observe and criticize, from whence will that worship be coming . . . for worship demands the presence of a number of genuine believers sincerely offering prayer and praise?'

There lies a confusion here, however. The 'worship' to be experienced and criticized in assembly – and Wilson was arguing for participation not just observation – can be in the content of the words and ritual, irrespective of whether they enable anyone in the room

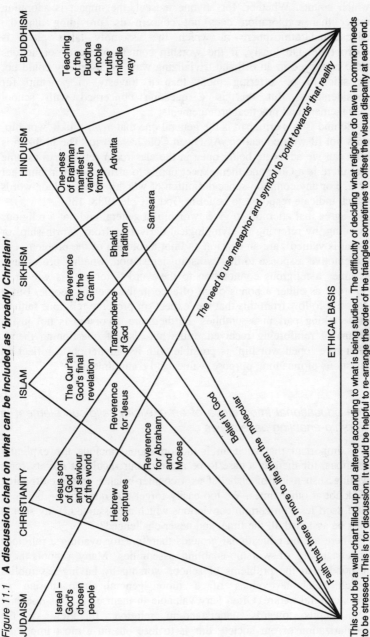

Figure 11.1 A discussion chart on what can be included as 'broadly Christian'

This could be a wall-chart filled up and altered according to what is being studied. The difficulty of deciding what religions do have in common needs to be stressed. It would be helpful to re-arrange the order of the triangles sometimes to offset the visual disparity at each end.

166 The Effective Teaching of Religious Education

actually to worship. It is the giving the opportunity, or permission for, which counts. Whether, for anyone present, the impact is adoration rather than exploration does not concern us, providing that the educational atmosphere in which the assembly takes place is appropriate. Obviously, if the worship content of words or actions were conveyed in an offhand trivializing way, the assembly could not be said to be offering more than a travesty of worship for consideration. But this is a question concerned with school management and practical arrangements.

Behind Cox's criticism is the general one that a word like 'worship' does not fit with education. As Owen Cole has put it: 'The problem is how can we advocate being open in the classroom refusing to assume that there is a God, and then expect pupils to affirm belief in him, her or it? For any common-sense definition of worship must include words which indicate response to belief in God.' (Cole 1988: 136).

I agree that attempts to give 'worship' a general and not a religious meaning, by referring to etymological derivation from 'worth-ship' or 'what is valued', are an evasion and not a solution of the problem. For the emotive response to the 'worship' legislation, whether pro or anti, assumes a religious connotation to the word – for that is why it is regarded as either a bonus or an offence in the eyes of people. But it does not follow from this that we 'expect' or presume religious faith in those taking part in assemblies. Furthermore, 'worship is not just a means of reinforcing received truths but also of questioning them'. Therefore 'open worship' is possible with its 'invitation to reflect on questions of meaning, purpose, values and commitments'.[7]

The educational importance of an explicitly religious element in worship-enabling assemblies

It is important that such an invitation should include the explicitly religious, for there is a case to be made in our secularist society for a willing suspension of disbelief as a counter-balance to the cultivation of doubt at other times. We too easily forget that questioning belief in God itself rests on certain convictions which are assumed. Why should they be assumed all the time, and never challenged?

There are no educational grounds therefore for evading a religious understanding of worship-enabling assemblies. Many schools have responded to the problems of school worship by having assemblies which celebrate values of a more general, humanitarian or cross-cultural nature. Often very valuable in themselves, this does not help pupils towards understanding religion. In view of the secularization of our society this is to lose out on a most important anti-indoctrinating activity. The need for this has been developed in Chapters 2 and 3 especially.

Provided the way in which it is presented is open and not assuming a particular response from participants, assemblies can present aspects of worship for serious consideration by pupils. This is how Derek Webster, lecturer in the University of Hull, expresses it:

School worship stretches pupils, asks them to look beyond themselves. If human society resembles a circle of people on a floating island, all looking inwards, then school worship is an opportunity to turn around and face an unknown, illimitable and mysterious ocean. Obviously worship is demanding of head and heart. It is like reading the *Phaedo*, for Plato asks his readers to ponder an argument and respond to the sweep of a vision which grants an eternal destiny. It is akin to heeding R.S.Thomas's words:
>   I had forgotten
>   the old quest for truth
>   I was here for. Other cares
>   held me.

(Webster 1991: 251)

The inspirational quality which worship-enabling assemblies should have calls for care with regard to practicalities to which I now turn.

Questions of organization

Who is responsible?

While it is the responsibility of headteachers to see that such assemblies are held, they do not have to lead them themselves. Indeed, it is educationally desirable that many others are involved; other staff, pupils and perhaps parents or local churches and religious communities. A team approach to the task of preparing assemblies is likely to be more productive as well as realistic in terms of time and energy needed. In many schools classes in turn are responsible for special assemblies in which they share some of the work they have been doing. It is also feasible to set up an 'assemblies committee' jointly of staff and pupils to plan, monitor and revise assemblies. Part of the task of such a committee is to test the temperature in the school with regard to assemblies and suggest ways in which they can become more integrated into the life of the school.

There has been increased use since 1988 of visiting speakers and leaders or worship from different religious traditions. There is also more awareness from the religious side of the need for careful preparation of such involvement.[8] The presence of outside visitors is valuable in making the assemblies more of an occasion, and giving variety and perhaps a religious visual aid, as it were, in the form of a person for whom religion is real.

Structure of assemblies

A great variety is possible. While some assemblies may be taken by particular classes and others led by visiting members of particular religious traditions, probably the 'bread and butter' assembly should require simpler planning and resources. It needs mostly to have at least five components:

1. some inspirational input: a reading, music, perhaps something visual;
2. space to reflect – a training in stillness and being able to be silent;
3. a specifically religious component in the form of an open invitation to take religion seriously;
4. a controversial element to remind everyone that a consensus is *not* assumed or looked for;
5. short sentences explaining and reminding people of the educational purpose of the assembly.

I have already discussed 3 so will comment on each of the others in turn, beginning with 4.

A controversial element

A controversial element should be present frequently, in order to avoid building up the mistaken impression that worship material is escapist or quietist in character. It does harm to worship as well as reflectiveness to pretend that everything in the garden is lovely and peaceful, while the real world is ignored where the difficult decisions have to be made and very awkward questions debated, and where people take sides often violently and certainly with emotion.

Again such an element may sound surprising to some people because of the dangers of controversy getting out of hand. This is where the total setting of the assemblies giving opportunity for worship is important. It links up indeed with the second component, that of space to reflect, to which I now turn.

Space to reflect

Space is important for many reasons including giving an opportunity to understand and control emotional responses to things, and as a means of beginning to undo the effects of indoctrination. It is a time when people can actually be on their own wavelength and not on somebody else's, and from that perspective they can begin to see things rather differently sometimes. The sting can be taken out of some negative emotions for example, and ideas towards breaking a deadlock or getting round difficulties can often come to people when they are silent.

Stillness is not the same as quietism. It is more like the natural rhythm of breathing in as well as breathing out. Attention only to the latter causes tension and breathlessness. The activist nature of our society makes it particularly important to help pupils experience some silence. The very difficulties involved in this indicate quite how necessary and important an educational task it is.

This underlines the value of frequency of assemblies because to learn stillness needs time, structure and regular opportunities for practising it. This is one of the most valuable skills that a school can encourage. I would express it as an entitlement on the part of pupils to be enabled to become familiar with well-established techniques of this kind. The experiential approach to RE has much to offer in this respect (see Chapter 6).

Sharing the education focus
Short sentences explaining and reminding people of the educational purpose of the assembly are particularly important because the assembly must be *seen* as educational. Explicitly religious words and actions should be just as explicitly put into the context of a learning situation. Phrases such as 'let us pray' should be abandoned in favour of something more like the following:

1. 'Let us listen to this prayer and, if we want to, silently say Amen.'
2. 'Let us try to imagine what it is like to be a Christian/Muslim/ Hindu as we sing/say these words.'
3. 'Let us say this prayer/sing this hymn considering what we can, and what we cannot, personally agree with in it.'
4. 'No assumption is made about your reaction to this hymn/prayer. Interpret it in whatever way is sincere for you.'

It needs to be explained many times to everyone, other staff as well as pupils, that attendance at worship-enabling assemblies is a training in integrity. It involves actually thinking out an authentic response to the particular stimuli presented, and because the response is not to be articulated to anyone, this involves learning to have an inner dialogue with oneself. Such inner dialogue is in fact part of what reflective thinking is about. It can give strength to character, and be experienced as very fulfilling even though often tough work.

The three levels of participation open to people need to be articulated over and over again to overcome the danger of wrong impressions. It is not enough for teachers to understand this. It must be communicated first and foremost to pupils, but also both via them and directly to parents and religious leaders of faiths to which pupils happen to belong. The theory must not be behind the scenes for them. It is what worship-enabling assemblies are about.

Stimulus material for assemblies
There is a great deal available in published sources, much of it very recent. Publishers appreciate the need for fresh material. Besides explicit assembly material, there is a lot concerned with religion which can easily be adapted for use in assemblies. A helpful article by Nicola Slee in reviewing some more unusual possibilities concluded with this paragraph:

With such materials as these in the shops and on the shelves, there are no excuses for dull, introverted or narrowly monocultural acts of worship, and plenty of hints towards an interpretation of ERA's worship clauses which stays well within the letter of the law and, at the same time, fulfils all the criteria of good educational practice.

(Slee 1991: 5)

Concluding discussion: The pioneer role of worship-enabling assemblies

As discussed in Chapter 8, the holding of such assemblies in school where it is essential to cater for a wide range of pupils whose beliefs cannot be assumed – where several different religions and/or stances for living may be represented – demands pioneer thinking. If schools can take up this challenge, and encourage in pupils an openness which nevertheless engages with religion at its central point, they will be performing a crucial task in preparing pupils for the real world. To be able to face controversy creatively, and learn how to be committed without being dogmatic, are invaluable skills which schools generally do too little about.

Every effort ought therefore to be made to see that worship-enabling assemblies do offer help in developing these skills. Especially important is the capacity to be quiet, and engage in inner dialogue with oneself, or move beyond being at the mercy of whatever thoughts and ideas one happens to be exposed to at any given moment to a point of stillness when often a new perspective becomes possible. The ability to be still in this sense can help to release people from chains of conditioning of all kinds, as well as assisting the ability to think for oneself and make responsible decisions.

Dialogue between religions

One aspect of this role for assemblies is promoting creative dialogue between world religions. I give suggestions of extracts which could be used in assemblies relating to the themes listed on page 164. The first, truth through metaphor, lends itself to a wide number of possibilities at every level from infant to sixth form.

The metaphor of the ocean

The inadequacy of human concepts in speaking of the Divine – or in trying to understand the Mystery at the heart of reality – leads religious people into exploring metaphor. The ocean is one example. The idea of ocean as symbolic could be introduced with a brief reference to the Greek word from which the name derives: Oceanus which in Homer refers to the great river encircling the whole earth – the great outer sea as opposed to the Mediterranean. By the seventeenth century it had come to be used metaphorically of an immense or boundless expanse of anything.

Ocean is often used as a metaphor for life, as, for example, in these lines from Longfellow

> Ships that pass in the night, and speak each other in passing.
> Only a signal shown and a distant voice in the darkness;
> So on the ocean of life we pass and speak one another,
> Only a look and a voice, then darkness again and a silence.
> (Tales of a Wayside Inn[3])

Ocean stands for voyages of exploration, for courage in leaving the safe and familiar and moving into the unknown, as in the poem by Gide quoted in Chapter 6. Even more was this so in centuries before advanced nautical technology had made travel as fast and common as today. To cross an ocean used really to be an adventure when life was at risk.

In the realm of beliefs and values and commitments, the ambiguity and vulnerability of life preclude the possibility of 'terra firma' certainty. As the Danish Christian thinker, Kierkegaard, used to say: 'we must learn to live over 70,000 fathoms of water'.

Ocean is a symbol for Reality within many religious traditions, especially in Hinduism, Buddhism and Sikhism. One of the hymns in the Granth begins:

> Thou art the ocean, all-knowing, all-seeing:
> How may I a mere fish, know Thy extent?
> (Talib 1975: 37)

A prayer of the great Hindu scholar, Sankara, likens himself to a wave, rather than a fish:

O Lord, even after realizing that there is no real difference between the individual and Brahman, I beg to state that I am yours and not that you are mine. The wave belongs to the ocean and not the ocean to the wave.[9]

The imagery is also found in Christian hymns such as this by the seventeenth century writer John Mason. The third verse of his hymn 'How shall I sing that majesty' runs as follows:

How great a being, Lord, is thine,
Which doth all beings keep!
Thy knowledge is the only line
To sound so vast a deep.
Thou art a sea without a shore,
A sun without a sphere;
Thy time is now and evermore,
Thy place is everywhere.

A single verse of a hymn like this can do much to wean people away from naive concepts of 'God'.

The art of focusing
The second example relates to the themes of religion and spirituality and the problem of idolatry. Every religion experiences the need to guard against de-spiritualizing tendencies in religious practice itself. Idolatry of one form or another – whereby means and ends become muddled – is an ever-present danger. All the great religions are aware of this danger, and that true religion is a matter of the spirit and not of outward forms.

The effort to avoid idolatry, and appreciate the spiritual significance of all religious acts, is like peeling off layer after layer of an onion and finding still more beneath. Idolatry can come in all shapes and sizes, as idolatry of dress, ritual, food, buildings, leaders, books, hierarchy, particular beliefs, particular concepts, forms of social organization, and so forth. It needs constantly to be guarded against by religious people, as does the misunderstanding of seeing religion like this by those who are not religious. For all the items just mentioned are intended to point beyond themselves. There are many passages in all the scriptures of the different religions which express awareness of this.

As a theme for an assembly, the art of focusing in religion could be helpful. The way in which a window exists in order that people can look *through* it, not just – indeed hardly at all – AT it, can illustrate the difference between something being in one's line of vision, and actually focusing on something. As the hymn by George Herbert puts it:

A man that looks on glass
On it may stay his eye;
Or if he pleaseth, through it pass,
And then the heaven espy.[10]

This is a quotation from a Russian Orthodox Christian, Metropolitan Anthony of Sourozh. When writing about prayer, he notes the importance of learning how to focus:

You cannot focus on things which are less than God. The moment you try to focus on an imaginary god, or a god you can imagine, you are in great danger of placing an idol between yourself and the real God. This is a thought which was expressed as early as the fourth century by St Gregory of Nazianus. He said that the moment we put a visible sign in front of ourselves, whether it be a crucifix, a tabernacle, an icon or an invisible image – God as we imagine Him – and we focus our attention on that, then we have placed a barrier between ourselves and God, because we take the image which we have formed for the person to whom we address our prayer. What we must do is to collect all the knowledge of God which we possess in order to come into His presence, but then remember that all we know about God is our past, as it were, behind our back, and we are standing face to face with God in all His complexity, all His simplicity, so close and yet unknown. Only if we stand completely open before the unknown, can the unknown reveal itself, Himself, as He chooses to reveal Himself to us as we are today. So, with this open-heartedness and open-mindedness, we must stand before God without trying to give Him a shape or to imprison Him in concepts and images, and we must knock at a door.

(Anthony of Sourozh 1986: 146f)

A passage like this is worship-enabling, but yet open and informative about religion for someone on the outside. It is also couched in language which transcends confinement within one particular tradition, and yet it does so in a way which illuminates the tradition which gave it birth. The passage, short as it is, touches on themes of prayer, of the need to get beyond concepts, of the dangers of mistaking external features of religion for the purpose of religion, and on an insight claimed by most religions – that of the need for revelation, for the Divine has ultimately to be revealed, not worked out by human reasoning.

Notes

1. As the CEM School Worship File puts it, Summer, 1992, p. 2.
2. Baroness Caroline Cox: 'We have a Gospel to proclaim . . .', in *The Methodist Recorder*, 16 March 1989 p. 8.
3. Watson, 1987, *Education and Belief*, ch. 14 esp. 192ff; and O'Keeffe, 1988, 'Children at school: a worshipping community? esp. p. 109f.
4. This is a point taken up for example in Guidelines for Visiting Speakers, 1989, published by the Free Church Federal Council entitled 'Worship in county schools: so you've been asked to take assembly?'
5. See for example the *Handbook for Agreed Syllabus Conferences, SACREs and Schools*, REC, 1990.
6. See the booklist in note 8 of Chapter 8. A report on inter-faith services and worship, published in March 1980 for the Archbishops of Canterbury and York spoke of the bond between religions created by 'common humanity, shared ethical interests and recognition of the Transcendent which is . . . always greater than our understanding'.
   On the possibility of inter-faith worship see for example *Multi-faith Worship* by the Inter-Faith Consultation Group published by Church House Publishing, 1992; Ghulam Sarwar, 1989, *What can Muslims do?* Collections of prayers from different religions have encouraged such

thinking, for example *God of a Hundred Names*, Gollancz, 1962; *With one Voice*, Hedges, 1970; *The Oxford Book of Prayer*, Appleton, 1985.
7. Christian Education Movement, Summer 1992, 'School worship file'.
8. Cf. the short leaflet already referred to under note 3. This gives excellent advice concisely and clearly briefing such visitors.
9. From T.M.P. Mahadevan (ed.), 1970, *The Hymns of Sankara*, Ganesh & Co. Madras.
10. From George Herbert, 'The Elixir'.

CHAPTER 12

What is it all about? RE and the rest of the curriculum

For teachers in England and Wales, the Education Reform Act and the recommendations of the National Curriculum Council are a required reference point. For those not bound by these particular regulations and guidelines, there is much of interest and importance to be gained from a discussion of their impact on RE, for such comment can highlight what educationally its role should be with regard to the curriculum as a whole. How should RE relate to all the other subjects?

The Education Reform Act has given a special status to RE of 'basic'. It is unclear whether this is meant as a compliment to the subject or to exclude it from the ranks of the 'core' and 'foundation' subjects. By calling it 'basic' the Act can be interpreted as paying its quota of lip-service to RE in order thereafter to ignore it and attend to 'what really matters'![1]

Whether or not this impression of the 1988 legislation is correct, it is very unclear to most people what 'basic' here means, and how RE can be it anyway. This chapter will discuss a possible valid meaning to be given to the term.

The need for education in beliefs and values

Picasso once remarked that 'museums are just a lot of lies'. He was referring to the way in which artists become compartmentalized into schools and graded in importance in a way which no-one thinks of questioning. An article in *The Independent* entitled 'Hung and quartered' quoted this and added: 'Every museum offers a hierarchy made visible'.[2] Every school curriculum similarly offers a hierarchy made visible. In order to operate at all a set of values is presupposed and arranged quite definitely in order of importance.

Attitudes, assumptions and outcomes

There are at least three ways in which what happens in the curriculum as a whole affects every subject including RE: attitudes, assumptions and outcomes.

Attitudes

Value-free teaching is not possible in any subject. Teachers cannot operate without promoting some values and discouraging others. Most teachers today would, I think, include the following in any list of desirable attitudes: openness, toleration of others as people with a right to their own opinions, self-esteem, honesty, courage, integrity, fair-mindedness, concern for justice, attentiveness, perseverance, unselfishness, generosity, compassion or love, sense of humour. These relate to the five-fold quality of respect argued for in Chapter 1 as educationally helpful, developing especially the capacity for autonomy, empathy potentially for all other people, responsibility, a sense of wonder, concern for truth, and willingness to be reflective.

Assumptions

Values are in fact based upon assumptions about what is right or desirable or both. Picked up from all over, they are often a question of historical accident. Some assumptions which people make may in fact be contradicted by others which they hold, and there may be many reasons why agreement cannot be reached about them. What is important, however, is to engage in reflection on them.

Some assumptions are essential for a subject to be engaged in at any level. For example, science is based on assumptions which include rationality, intelligibility, orderliness, uniformity, and the desirability of the pursuit of knowledge (e.g. Poole 1990b: 27).

The National Curriculum Council's outline of Technology supports the view that certain values are fundamental for Technology if it is properly taught:

1. that quality of life is important – it is more than a comfortable standard of living;
2. that people's needs matter because people have unique significance;
3. that aesthetic considerations matter – beauty is not an optional extra;
4. that pupil's self-esteem and self-responsibility should be encouraged;
5. that understanding of different cultures matters, as well as a sense of history;
6. that the development of moral sensitivity is vital.

Outcomes

The content and methods used in each subject produce outcomes which may be helpful or harmful. Here for example is a list of some possible outcomes in technology:

*   responsible attitude   *or*   consumerist greed and
    towards the environment   increasing pollution

- intelligent democratic   *or*   political repression
  citizenship

- aesthetic awareness   *or*   creation of ugliness

- enhanced status given   *or*   devaluing of persons
  to all people

The responsibility which teachers have is considerable, indeed awesome. Richard Pring, in his inaugural lecture as Professor of Educational Studies at Oxford (8 May 1991) argued the importance of the teacher's role – for them 'to uphold the standards which are at the centre of the best of liberal learning'. He sums this up by a letter from the head of a large high school in Boston, USA, which was sent to new teachers in her school.

Dear teacher,
I am a survivor of a concentration camp. My eyes saw
what no man should witness:
gas chambers built by learned engineers
children poisoned by educated physicians
infants killed by trained nurses
women and babies shot and burned by high school and
college graduates
so, I am suspicious of education.
My request is: help your students become human.
Your efforts must never produce learned monsters,
skilled psychopaths, educated Eichmanns.
Reading, writing, arithmetic are important only if
they serve to make our children more human.

(quoted by Pring 1992: 37f)

Pring comments: 'That ultimately is what we are preparing our students for. 'And this is written into the beginning of the Education Reform Act: schools are to 'promote the spiritual, moral, cultural, mental and physical development of pupils at the school and of society' (1.2.). Figure 12.1 shows how each subject bears some responsibility for fulfilling this vision.

Geography may serve as an example. A leading geographer, Patrick Bailey, has commented:

I see geography as a very effective vehicle for raising issues and questions which go beyond purely materialistic considerations and far into the dimension which I would term spiritual . . . Love is a tremendously powerful principle of life and practising it will inevitably lead to actions which are of interest to geographers, concerned as they are to explain the observable effects of human behaviour.

As an example he refers to urban studies which form a part of almost every school geography course and how

Figure 12.1 **The total curriculum** *(as discussed on pp. 175–7)*

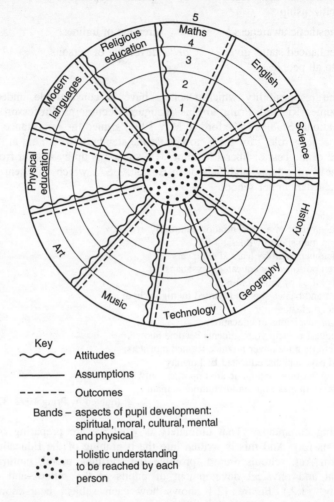

Key

∿∿∿ Attitudes

——— Assumptions

------ Outcomes

Bands – aspects of pupil development:
spiritual, moral, cultural, mental
and physical

Holistic understanding
to be reached by each
person

the point is seldom made that all town development expresses the accepted values of societies . . . We do not have to invoke a spiritual dimension when we teach about the problems of cities; but to omit it is to leave out the most cogent reason why we should do something about the evils we describe.[3]

This is why the proposals of Kenneth Clark in January 1991 to backtrack on the National Curriculum Council's intention of including education in beliefs and values within the history and geography curriculum were so serious (see p. 27). The attempt to make geography lessons only deal with facts and not concern themselves with opinions or attitudes or beliefs is impossible. For there are no facts without interpretation. It is as impossible to try to teach 'knowledge and understanding' without reinforcing or promoting certain values and attitudes, as it is to have poached eggs without cooking them. The fact/belief divide is a phoney one (see Chapter 3). The great merit of the National Curriculum geography proposals was that attention was drawn to this unavoidable aspect of learning. Regurgitation of so-called facts, assumed to be accurate and in any case selected by the teacher, is appropriate for the teaching of parrots not citizens of a democracy living in a dangerous world where values and attitudes matter more than ever before.

History or geography from which any serious consideration of beliefs and values has been removed will not only tend to be superficial but also be likely to indoctrinate into particular current interpretations and emphases. Similarly, science-teaching which ignores education in beliefs and values can not only do great harm unintentionally to pupils' development in other areas by giving the impression that everything outside scientific knowledge is mere subjective opinion, but it can also fail in helping pupils understand what science is *per se.* (see discussion in Chapter 3, pp. 27–8, and booklist on p. 202 note 1). Physical education and health education have very important links with moral and psychological maturity and with the total framework of ideas about the nature of the world which people need to think about. There are moral and spiritual dimensions to language-learning and technology no less than to music, and so forth.

Can RE be basic to the curriculum as a whole?

In the diagram of the Curriculum Wheel (Fig. 12.1), RE is not regarded as basic, but as one among many subjects. A possible exercise could be devised to try to construct another model in which RE is basic. Would it be educationally valid and applicable to all schools and not just perhaps to those founded by religious organizations? Readers may like to refer to an article entitled 'RE – the hub of the curriculum' by Jack Priestley[4] which discusses this question in an illuminating way and gives alternative diagrams.

At least four reasons can be put forward as to why religious education should have a central, and not an optional or peripheral, role in today's schools. No special pleading is involved, for these reasons start from within the de-religionized setting itself, that is, from the assumptions upon which education is based.

Links between religion and beliefs and values

While not to be identified with education in beliefs and values in the way that some tend to argue,[5] RE undoubtedly has very close connections with it and can bring the insights of major traditions to bear upon current debates. It can offer much material for discussion about both *what* values should be encouraged and *why* and also *how* they can be achieved.

It is certainly not the case that to hold theoretically to the beliefs and values of a major world religion is sufficient to ensure that the ideals are put into practice. All religions – as pointed out in Chapter 8 – produce a wide gap between the beliefs which are expressed verbally and those by which people – including religious people – actually live. Nevertheless the articulation of high beliefs supported by strong arguments – which all religions do supply – plays a not insignificant part in curbing selfishness. Hatred for example can show its face anywhere, but if it is also officially promulgated, as in Stalinist Russia, then the chances of creating a loving, caring and open community are much less.

Similarly, while it is undoubtedly true that high moral beliefs and values can be held and lived by without the support of religious faith, yet the links between religion and morality cannot be so readily cut as some assume. What is the source, for example, of the sense of moral *obligation*? To ground human rights, in a belief in a Transcendent Moral Order which is concerned about justice and love arguably puts values on a much firmer basis than when they rest on pragmatic grounds or on faith in humanity – a trust which can easily be betrayed except for those gifted with boundless optimism.

The religious heritage argument

Some press this strongly. (See, for example, Burn and Hart. 1988.) Others regard it as irrelevant or mistaken, as in this comment: 'we view RE like any other curriculum area. No special pleading that ours is a Christian country or that Christian bodies were the first providers of education' (Owen Cole and Evans-Lowndes 1991: 91).

Yet the reference to history cannot just be dismissed in this way, for it concerns both empirical and psychological realism. It is not a desire to be bound by the past which seeks to relate pupils to this, but a concern for rootedness. It takes seriously the organic connection which must exist between a living society and its past. Unavoidably, the values on which current thinking relies are bound up, both historically and philosophically, with what is inherited. For a society simply to live off its capital accumulated by previous generations is a dangerous thing to do, especially in a world facing unprecedented change and the need for flexibility and creative thinking.

To leave pupils to work out a value system on their own is in fact an abdication of responsibility. We do not expect them to go back literally to pre Stone Age know-how in technological matters and work out how to make fire for themselves, and so on. We hand on understanding. The same must happen with regard to values, and these have been, and for many still are, governed by religious belief.

It may perhaps be asked, 'Can't we generate new values?' Yes, it is possible, but to be enduring and fair these should not just be dreamed up today but be tested against tradition and sustainability among other criteria. The example of Marxism implanted in Russia provides a warning. Only on the basis of understanding of all that is best about the past can sufficient stability be found for necessary change and development to be effective.

To teach understanding of Judaeo-Christian beliefs and values is therefore fundamental to whatever else is attempted. The fact that these are mostly reinforced also by the teaching of other religions now represented in Western societies underlines the non-narrowness of focus here.

The objection is often made by Humanists that the religious contribution to inherited values has been overplayed, while that to Renaisssance values has been under-acknowledged.[6] While it is true that other traditions have contributed at every stage to the development of modern Western societies, it remains the case that Western societies have been predominantly impregnated with values associated with a religious matrix. The protest is, however, valuable as a warning against triumphalism – the view that *my* or *our* views are better than anyone else's – a view which seeks to win converts for one's own point of view. Christianity has often been viewed as triumphalist. This impression is easily conveyed when values like caring which almost all people hold, are termed 'Christian values'. Within a Christian setting it is true that Christianity teaches caring, but it should not claim exclusive ownership of this virtue. It needs to be remembered, however, that such a danger is not a prerogative of Christianity alone; it tends to exhibit itself whenever an ideology or religion has been very influential and long-lived.

The point is seldom made that intolerance is in fact un-Christian, however much practised in a society claiming to be Christian. It is therefore particularly important that teaching concerning religious heritage develops pupils' skills of discernment at all seven levels discussed in Chapter 7 (pp. 93–101).

This relates to how essential it is that RE is conducted in a way which is not itself guilty of indoctrinating tendencies. Religious indoctrination is no better than secularist indoctrination. Such would be, in any case, an impossible task from the point of view of genuine religious faith, for a prior requirement for authentic personal commitment is freedom.

The importance of the questions which religion considers

Religious education deals with what is potentially the most important of all subject-matter. It raises questions of ultimate meaning, and can have a most exciting and integrative effect on pupils' total learning, whether or not they subscribe to belief in God. It is a fascinating area for debate and search. The challenge is well summarized by Bishop Hugh Montefiore:

> Christians believe that the Christian faith provides a more adequate basis for life and thought than a secular world-view which regards the world as lacking an ultimate purpose and values other than those which individuals may ascribe to it.
>
> (Montefiore 1992: 10)

Pupils can hardly be said to be educated unless they have realized the force of such a possibility and gone some way forward in considering it seriously. For 'Christians' read 'religious people' as in his original version, later altered because writing in the context of discussion specifically about Christianity. This offers a good example of the importance of appreciating the context in which statements are made: when talking to Christians or about Christianity, it is appropriate to speak of faith or values as 'Christian' (cf. discussion on pp. 98–9), but when a wider audience is listening such language can convey an unintended exclusivism.

A sense of overall purpose and value promotes personhood, and this is what education is about. Becoming a real person – finding one's own authentic self – is bound up with developing a coherent and perceptive attitude to life. Conviction and commitment – 'I know' and 'I choose' – are inescapably part of what it means to be fully human. Religious education focuses precisely on such capacities for personal reflection and personal responsibility. By emphasizing the spiritual it makes possible for each individual a comprehensive 'wholeness' to life. A person cannot be fragmented, nor can the spirit. Serious thought given to the latter can therefore safeguard the development of the former. Chapter 6 has discussed this at some length.

The anti-indoctrinating role of RE

I think that the points just discussed would normally be conceded if it were not for fear of indoctrinating something which is fundamentally controversial. The paradox is that in our current society not to present religion is to indoctrinate into secularism and a secularist view of values. RE therefore has a basic task to perform in challenging the prevailing form of indoctrination.

A prime objection that many religious groups have against Western education is that they perceive it, in the name of tolerance and openness, to give the cold shoulder to religion. The assumption that religious belief is unnecessary is one which, as Chapter 3 has shown, is challengeable. In order, therefore, to avoid indoctrination into secularism, it is essential that religious beliefs are discussed fairly.

An example from technology
How might the anti-indoctrinating role of RE work? I take an example almost entirely at random from the Technology Guidelines drawn up by the National Curriculum Council: the suggestion, under the Programme of Study for Key Stage 3, Levels 3–7, that pupils be set the task of: 'Finding the maximum load for a carrier bag.'

This apparently innocuous and straightforward task *can contribute*, under the impact of various factors, such as those referred to on p. 121, to pupils' indoctrination into a utilitarian, mechanistic, instrumentalist view of life, even though largely unintentionally. The recurrency factor, for example, refers to the way in which such tasks are typical not just of technology education but right across the curriculum, as well as in general life experience. If this kind of thing is repeated constantly, while values such as aesthetic or spiritual ones are rarely or never mentioned (the default factor), then for the pupil it reinforces a particular way of life.

What might an RE perspective offer if applied to the carrier-bag task? Very little, some may consider, unless reference is made to the carrier-bag containing food for a Sikh gurdwara or a church social! Yet its major contribution would be in raising the meta-questions: why should such tasks be thought important? why develop such skills? Carrier-bags suggest, for example, shopping or the conveyance of goods; in an acquisitive and consumerist society it matters very much that some interrogation of these values takes place. Pupils need to consider perhaps what difference it might make to how such tasks were performed if a person believed in the sacramental significance of everything that happens in this world.

In fact it would make a great deal of difference to both intention and practice. Such considerations affect not only assumptions but attitudes and outcomes also. Muhammad Akram Khan, for example, writes about the difference in both intention and practice which can or should exist regarding consumer behaviour in an Islamic economy which is shaped by Muslim beliefs and values. Of the seven points he cites, four are especially relevant:

i) Belief in the day of judgement extends the time horizon of one's decisions. Immediate utility of a product is replaced by considerations of reward in the *Akhira*;

ii) The *qur'än* speaks of the material resources of the world as *hasanät, tayyibät, fadl Allah* and *ni'ma*, but they are basically a means to lead life in this world. They are not an end in themselves . . . The Prophet taught contentment (*qana'*) and thanksgiving (*shukr*), and subdued demand for material resources;

iii) The *Qur'an* has condemned both extravagance (*'israf*) and niggardliness (*bukhl*) and has enjoined us to adopt an attitude of moderation in consumption;

iv) The *Qur'an* has condemned emulation in consumer behaviour . . . do not covet the bounties which God has bestowed more abundantly on some of you than others . . . Resources are a 'trial' for everyone, implying thereby that one who has lesser endowments faces a softer accountability.

Implementing RE as basic

How RE exercises this basic role is chiefly through either explicit dialogue with other subject-areas or through involvement in some form of integrated or cross-curricular work.

Explicit dialogue between RE and other subjects

The possibility of misunderstanding and misrepresentation – either of religion within other subjects, or of other subjects within RE – calls for times of explicit dialogue between subjects. It is easy, for example, for the teaching of evolution in science to cause pupils to dismiss the concept of creation, unless attention is specifically drawn to the danger. This argues for some close links between RE and science. The same can be said about history and RE, and all the other subjects in turn.

Watertight compartmentalism has never been possible. For example, a textbook for history within the 9–13 range, chosen almost at random from a display in Blackwells, Oxford, entitled *The Roman Empire* by Simon Mason,[8] has 4 pages out of 80 directly on religion. What is selected for inclusion, and the slant given to it, is bound to influence pupils. This particular book gives some useful information, and from within an open framework. The activity given to the children was to develop the point of view of a Christian in Rome in AD 95. This could lead directly into valuable discussion with RE, as could a more controversial point: the time-chart on the back of the book divides the Roman Empire into political, economic and scientific, social and religious, and cultural sections, thereby implying that religion is adequately understood as an aspect of social history. Yet this is to convey an extremely misleading impression of religion.[9] This assumption parallels the way that in school timetabling RE is often assumed to be one of the humanities subjects, or part of PSE or social sciences. This assumption does need to be pointed out and challenged.

Starting points for such dialogue would do well to emphasize what is held in common so that the dialogue can be seen to be authentically a part of what each subject needs to be doing anyway. Table 12.1 suggests some of the ways in which effective RE can be helped, through work intrinsic to the separate disciplines.[10]

Table 12.1 **How subjects can promote effective religious education**

From maths: Skills of logic. Use and danger of statistics	From science: Skills of investigation, plus knowledge of the natural world to relate to religious questions	From technology: Awareness of human needs and practical means to help, plus a growing ability to use information technology and computers
From English: In addition to the ability to read, write, listen and take part in discussion, awareness of metaphor, symbolism, poetry and various forms of narrative, plus some knowledge of literature and experience of drama, and the way these can raise questions of ultimate significance	**From every subject: A sense of wonder, concern for integrity, openness, search for truth, and development of responsible attitudes towards other people**	From history: Awareness of the nature of historical evidence, plus some knowledge of particular periods of significance for religious history
From PE: Concern for the physical basis of life and proper attitudes of self-affirmation, fair play, and co-operation with others, as well as some awareness of the use of dance-form as a vehicle for expressing ideas	From art: A growing capacity to express ideas and feelings, as well as increasing visual awareness	From geography: Awareness of the importance of place, plus some knowledge of major countries of the world
From music: Some experience of the evocative nature of music and especially the way that it can point beyond itself as a vehicle for expressing a spiritual dimension		From modern languages: Awareness of the nature of language, problems of translation and the importance of context for understanding

Table 12.2   **Maslow's hierarchy of human needs**

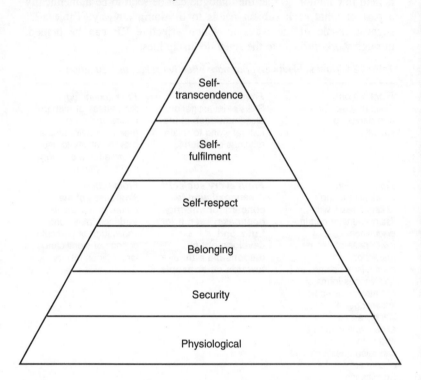

RE can relate, for example, to the National Curriculum Council Technology requirements themselves. The Technology Attainment Target 1 concerns people's needs and this affords excellent opportunities for opening up discussion within a broader agenda. Abraham Maslow drew up a fascinating hierarchy of human needs which can be represented in a triangle as in Table 12.2.

Kenneth Adams has argued that this is a very misleading way of looking at human needs:

Those physiological needs are vital and basic, but, although they are essential, they are in fact limited. I can only eat so much food, drink so much water, breathe so much air. The same is true at the next levels of need: I can only live in one room at a time, there is a limit to my security needs and to my belonging needs because I can only relate to a limited number of people. But as I ascend in that hierarchy the picture changes and as I break into my self-fulfilment and self-transcendence needs the limiting factors seem to fall away. My needs in those areas do, in fact, feel to me to be limitless. So you see, the picture of our needs is much more like this. (Adams 1990: 832f)

Table 12.3 **Adams' hierarchy of human needs**

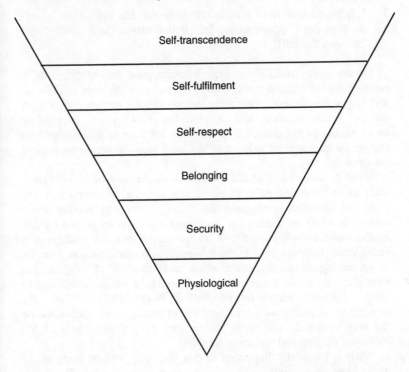

He then stands the triangle on its head – see Table 12.3.

Considerations like this offer a framework for deepening and broadening learning. RE has more and more to offer as the needs at the top of Adams' triangle are taken seriously.

Contribution of RE to integrated work

Recent years have seen a great deal of experimenting with integrated forms of teaching. Indeed in the primary school some such approach is almost taken for granted for much of the school week. Problems of organization in secondary schools mean that the integrated approach has had a more checkered career there.

The integrated approach ought ideally to be welcomed by RE. It should have the effect of encouraging cooperation and reducing competitiveness between subjects, and all subjects including RE will be the gainers. The specific advantages for RE of integrated work include these:

1. it ends the sense of isolation, of RE as something different;

2. it shares resources including speakers and the possibility of local fieldwork;
3. it helps religion to be seen in the context of life as a whole;
4. it provides opportunities for collaboration and cooperation between the staff.

On the other hand RE has experienced a great deal of difficulty in entering into integrated work as an equal partner with more established and larger departments. Often the themes chosen for integrated work are not really suitable, and religion has either to be dragged in inorganically or bypassed. Often too there has been an inhibiting effect due to the presence of other teachers who may be secularist in their orientation.

What is needed is that RE teachers must be sure of themselves – clear as to what is distinctive about religion, and that their teaching style and approach is educationally valid. In this way a more active role in deciding on themes for integrated work can be played by RE. Furthermore, even if landed with inappropriate ones, RE teachers who really know their subject can show ingenuity in relating them, even so, to something which is central to an understanding of religion. For example, a theme on American football could, by using something like Michel Quoist's prayer on Football at Night (Quoist 1966: 73f), develop some useful work on the power of analogy and symbol and on the way in which religion is inextricably part of the whole of life including playing and watching football.

What is especially important is that the many pitfalls lying in the way of seeing a superficial link with a theme are avoided. The theme of journeys for example might immediately make someone think of pilgrimage, and indeed this could be valuable RE, but not unless the question as to why people go on pilgrimage is explored *in depth* and related to specific religious belief.

Taking part in and generally fostering non-subject-based cross-curricular work is important also. This includes dimensions such as personal and social development, and all aspects of equal opportunities and multi-cultural education. Particular cross-curricular themes have been put forward by the National Curriculum Council to include economic and industrial understanding, careers education and guidance, education for citizenship and environmental education (see Table 12.4 on possible RE input into these cross-curricular themes).

It would be helpful for RE teachers sometimes to get a particular theme studied in a cross-curricular way which is readily congenial to discussion of religious views. The following chapter gives an example of such a theme.

Table 12.4 **Religious education: its contribution towards cross-curricular themes and dimensions (Year 7, Key Stage 3)**

Content	Economic awareness	Citizen-ship	Careers	Environ-mental education	Health education	PSE/equal oppor-tunities
Work on St Francis referred to in Chapter 6	Raises very profound questions about the money-economy, and the dangers of possess-iveness and what to do about it	Engages with this through relation-ship to the church of his day; the need for reform yet staying within the church encour-aging it to be more authentic – much more difficult but in the end effective. This relates specifically to questions of citizenship	On what basis do we choose our career? How do we decide it? Why does it matter? The story of St Francis raises these questions in an acute form	St Francis could perhaps be the patron saint of environ-mental education	Raises very interest-ing questions about the pursuit of health, the power of mind over body, etc.	His respect for Clare and the impact of the Francis-can way of life on women today. For example the CPS ashram in Pune, India, plus the profound effect of his teaching and example on spirituality

Notes

1. The HMI overview of the first year in which the ERA was put into effect (DES 1991) expressed concern at the 'generally unsatisfactory' quality of RE in many primary schools, while being more optimistic about the RE in secondary schools, especially in Years 10 and 11. The weighting given to subjects, however, is effectively underlined in the Appendix which states the evidence on which the Report is based: thus they visited 373 secondary schools for maths, 231 for science, 257 for technology, but only 87 for religious education.

2. Andrew Graham Dixon in The Independent, Tuesday 23 January 1990, p. 15.

3. Patrick Bailey – lecturer in Geography in the University of Leicester School of Education and a past president of the Geographical Association. The article, entitled 'The spiritual dimension' appeared in the *TES* on 5 December 1986, p. 40

4. Priestley, in *Religious Education Today*, Summer, 1991, p. 8f. The article is part of an address given to the Welsh Association of RE Teachers at Aberystwyth in July 1990.

5. E.g. see Cole and Evans-Lowndes, 1991 p. 91–5.

6. E.g. A recent article by Christine and Herman Bondi on 'Humanism is the source of our values', in *Newsvalues* NAVET, Spring, 1992, issue no. 8.

7. Muhammad Akram Khan, 1985, 'Resource allocation in an Islamic economy', *The Islamic Quarterly*, vol. XXIX, no. 4: 243 . See also two articles in *British Journal of Religious Education*, Autumn 1990, vol. 13, no.1: Ruth Conway, 'The influence of beliefs and values on technological activities – a challenge to religious education' pp. 49–55 and Anne Riggs 'Biotechnology and religious education' pp. 56–64. A Borgmann, 1991, gives a scholarly analysis of the nature of technology: *Technology and the Character of Contemporary Life: A Philosophical Inquiry*. University of Chicago Press.

8. In Jon Nichol (ed.), 1991, *Thinking History Series*, published by Blackwell.

9. See, e.g. discussion in Chapter 3 on p. 30.

10. See e.g. an article by Stephen Bigger on 'National curriculum geography and history proposals: an RE perspective' *Journal of Beliefs & Values*, vol. 11, no. 2, pp. 9f, and articles in *Religious Education Today*, Summer, 1992 which is devoted to work with history and RE. See also an article by B.V. Hill, 1989, on 'Spiritual development in the education reform act'. Mark Roques offers a critique of current practice within different subjects in *Curriculum Unmasked*, 1989.

CHAPTER 13

Theme for the classroom on 'seeing and knowing'

This chapter gives some suggestions and background material for cross-curricular work which ideally could involve in a secondary school all subject areas – perhaps a whole day, week, or indeed fortnight devoted to it – and in a primary school could be wholly integrated work. If it is just used as part of RE, it could form a theme to which one comes back from time to time over the year.

Purpose of the unit of work

Its purpose is to draw attention to the importance of our being aware

1. that we have each of us a particular perspective – particular things which we take for granted and which our experience reinforces, and which make it difficult for us to consider any other ways of looking at things, especially if that would be uncomfortable or unsettling to our set way;
2. that there may be such another way of looking which makes more sense of the whole of our own experience and that of everybody else's – a way of looking which requires imagination to understand it;
3. that if there is, we shall need to draw upon *all* the ways of knowing open to us to enable us to see this, otherwise our outlook may be just a flat two-dimensional one.
4. that we cannot in such matters *prove* we are right in such a way as to compel others to agree with us. Nor can they *prove* their way is right.

By opening up these questions the work should help encourage a fresh perspective on religion, as well as moral and social issues, and enable some perhaps to see the possibility of a spiritual dimension to life.

The unit of work

Sections A, B and C in the following pages can be used with younger children as well as upper primary and secondary. Section D lends itself to upper secondary school work but could be adapted for younger pupils.

The work in Section A is based on Edwyn Abbott's story of 'Flatland'. Written over a hundred years ago and published in Penguin Science Fiction Library (1987), the story focuses on a land that is entirely flat, and the difficulties which one of its inhabitants, a Square, met in trying to conceive of any other possible world. It is a penetrating sociological as well as religious allegory.

The story could become the focus for considerable cross-curricular work. Possibilities include:

Mathematics: the geometry of how a Flatlander could recognize the appearance and movement of shapes.

Science: beginning to understand the theory of relativity – the story was reprinted primarily as an excellent introduction to this.

History: going backwards in time, and what this involves and what we cannot find out about.

Art: work on perspective: what Flatlanders can see; what we see is actually governed by what we already know and take for granted.

English: problems in communication – the meanings given to words, literal and otherwise.

Social Studies: expression and discussion of values which the Flatlanders had, for example sexism, elitism, and so on.

Application to RE

The Flatland story challenges the secularist assumption which is so prevalent today, without being dogmatic on the part of religion. It invites questions such as: Is there a 'more-than-sphere' world? How can we find out? What might convince us? The Flatlanders are like us who live in a world of time and space in which we find out about things through our five senses using our brains and how we feel about things. The sphere-world for them is like the more-than-sphere world for us to which religion points – a spiritual world which can be related to, but is radically different from our world here, the existence of which we are unable to grasp with our senses, brains and emotions. How can we know about it, supposing just for a half a second that it actually exists?

There are many suggestions in the story:

1. the Square has a grandson who almost gets to the point of working out by mathematics that a Sphere-world exists;
2. the Square then has a dream of Lineland;

3. later, a visitor from the Sphere-world appears in Flatland who also appeals to reason trying to teach the Square but without success;
4. he works miracles which again fail to convince;
5. eventually, as a last resort, he actually allows the Square to have a vision which does convince;

This has parallels with religion. The ways in which religious people believe they become aware of another reality, can be listed as follows.

Flatland story	*Religious revelation*
1. Reasoning power using analogy	wisdom/teaching, especially through story and parable
2. Dreams and imagination	feelings and experiences which cause people to consider a different way of looking at things.
3. Presence of people who do see and understand	saints, sages, gurus . . .
4. Unusual happenings	miracles
5. Special experience	visions

Do these help to suggest that there might be *other* ways of coming to know the truth about life other than just through our five senses, or by means of straight logic? The fact of religion encourages the view that there is more to life than meets the eye. Can we be *sure* there is not, and that religion is wrong? Or *sure* that there is, and that religion is right?

This question is a fundamental one, and if RE teachers can help pupils to see its force, then they have achieved something very, very valuable indeed. It is not for them to try to reinforce *answers*, but it is for them to raise questions which are really meaningful and which open up enquiry and discovery. Such questions can engage people's attention for a lifetime.

The story could lead on to work on the science and religion debate. Why is it that religion tends to be looked down on today? Why is it that science is looked up to? Does it disprove religion?[1] (*Note*: The story was written by a headteacher who was a theologian as well as a mathematician, scientist, and acute observer of society. The theological interpretation of the story is therefore not fanciful.)

Section A: Imagining a different kind of world

Ask the children to imagine a world in which there is no height, only breadth and length. All the objects and buildings in this world are flat, just like the people. People are different shapes, and there is variety between people as with human beings, though to the more limited extent possible for them because, unlike us who have height, they are just flat. Draw a picture of this world as it might appear to someone looking at it from above, with shapes for people and buildings.

The following questions could be put:

1. What would it appear like to the Flatlanders themselves? What would they see? What would a person coming towards them for example look like to them? What would a house which they were approaching look like to them? (Just flat, different sized shapes advancing or receding. Could they tell, for example, whether someone was a circle, or a square, or a triangle, or a pentagon?)
2. How might they know which was a house, and which a person, if they both were the same shape, for example both square? (Touch or feel? Might they also *see* a difference?)
3. How would they recognize each other? (Might they talk to each other and touch each other and see who is who?)
4. Imagine a day in the life of a Flatlander.
5. Suppose one day a visitor from another world came to see them – a sphere – would the Flatlanders recognize this person as a sphere?
6. Could the sphere-shaped visitor do anything to convince the Flatlanders of his or her presence? (Talk to them – would they be likely to take any notice? Land on them, perhaps even knock them out! Touch them – how might they interpret that? Try to prove things to them – work miracles, doing what they could not do themselves and seeing what they could not see.)
7. How successful do you think the visitors would be? What might really work? (Take them out of their world, perhaps in a dream? in a vision?)
8. Supposing that as a result of this dream or vision they came to believe that there is such a thing as height, and that there are people like this sphere-visitor, would they be right or wrong to think this? (They would be right because the existence of our world provides such an example.)
9. Could Flatlanders who had become convinced of this sphere-world explain it to their friends in such a way that they too would necessarily come to believe it? (Why? Why not?)
10. Does the difficulty of convincing other people mean that a person is wrong, or that the others are blind, dull or ignorant? (It could be difficult because neither side can *prove* their point of view is

right. Given that this is so, how could anyone choose who was right? To whom would you give the benefit of the doubt, and why?)

11. Can you think of any ways in which we who live in sphere-world might be like the Flatlanders? Are we limited like them? (Think of some of the things we cannot do, we can't find out about. Imagine what perhaps the human race could evolve into in a million years' time.)

12. Do you think there is a 'more than sphere'-world? Why? Why not?

13. If you think there is, try persuading someone in the class who does not. If you do not think there is, try persuading someone in the class who does. In both cases, let a third person make notes on what is said.

14. Discuss what was said and whether it was convincing or not – and if it was, why?, and if not, why not? (Discuss with the class the arguments used. Do they make sense?)

General note to teacher on Section A
The approach here is a simplified way in for younger children. Older pupils may appreciate the full story. All kinds of developments and spin-offs may ensue from the use of the 'observer' technique in which a group consists of at least three people – one standing up for the idea of 'more than sphere'-world, one denying it, and one observing the discussion. Does B listen to what A has said? Can B repeat what A has said in reply in such a way that A is satisfied, and so on.

It is important to help pupils analyse the arguments used because this then leads on to the question of whether the arguments are sound and sensible or not, and this is to move significantly beyond the simple stage of exchange of opinions. This unfortunately is where much RE tends to stay. The 'What do you think?' is really only a curtain-raiser, otherwise it simply conveys the view to pupils – even though unintentionally – 'Well, it's all just a matter of opinion, no-one can be right or wrong.' This is a form of indoctrination into beliefs associated with cultural relativism. Such an outlook, while it has a number of things going for it, is in fact deeply flawed. (See Chapter 3, pp. 29–31 on this.)

The question of a 'more-than-sphere' world is clearly related, though not in name, to the possibility of a spiritual/religious world. All the religions speak of such a reality which is more than this world of time and space. The denial of such a reality is what constitutes secularism – the view that religion is wrong and that this world is all there is. See Chapter 2, pp. 16–18 for more on this, and on how this view is constantly put across today.

Section B: On what we see

Quite young children, as well as older pupils, could do work on Blake's verse:

> To see a world in a grain of sand
> And a heaven in a wild flower,
> Hold infinity in the palm of your hand
> And eternity in an hour.[2]

1. Ask a few of the pupils to bring some wild flowers or grasses, enough for everyone in the class to have one. Ask them to put one in the palm of their hands and look at it and think about it (stopwatch a time). What do they feel about it, what ideas does it bring into their mind?

2. They could be asked which three things in this poem we can see and touch. Why doesn't Blake simply say, 'see a grain of sand'? What does he say we can see? Can you see a world? What does it look like? How big is it? What does 'world' really mean? What other words are there like 'world' in this poem? Does heaven mean a place? Look at a wild flower – can everyone see that? Can they all see heaven in it? Can they see heaven in anything else? If so, in what? Does everyone in the class agree? Can we see an hour in the same way as a wild flower? Why/why not? What do they think words like 'eternity' and 'infinity' mean?

3. With older children we can move on to another verse from Blake:

> This life's five windows of the soul
> Distorts the Heavens from pole to pole
> And leads you to believe a lie
> When you see with, not through, your eye.[3]

Question and answer techniques should be able easily to establish what the five windows are, and children could be asked to suggest examples of mistakes in seeing, or hearing, or touching, and so on. What does Blake mean by seeing *with* or seeing *through* in the last line? They could be helped if necessary by two more short verses, the first again from Blake:

> The tree which moves some to tears of joy,
> is in the eyes of others only a green thing
> that stands in the way.[4]

> Two men look out through prison bars
> The one sees mud, the other stars.[5]

In the Jewish and Christian scriptures there is an unusual phrase about people who 'see, yet see not, and hear, yet hear not'. What is that really saying? Can you think of an example?

4. Tell the story of the blind men and the elephant, perhaps in the form of this poem:

'The Blind Men and The Elephant'

It was six men of Hindustan
To learning much inclined,
Who went to see the Elephant
(Though all of them were blind;)
That each by observation
Might satisfy his mind.

The First approached the Elephant,
And happening to fall
Against his broad and sturdy side,
At once began to bawl,
'Bless me, it seems the Elephant
Is very like a wall!'

The Second feeling of his tusk,
Cried 'Ho, what have we here –
So very round and smooth and sharp?
To me 'tis mighty clear
This wonder of an Elephant is very like a spear.'

The Third approached the animal
And happening to take
The squirming trunk within his hands,
Thus boldly up and spake:
'I see,' quoth he, 'the Elephant
Is very like a snake!'

The Fourth stretched out his eager hand,
And felt about the knee:
'What most this mighty beast is like,
Tis mighty plain,' quoth he,
'Tis clear enough the Elephant
Is very like a tree.'

The Fifth, who chanced to touch the ear,
Said: 'Even the blindest man
Can tell what this resembles most;
Deny the fact who can,
This marvel of an Elephant
Is very like a fan!'

The Sixth, no sooner had begun
About the beast to grope,
Than, seizing on the swinging tail
That fell within his scope,
'I see,' quoth he, 'the Elephant
Is very like a rope.'

And so these men of Hindustan
Disputed loud and long,
Each in his own opinion
Exceeding stiff and strong.
Though each was partly in the right
And all were in the wrong!'

When tired of holding to their view
The six blind men were silent;
They thought of what the other knew
And shared what each had learnt
Till all of them began to know
The real Elephant.[6]

This lends itself well to work in art, drama, dance or role-play.
Other examples of mistaken identity, through jumping to conclusions
too soon from just one's own limited point of view, could be
discussed. How might the blind men be able to get a better picture in
their mind's eye of the elephant? Points which could be made include:

1. the need for cooperation between people, because no-one by
   themselves can know everything;
2. the need to be interested in learning from other people's
   experience;
3. the way we can trust our own experience – our own contact with
   the real elephant – but we may interpret and express it wrongly;
4. the way that metaphor and similes are only helpful so long as we
   remember that that is what they are. The little word 'like' is
   extremely important.

Section C: On taking things for granted

How far the blind men might be successful in taking a broader
perspective depends on their examining what they take for granted.
This is extremely important for everyone.

We need to clarify what we, pupils and teacher, happen to take for
granted. We might start by some direct questioning or discussion, but
this is likely not to get very far because what we take for granted is on
the whole what we never think about – of what we are almost
certainly unaware. It might help to draw on the analogy of a journey.
To look up a route on a map, it is obvious we must know where we're
starting from! That's actually not so easy a question, however, if our
journey is a mental, personal or spiritual one – if we are interested in
going places as regards what we think and feel about the world, and
about the kind of direction we want our lives to take. If we ask
ourselves where we are now on our mental map, we may find
ourselves in for some surprises.

Class discussion or in groups, or individual written work, might include some of the following, according to age, ability and interest:

1. list some things you feel absolutely certain about;
2. list some things you feel very uncertain about;
3. why do you feel uncertain about them? – Is it because of your lack of experience or skill, or is it because no-one can be certain of them?
4. if no-one can be certain of them, why?
5. how do you rate the relative importance of the kind of things you have put down under 1 with what you have put down under 2?
6. on what grounds did you rate their importance?
7. do you feel sure you're right in considering some things more important than others? How do you know you cannot be mistaken? And if you do not feel sure, does this matter?
8. is it possible to doubt everything all the time?
9. a great scientist and thinker of the seventeenth century, Pascal, once remarked: 'Few speak of doubt doubtingly'.[7] Think of an example of the point he was trying to make. (Here's one to get you started: 'Your view is just opinion', announced Mary with great conviction and emotion.)
10. when we express strong doubts with such certainty we are taking certain things for granted – we are assuming something in the background which is beyond doubt. List some things you take for granted;
11. list some things which someone you know or whom you have seen on television might take for granted;
12. list some things which a Muslim, or Humanist, or Hindu might take for granted? In each case say why or why not;
13. does it matter what people take for granted? Why? Why not?
14. if you answered 'No' to question 13, what would you say to someone who does not take human rights for granted but regards it as perfectly in order to torture and kill people? If you answered Yes to question 13, try to express the dilemma to which this gives rise.

Grounds for beliefs and assumptions
Many different kinds of reasons for assumptions are possible, and if we are to exercise any choice as to what we believe and value – on what we build our lives – it is important to be aware of these reasons. Pupils can be asked for their views on this not only with regard to what they believe (disregarding for the moment the content of the beliefs) but also why other people believe as they do.

Figure 13.1 suggests a number of reasons which can evoke quite a lot of discussion at any age or ability level. It can be asked whether all these reasons are equally satisfactory.

*Figure 13.1 **Grounds for holding a belief***

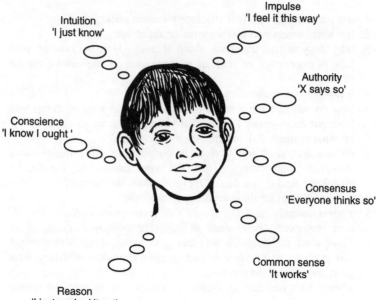

1. are there snags with any of them? – with all of them perhaps?
2. if so, on what basis can anyone *choose* a value or belief? or are we all just hemmed in tightly to whatever our parents or teachers or peer groups or the media or the government or a religious authority, might say?
3. what in any case does this variety of possible authorities mean for people's freedom to begin to choose for themselves?
4. are there dangers in 'going it alone' with regard to what we believe and value?
5. does what we believe depend on what we see?

Section D: Different kinds of seeing: an example from Hinduism

Work on seeing and knowing can easily be related to a study of specific religions. A course on Hinduism, for example, might refer to pilgrimage to a holy place like Varanasi. The question could be posed: What do Hindus see there? Do they see what, for example, tourists might see? Or an artist? Or a person interested in social studies or in history? If we imagine a visit to Varanasi, at least three points of view are possible for even the quite casual visitor – these are given below under points 1–3. What might the Hindu, especially the devout Hindu, see more?

The same kind of questions and discussion could be applied to a holy site nearer home. How can anyone gauge who is right? *Suppose* the genuinely devout religious person is right, how might other people come to know that?

Pilgrimage to Varanasi

It should be explained that the most ancient name for the city of Benares, today officially called Varanasi, is Kashi (from the Sanskrit word *Kash* which means 'to shine'). And so Hindus know Varanasi as 'the city of light'. But in what respects for them is it the city of light? Three observers might give three different answers:

1. 'It's because of the beautiful way the sun bathes the city in light especially in the early morning. Crescent-shaped, the river-front receives uninterruptedly the rays of the sun from sunrise to mid-afternoon.'

2. 'Yes, but it's also because the city is full of visual objects which remind them of their religion: wherever you turn you can see a picture of a god or goddess, a shrine sprinkled with holy water and flowers, people praying or meditating, *sadhus* (holy people) in their faded orange robes with staff and water-pot who have renounced ordinary life.'

3. 'Yes, but there's more to it than that. Varanasi is a city whose colourful vitality attracts people like a magnet, or like a moth to the light. You just feel more alive here.'

These three ways of looking at Varanasi are available to even the casual sight-seer. Just viewing a few slides can give this impression. But the Hindu sees far more, and the devout Hindu far more still. It is not easy for the outsider to see through Hindu eyes, and yet if we are to try to understand anything about Hinduism, the attempt must be made.

A Hindu text notes that 'In Benares there is a sacred place at every step'.[8] The city has been renowned for its sacredness for over 2500 years and, although it has seen many changes and disruptions over the centuries, the many myths, legends and traditions are still 'in the air'. Any one Hindu may not know many of these stories and rituals but, brought up in the atmosphere of Hinduism, Hindus unconsciously see Varanasi through their prism, and come there to take part in it. To see as a participator is very different from seeing as an observer, because there are many things which can only be known by doing them. The more devoutly and consciously they are done, the more they are known. So it is with Hinduism.

Hindus come to Varanasi for *darshana* which means 'seeing' 'not sight-seeing but sacred sight-seeing'[9] – *darshana* in three respects:

1. *Darshana* of the gods. Thus Hindus go into a temple to see the divine image, whether it be the elephant-headed Ganesh, the four-armed Vishnu, the *lingam* of Shiva or any other of the many, many forms in which they believe that *Brahman*, the One Being, can be expressed. Hindus do not therefore just see the visual object but they see it as a symbol or pointer towards the One. The image is a lens through which God is 'seen' with the 'eye' of the inner self.

2. *Darshana* of teachers and holy people. Students of all ages therefore come to Varanasi to sit at the feet of a *guru* who can become for them the visible embodiment of their spiritual aspirations. Here they pursue Sanskrit studies and learn more of the Hindu scriptures. Many come too, not to study so much as simply to bask in the presence of some deeply religious person.

3. *Darshana* of the city as a whole which for Hindus is a gateway to *moksha*, liberation from the round of rebirth. Symbolically its winding streets, lanes and teeming activity represent the constant ebb and flow of *samsaric* life, while the calm and majestic waters of the Ganges lift the veil and enable the devout beholder to see beyond to that which does not change and die, to Being Itself.

Notes

1. Short book-list: M. Poole, 1990, *Guide to Science and Belief*, Lion; M. Poole, 1992, *Miracles – Science, the Bible and Experience*; R. Stannard, 1989, *The Time and Space of Uncle Albert*; D. Sankey, D. Sullivan, and B. Watson, 1988, *At Home on Planet Earth*; V. Blackmore and A. Page, 1989, *Evolution: the Great Debate;* C. Humphries, 1985, *Creation and Evolution*.
2. Blake, 'Auguries of Innocence', (See *The Complete Writings of William Blake*, edited by Geoffrey Keynes. OUP. 1966: 431.)
3. Blake, 'The Everlasting Gospel'. (*ibid*: 753.)
4. Blake, from the *Faber Book of Aphorisms*, p. 29.
5. Frederick Langbridge, 'Cluster of Quiet Thoughts'. See *A Dicitionary of Famous Quotations* compiled by Robin Hyman. Pan, 1983: 193.
6. This rendering in verse is by J.G. Saxe 1816–87. The last verse was added by K. Earl, 1977.
7. Pascal, *Pensees*, 427.
8. The *Padma Purana*.
9. D.L. Eck, 1984, *Benares, City of Light*, Routledge and Kegan Paul, p. 20.

GLOSSARY

Adi Granth	the principal Sacred Book of the Sikhs, compiled by the Fifth Guru, Arjan, and venerated as the embodiment of the eternal Guru
Akhira	the Muslim term for the afterlife, contrasted with this present life (dunya)
anatta	literally "no self", and refers to the consequences of the Buddhist concept of anicca, namely, that nothing whatever has the capacity to endure
anicca	literally, "non-permanence", and used in Buddhism to denote the radical condition of constant change in this world
ashram	the Hindu term for a hermitage or religious community, usually centred round a guru or other holy person
Bhagavad Gita	literally "Song of God" – and refers to what is probably the most well-known of all the Hindu scriptures
Brahman	the Hindu concept of cosmic or all-pervading power, the ground of all being, the Absolute, the Supreme
Buddha	the Enlightened or Awakened One – a term pre-eminently given to Gautama, the founder of Buddhism
darshana	literally "seeing", and hence denotes the Hindu concept of vision, or the insight conveyed in the presence of God or of a saint
dharma	comes from the word meaning "to uphold, support", therefore used in Hinduism for teaching, doctrine, law, custom, duty, or morality
guru	spiritual guide or teacher (Hinduism)
jihad	literally "struggle" – the term used in Islam to denote "holy war" or the spiritual struggle against forces of evil including in oneself
karma	literally "action" – denotes the Hindu notion of acts done in a previous life having consequences in this life
lingam	phallic symbol and emblem of the Hindu god Siva
Mahayana	one of the main traditions of Buddhist thought and practice going back to the first century CE, becoming

	the dominant form of Buddhism in the Far East
mantra	the Hindu concept of sacred words being chanted as an aid to devotion – often a verse from the scriptures
moksha	literally "liberation" and used in Hinduism to denote release from the continuing round of rebirths – the final goal of Hindu spirituality and devotion
neti-neti	literally "not this, not this", which refers to the way in which Hindus consider that it is easier to say what Brahman is *not* (cf. the *via negativa* of Christian theology)
Nirvana	literally "Extinction" and refers to the Buddhist concept of a state of being free from all that causes suffering, that is from egoism associated with greed, hatred and delusion
Qur'an	the Muslim scriptures given to the prophet Muhammad and believed by Muslims to be the final revelation of Allah
samsara	comes from "to flow" and refers to the Hindu concept of a cycle of rebirths or continuity of existence through many lives
Shunyata	the Void, beyond concepts of any kind (Buddhism)
Theravada	literally "The Teaching of the Elders" and it refers to the earliest surviving school of Buddhism claiming to preserve the earliest teachings of the Buddha. It is strong today in Sri Lanka and South East Asia
Upanishads	important Hindu scriptures in the form of philosophical treatises

REFERENCES AND RECOMMENDED READING

Abba, R. 1983. *The Nature and Authority of the Bible*. James Clarke.

Abbott, E. 1987. *Story of Flatland*. Penguin.

Adams, K. 1990. Changing British attitudes. *Royal Society of Arts Journal*, vol. CXXXVIII, no. 5412: 826–34.

Ainsworth, D. 1968. *Aspects of the Growth of Religious Understanding in Children aged 5–11. Unpublished thesis for Advanced Diploma in Education, Manchester University*.

Anderson, N. 1973. *A Lawyer Among the Theologians*. Hodder & Stoughton.

Anthony of Sourozh. 1986. *The Essence of Prayer*. Darton, Longman & Todd.

Appleton, G. 1985. *The Oxford Book of Prayer*. Oxford University Press.

Ashton, E. 1989. *Religious Education and the Unconscious*. University of Durham unpublished MA thesis.

Association of Religious Education Advisors and Inspectors (AREAI) 1989. Religious education for ages 5 to 16–18.

Bakhtiar, L. 1976. *Sufi: Expressions of the Mystic Quest*. Thames & Hudson.

Barfield, O. 1971. *What Coleridge Thought*. Wesleyan University Press.

Barnes, M. 1991. *God East and West*. SPCK.

Barnes, M. 1989. *Religions in Conversation*. SPCK.

Barton, J. 1991. *What is the Bible?*.

Beck, C. 1990. *Better Schools: a Values Perspective*. Falmer.

Begbie, J. 1992. The gospel, the arts and our culture, in Montefiore, 1992.

Berger, P. 1969. *A Rumour of Angels: Modern Society and the Discovery of the Supernatural*. Pelican.

Bigger, S. 1991. Assessing religious education. *Journal of Beliefs and Values*, vol. 12 no. 1: 1–4.

Bigger, S. 1990. National curriculum geography and history proposals: an RE perspective, *Journal of Beliefs and Values* vol. 11, no. 2: 9f.

Black, M. 1971. Models and metaphors. in Ramsey, 1971.

Blackmore, V. and Page, A. 1989. *Evolution: the Great Debate*. Lion.

Bobrinskoy, B. 1986. Revelation of the spirit; language beyond words. *Sobornost*, vol. 8, no. 1: 6–14.

Bondi, C. and Bondi, H. 1992. Humanism is the source of our values, *Newsvalues*, National Association for Values in Education and Training Spring, 8.

Bookless, D. 1991. *Interfaith Worship and Christian Truth*, Grove Worship Series 117. Grove Books.

Borgmann, A. 1991. *Technology and the Character of Contemporary Life: A philosophical Inquiry*, University of Chicago Press.

Borowitz, E.B. 1979. *Understanding Judaism*. Union of American Hebrew Congregations, New York.

British Council of Churches. 1989. *Worship in Education*. BCC London.

Brown, A. (ed.) 1987. *SHAP handbook on world religions in education*. Commission for racial equality.

Brown, J.M. 1980. *Men and Gods in a Changing World. SCM.*

Brown, S.C. 1979. *Philosophical Disputes in the Social Sciences.* Harvester.

Buber, M. 1985. Heart searching and the particular way, in Garvey, 1986.

Burke, C. 1967. *God is for Real,* Fontana Books.

Burn, J. and Hart, C. 1988. *The Crisis in Religious Education.* The Educational Research Trust, London.

Capra, F. 1982. *The Turning Point – Science, Society and the Rising Culture*. Flamingo.

Centre for Religious Education Development and Research. (CREDAR) Grimmitt, M., Grove, J., Hull, J. and Spencer, L. 1991. *A Gift to the Child*. Simon & Schuster.

Chappell, K.R. 1991. *Investigating Jesus.* Edward Arnold.

Charlesworth, J.H. 1991. *Jesus within Judaism.* SPCK.

Claxton, G. 1990. *Teaching to Learn.* Cassell Educational.

Clifford, R. 1991. *Leading Lawyers Look at the Resurrection.* Lion.

Cohn-Sherbok, D. 1991. *A Dictionary of Judaism and Christianity.* SPCK.

Cole, W.O. 1988. 'Religious Education after Swann' in O'Keefe

Cole, W.O. and Evans-Lowndes, J. 1991. *Religious Education in the Primary Curriculum: Teaching Strategies and Practical Activities.* RMEP Norwich.

Cole, J. 1988. *God in his World Today*, Amate Press.

Coles, M.J. and Robinson, W.D. (ed.) 1989. *Teaching Thinking.* The Bristol Press.

Conway, R. 1990. The influence of beliefs and values on technological activities – a challenge to religious education. *British Journal of Religious Education*, vol. 13, no. 1, 49–55.

Cooling, M. and Cooling, T. 1992. Christianity in the primary school, *Resource*, vol. 14, no. 3.

Copley, T. 1989. *Worship, Worries and Winners*. National Society/Church House Publishing.

Copley, T. 1991. *About the Bible*. Bible Society.

Corless, R. and Knitter, P.F. 1990. *Buddhist emptiness and Christian trinity*. Paulist Press.

Cracknell, K. 1986. *Towards a New Relationship – Christians and People of other Faith*. Epworth Press.

Crossan, J.D. 1991. *The Historical Jesus: the Life of a Mediterranean Jewish peasant*, Clark, Edinburgh.

D'Costa, G. 1988. *Faith meets Faith – Interfaith Views on Interfaith*. British and Foreign Schools Society RE Centre, London.

D'Costa, G. 1990. *Christian Uniqueness Reconsidered*. Orbis Books, Maryknoll, New York.

Department of Education and Science (DES). 1977. *Supplement to Curriculum 11–16*. HMSO.

Department of Education and Science (DES). 1991. *Education observed: the implementation of curricular requirements of the ERA*. HMSO.

Desforges, C. 1989. Understanding learning for teaching. *Westminster Studies in Education*, vol. 12.

Dunne, J. 1991. *The Partings of the Ways: Between Christianity and Judaism and their Significance for the Character of Christianity*. SCM/TPI.

Egan, K. 1988. *Primary Understanding*. Routledge.

FARE, 1990. *Forms of Assessment in RE*. Exeter University, School of Education.

Fisher, J. 1986. *Interface: Essential Life-issues Explored Through Contemporary Fiction*. Lion Publishing.

Fisher, R. 1990. *Teaching Children to Think*. Basil Blackwell.

Francis, L.J. and Thatcher, A. 1990. (ed.) *Christian Perspectives for Education*. Gracewing.

Free Church Federal Council, 1989. *Worship in County Schools*. (leaflet).

Fuller, P. 1990. *Images of God*. The Hogarth Press.

Garvey, J. 1986. *Modern Spirituality: an Anthology*. Darton, Longman & Todd.

Goldman, R. 1964. *Religious Thinking from Childhood to Adolescence*. Routledge & Kegan Paul.

Goldman, R. 1965. *Readiness for Religion*. Routledge & Kegan Paul.

Gollancz, V. and Greene, B. 1962. *God of a Hundred Names*. Victor Gollancz.

Griffiths, B. 1982. *The Marriage of East and West*. Collins.

Griffiths, B. 1989. *A New Vision of Reality: Western Science, Eastern Mysticism and Christian Faith*. Collins.

Grimmitt, M. 1973. *What can I do in RE?*. Mayhew-McCrimmon.

Grimmitt, M. 1987. *Religious Education and Human Development: the Relationship Between Studying Religions and Personal, Social and Moral Education*. McCrimmon.

Grimmitt, M., Grove, J., Hull, J., and Spencer, L. 1991. *A Gift to the Child*. Simon & Schuster.

Gunton, C. 1992. Knowledge and culture: towards an epistomology of the concrete, in Montefiore, 1992.

Habig, M.A. 1972. *St Francis of Assisi – Omnibus of Sources*. SPCK.

Hammond, J., Hay, D. *et al*. 1990. *New Methods in RE Teaching – an Experiential Approach*. Oliver & Boyd.

Hampson, D. 1990. *Theology and Feminism*. Basil Blackwell.

Hanson, R.P.C. 1984. *The Making of the Doctrine of the Trinity*. Anglican and Eastern Churches Association.

Harries, R. 1987. *Christ is Risen*. Mowbray.

Harris, J.G. 1989. *GCSE Religious Studies Coursework*. Longman Group.

Harris, M. 1988. *Women and Teaching*. Paulist Press.

Hay, D. 1990. *Religious Experience Today: Studying the Facts*. Mowbray.

Hay, D. and Hammond, J. 1992. When you pray go to your private room – A critical reply to Adrian Thatcher. *British Journal of Religious Education*. Summer: 145–50

Hebblethwaite, B. 1988. *The Ocean of Truth – A Defence of Objective Theism*. Cambridge University Press.

Hedges, S.G. 1970. *With one Voice*. Religious Education Press.

Hick, J. 1990. *Philosophy of Religion*, 4th edn. Prentice-Hall.

Hill, B.V. 1989. Spiritual Development in the Education Reform Act. *British Journal of Educational Studies*, vol. 37: 169–82.

Hill, B.V. 1990. Will and should the religious studies appropriate to schools in a pluralistic society foster religious relativism? *British Journal of Religious Education*, vol. 12, no. 3: 126–36.

Hinnells, J.R. 1984. *A Handbook of Living Religions*. Penguin.

Hinnells, J. 1990. Religion and the arts, in King, 1990.

Hodges, W. 1977. *Logic*. Penguin Books.

Hodgson, P.E. 1984. *The Implications of Quantum Physics*, Farmington Institute for Christian Studies, Oxford.

Hollis, M. and Lukes, S. (ed.) 1982 *Rationality and Relativism*. Basil Blackwell.

Holloway, R. 1988 *Crossfire – Faith and doubt in an age of certainty*. William Collins.

Holloway, R. (ed.) 1991 *Who needs Feminism?*. SPCK.

Hooker, R. 1989 *Themes in Hinduism and Christianity* Verlag Peter Lang, Frankfurt.

Hooker, R. and Sargant, J. (eds) 1991. *Belonging to Britain*. British Council of Churches/Council of Churches of Britain and Ireland.

Houghton, J. 1988. *Does God Play Dice? A Look at the Story of the Universe*. Inter-Varsity Press.

Hull, J. 1989. *The Act Unpacked*. Christian Education Movement, Birmingham University.

Hull, J.M. 1991. *God-talk with Young Children*. Christian Education Movement, Birmingham University.

Hull, J. 1992. *Mishmash; Religious Education in Multi-cultural Britain: a Study in Metaphor*. Christian Education Movement, Birmingham University.

Hulmes, E. 1979. *Commitment and Neutrality in Religious Education*. Geoffrey Chapman.

Hulmes, E. 1989. *Educational and Cultural Diversity*. Longman Group UK.

Humphries, C. 1985. *Creation and Evolution*. Oxford University Press.

Hyde, K.E. 1991. *Religion in Childhood and Adolescence*. Religious Education Press, Birmingham, Alabama.

Inter-Faith Consultation Group. 1992. *Multi-faith Worship?* Church House Publishing.

International Religious Foundation. 1991. *World Scripture: a Comparative Anthology of Sacred Texts*. Paragon House.

Islamic Academy. 1991. *Faith as the Basis of Education in a Multi-faith, Multi-cultural country; Discussion Document II*. Islamic Academy.

Ives, E. 1992. The Gospel and History, in Montefiore 1992.

Jackson, R. 1989. *Religions Through Festivals: Hinduism*. Longman Group UK.

Jackson, R. 1987. *Religious education – a middle way*, in Brown 1987.

Jackson, R. and Starkings, D. 1990. (eds) *The Junior RE Handbook*. Stanley Thornes.

James, M. 1989. Principles for profiling and recording pupils' achievement: their implications for religious education. unpublished paper. Keswick Hall Trustees.

Jeremias, J. 1971. *New Testament Theology: Volume One*. SCM.

Kandinsky, W. 1977. *Concerning the Spiritual in Art*. Dover Publications, New York.

Kelsey, M. 1991. *Myth, History and Faith*. Element Press.

Khan, M.A. 1985. Resource allocation in an Islamic economy. *The Islamic Quarterly*, vol. XXIX, no. 4: 241ff.

King, U. (ed.) 1990. *Turning Points in Religious Studies*. T. & T. Clark.

Kingaid, M. 1991. *How to Improve Learning in RE*. Hodder & Stoughton.

Kirkwood, R. 1990. *Looking for Proof of God*. Longman Group UK.

Knitter, P.F. and Corless, R. 1990. *Buddhist Emptiness and Christian Trinity*. Paulist Press.

Lawton, D. 1989. *Education, Culture and the National Curriculum*. Hodder & Stoughton.

Levering, M. 1989. *Rethinking Scripture: Essays from a Comparative Perspective*. State University of New York Press.

Lipman, M., Sharp, A.M. and Oscanyan, F.S. 1980. *Philosophy in the Classroom*. Temple University Press.

Lloyd, B. 1990. *Education Plus Training*, vol. 32, no. 3. MCB University Press.

Macquarrie, J. 1968. *New Directions in Theology Today: Volume 3, God and Secularity*. Lutterworth Press.

Mahadevan, T.M.P. 1976, *Ramana Maharshi and his Philosophy of Existence*, 3rd edn. Venkataraman, Tiruvannamalai, S. India.

Mahadevan, T.M.P. 1977. *Ramana Maharshi, the Sage of Arunacala*. Unwin Paperbacks.

Matthews, G.B. 1980. *Philosophy and the Young Child*. Harvard University Press.

Mitchell, B. 1980. Religious education. *Oxford Review of Education* vol. 6, no. 2: 133–9.

Mitchell, B. 1990. *How to Play Theological Ping Pong*. Hodder & Stoughton.

Moberly, W. 1992. 'Old Testament' and 'New Testament': The propriety of the terms for Christian theology. *Theology*, vol. XCV, no. 763: 26–32.

Montefiore, H. 1992. *The Gospel and Contemporary Culture*. Mowbray.

Moorman, J.R.H. 1963. *Saint Francis of Assisi*. SPCK.

National Curriculum Council (NCC). 1991a. *Analysis of SACRE Reports*. NCC.

National Curriculum Council (NCC). 1991b. *Religious Education: a Local Curriculum Framework*. NCC.

Newman, J.H. 1979, *A Grammar of Assent*. University of Notre Dame Press.

Newton, D. 1990. Shattering the dream of a post-patriarchal Christianity: can not even feminists redeem Christianity? *Journal of Beliefs and Values*, vol. 11, no. 2: 2–8.

Nichols, A. 1990. *From Newman to Congar*. T & T Clark.

O'Keeffe, B. (ed.). 1988. *Schools for Tomorrow: Building Walls or Building Bridges*. The Falmer Press.

Orchard, S. 1991. What was Wrong with Religious Education? *British Journal of Religious Education*, vol. 14, no. 1, Autumn: 15–21.

Osborne, A. 1970. *Ramana Maharshi and the Path of Self-knowledge*. Rider & Co.

Palmer, M. 1991. *What Should we Teach? – Christians and Education in a Pluralist World*. WCC Geneva.

Parrinder, G. 1990. *A Dictionary of Religious and Spiritual Quotations*. Routledge.

Petrovich, O. 1989. *An Examination of Piaget's Theory of Childhood Artificialism*. University of Oxford unpublished PhD thesis.

Phillips, J.B. 1932. *Your God is too Small*. Epworth Press.

Plunkett, D. 1990. *Secular and Spiritual Values*. Routledge.

Polanyi, M. 1964. *Science, Faith and Society*. University of Chicago Press.

Poole, M. 1990a. *A Guide to Science and Belief.* Lion Publishing.

Poole, M. 1990b. Beliefs and values in science education: a Christian perspective, Part 1. *School Science Review,* March 1990, point 71 (256): 25–32.

Poole, M. 1990c. Beliefs and values in science education: a Christian perspective, Part 2. *School Science Review,* June 1990, point 71 (256): 67–73.

Poole, M. 1992. *Miracles – Science, the Bible and Experience.* Scripture Union.

Priestley, J. 1991. RE – the hub of the curriculum. *RE Today,* Summer 1991, 8f.

Priestley, J. 1992. Whitehead revisited: religion and education – an organic whole, in Watson, 1992.

Pring, R. 1992. *Academic Respectability and Professional Relevance.* Clarendon Press.

Pring, R. 1984. *Personal and Social Education in the Curriculum.* Hodder & Stoughton.

Quoist, M. 1966. *Prayers of Life.* Logos Books.

Raban, K. 1990. Guided imagery and religious education, in Hammond, Hay, *et al.* 1990.

Raeper, W. and Smith, L. 1991. *A Beginners' Guide to Ideas.* Lion.

Ramsey, I.T. 1971. *Words about God – The Philosophy of Religion.* SCM.

Read, G., Rudge, J., and Howarth, R. 1986. *How do I Teach RE?.* Stanley Thornes & Hulton.

Read, G., Rudge, J., and Teece, G. 1992. *How do I Teach RE?.* Westhill Project Teachers' Manual.

Religious Education Council, (REC) 1991. *RE, Attainment and National Curriculum.* REC.

Religious Education Council, (REC), 1990. *Handbook for Agreed Syllabus Conferences, SACREs and Schools.* REC

Richards, I.A. 1936. *The Philosophy of Rhetoric.* Oxford.

Riggs, A. 1990. Biotechnology and religious education. *British Journal of Religious Education,* vol. 13, no. 1, 56–64.

Roques, M. 1989. *Curriculum Unmasked.* Monarch Publications.

Rose, D. 1992, *Towards an Understanding of Religious Diversity in School.* Fulton/Roehampton.

Ross, C. 1991. *Leading Lawyers Look at the Resurrection.* Lion.

Ryeland, G. (ed.) 1991. *Beyond Reasonable Doubt.* The Canterbury Press.

Sacks, J. 1991. *The Persistence of Faith.* Weidenfeld & Nicolson.

Sanders, E.P. 1992. *Judaism – Practice and Belief 63 BCE – 66 CE.* SCM/TPI.

Sankey, D., Sullivan, D., and Watson, B. 1988 *At Home on Planet Earth.* Basil Blackwell.

Sarwar, G. 1989. *What can Muslims do?.* Muslim Educational Trust.

Schools Council. 1971. *Religious Education in Secondary Schools*: Working Paper 36. Evans/Methuen.

Sherley-Price, L. 1959. *St Francis of Assisi*. Mowbray.

Slee, N. 1989. Conflict and reconciliation between competing models of religious education: some reflections on the British scene. *British Journal of Religious Education*, vol. 11, no.3: 126–35.

Slee, N. 1991. Windows on worship: a review of some recent resources for assembly. *Journal of Beliefs and Values*, vol. 12, no.2: 5f.

Smart, N. 1989. *The World's Religions: Old Traditions and Modern Transformations*. Cambridge University Press.

Smith, H. 1991. *The World's Religions*. Harper.

Soskice, J.M. 1985. *Metaphor and Religious Language*. SCM.

Stannard, R. 1985. *Science, Psychology, and the Existence of God* Occasional paper 19. Farmington Institute for Christian Studies, Oxford.

Stannard, R. 1989. *The Time and Space of Uncle Albert*. Faber & Faber.

Starkings, D. 1993. *Religion and the Arts in Education: Dimensions of Spirituality*. Hodder & Stoughton.

Stewart, I. 1989. *Does God Play Dice – The New Mathematics of Chaos*. Penguin Books.

Swinburne, R. 1986. *Evidence for God*. Mowbray.

Talib, G.S. 1975. *Selections from the Holy Granth*. Bell Books Vikas.

Taylor, J.V. 1978. The theological basis of inter-faith dialogue. *Crucible*, January/March: 4–16.

Taylor, M. 1991. *SACREs: their Formation, Composition, Operation and Role on RE and Worship*. NFER/NCC.

Teasdale, W. 1987. *Towards a Christian Vedanta*. Asian Trading Corporation, Bangalore.

Thacker, J., Pring, R., and Evans, D. 1987. *Personal, Social and Moral Education in a Changing World*. NFER-Nelson.

Thatcher, A. 1991. A critique of inwardness in religious education. *British Journal of Religious Education*, vol. 14, no.1: 22–7.

Thiede, C. 1991. *Jesus: Life or Legend*. Lion.

Thouless, R.H. 1953. *Straight and Crooked Thinking*. Pan Books.

Trigg, R. 1989. *Reality at Risk: a Defence of Realism in Philosophy and the Sciences*, 2nd edn. Harvester, New York.

Underhill, E. 1985. Spiritual Life, in Garvey, 1986.

Upitis, R. 1990. *This too is Music*. Heinemann Educational.

Vardy, P. 1988. *And if it's True?*. Marshall, Morgan and Scott.

Walker, A. 1988. *Different Gospels*. Hodder & Stoughton.

Ward, K. 1989. *Images of Eternity*. Darton, Longman & Todd.

Ward, K. 1991. *A Vision to Pursue*. SCM.

Ward, K. 1990. The study of truth and dialogue in religion, in King 1990.

Watson, B.G. 1987. *Education and Belief.* Blackwell.

Watson, B.G. 1988, Children at school: a worshipping community, in O'Keeffe, 1988.

Watson, B.G. (ed.) 1992. Priorities in Religious Education. Falmer.

Watson, J.T. 1988. *Recovery of Belief in God (A Journey to Belief)* Occasional Paper 21. Farmington Institute for Christian Studies, Oxford.

Webster, D. 1991. School Worship. *Theology* vol. XCIV, July/August, 1991, no. 760: 245–53.

Wenham, J. 1992. *The Easter Enigma*, 2nd edn. Paternoster Press, Guernsey.

Westhill College Regional RE Centre (Midlands) 1991 *Assessing, Recording and Reporting RE.* Birmingham.

Whaling, F. 1986. *Christian Theology and World Religions.* Marshall Pickering.

Whitehead, A.N. 1950. *The Aims of Educations.* 2nd edn. Ernest Benn.

Wilby, B. 1974 *Meeting the Occult.* Lutterworth Educational.

Wiles, M. 1992. *Christian Theology and Inter-religious Dialogue.* SCM.

Wilson, A.N. 1991. *Against Religion: Why We Should Try to Live Without it.* Chatto & Windus.

Wilson, A. (ed.) 1991. *World Scripture: a Comparative Anthology of Sacred Texts.* Paragon House, New York.

Wingate, A. 1988. *Encounter in the Spirit.* WCC Publications, Geneva.

Wink, W. 1990. *Transforming Bible study – a Teacher's Guide.* Mowbray.

Yeaxley, B. 1925. *Spiritual Values in Adult Education.* Oxford University Press.

Young, F.M. 1991. *The Making of the Creeds.* SCM.

It would be invidious to try to draw up a list here of the resources to which the RE teacher can turn. Such a list would soon be out of date anyway. What is more useful is to know how to keep abreast of what is happening. Basically there are three ways:

1. Contact through Teachers' Centres. Those of national significance concerned with RE include:

BFSS National RE Centre at
   West London Institute of Higher Education, Lancaster House, 1 Borough Road, Isleworth, Middlesex, TW7 5DU
National Society's RE Centre
   23 Kensington Square, London W8 5HN
Regional RE Centre,
   Westhill College, Selly Oak, Birmingham B29 6LL
RE–ME Enquiry Service
   St Martin's College, Lancaster, LA1 2TB
Religious Resource and Research Centre,
   Derbyshire College of Higher Education, Mickleover, Derby DE3 5GY
Religious Education Centre
   Avery Hill College, Bexley Road, Eltham, London W14 0BL
Welsh National Centre for Religious Education
   University College of North Wales, Lon Pobty, Bangor, Gwynedd, LL57 1DZ
York Religious Education Centre
   The College, Lord Mayor's Walk, York YO3 7EX

2. Through membership of one or more organizations which mail members. These include:
ACT
   Association of Christian Teachers, 2 Romeland Hill, St Albans, Herts. AL3 4ET
CEM – Christian Education Movement
   Royal Buildings, Victoria Street, Derby DE1 1GW

PCFRE
  Professional Council for Religious Education (available at the
  address given for CEM)
SHAP WORKING PARTY
  The Secretary, Bishop Otter College, College Lane, Chichester,
  West Sussex

3. Contact with various religious organizations

The Buddhist Society
  58 Eccleston Square, London SW1V 1PH
Catholic Educational Council
  41 Cromwell Road, London SW7 2DJ
Farmington Institute for Christian Studies
  Manchester College, Oxford
Islamic Cultural Centre
  146 Park Road, Regent's Park, London NW8
Jewish Educational Bureau
  8 Westcombe Avenue, Leeds LS8 2BS
Jewish National Fund
  Harold Poster House, Kingsbury Circle, London NW9
Minaret House
  9 Leslie Park Road, Croydon, Surrey, CR0 6TN
Multi-Faith Centre and Resource Unit
  1 College Walk, Selly Oak, Birmingham, B29 6LE
North of England Institute of Christian Education
  School of Education, Carter House, University of Durham, Durham
Ramakrishna Vedanta Centre
  Blind Lane, Bourne End, Bucks. SL8 5LG
Sikh Missionary Society
  10 Featherstone Road, Southall, Middx. UB2 5AA
Society of Friends
  Friends House, Euston Road, London NWI 2BJ
West London Synagogue
  33 Seymour Place, London W1
World Congress of Faiths
  28 Powis Gardens, London W11 1JG

Index